TALES OF THE CITY

A Study of Narrative and Urb ii ʲ ˣ

How do we picture urban life and formulate our experience of it? *Tales of the City* brings together the academics' abstract tales with the vivid stories about a particular city, Milton Keynes, and the often moving self-narrations of its residents. It explores the role of story-telling processes for the creative constructing of experience, with particular attention to personal narrations. The story that is now emerging, told by many individual actor-narrators, is of the city as a natural setting for human life, in stark contrast to the pessimistic anti-urban tales of many academic narrators. Drawing on narrative studies, cultural and linguistic anthropology and social theory, Professor Finnegan skilfully examines the narrative conventions and cultural implications of our multiple tales of the city, and relates them to profound mythic themes about urban life, community and the creative role of the active, reflecting individual.

RUTH FINNEGAN is Professor in Comparative Social Institutions at the Open University. Her many publications include *Limba Stories and Story-Telling* (1967), *Oral Poetry* (1977), *The Hidden Musicians* (1989) and *Oral Traditions and the Verbal Arts* (1992).

TALES OF THE CITY

A Study of Narrative and Urban Life

Ruth Finnegan

CAMBRIDGE
UNIVERSITY PRESS

PUBLISHED BY THE PRESS SYNDICATE OF THE UNIVERSITY OF CAMBRIDGE
The Pitt Building, Trumpington Street, Cambridge CB2 1RP, United Kingdom

CAMBRIDGE UNIVERSITY PRESS
The Edinburgh Building, Cambridge, CB2 1RU, United Kingdom
http://www.cup.cam.ac.uk
40 West 20th Street, New York, NY 10011–4211, USA   http://www.cup.org
10 Stamford Road, Oakleigh, Melbourne 3166, Australia

First published 1998

Printed in the United Kingdom at the University Press, Cambridge

Typeset in Concorde Regular 9.25/13 pt [VN]

A catalogue record for this book is available from the British Library

Library of Congress Cataloguing in Publication Data
Finnegan, Ruth H.
Tales of the city: a study of narrative and urban life/Ruth Finnegan.
    p.   cm.
Includes bibliographical references (p.   ) and index.
ISBN 0 521 62334 0 (hb). – ISBN 0 521 62623 4 (pb)
1. Milton Keynes (England) – Social life and customs – Historiography. 2. Milton Keynes (England) – Social life and customs. 3. City and town life – England – Milton Keynes. 4. Storytelling – England – Milton Keynes. 5. Narration (Rhetoric)
I. Title.
DA670.M66F56   1998
942.5'91'0072–dc21   97–35263   CIP

ISBN 0 521 62334 0 hardback
ISBN 0 521 62623 4 paperback

Contents

Figures

Preface

This study started from my curiosity about the notion of the city and about how people living in my own town conceived of this – 'ordinary' people, I thought, as distinct from the academics. This rather unformulated curiosity first led me into investigating some local life stories. Then the narrative element in these personal tales became an additional focus, feeding into my long-standing interest in story-telling. And I began to realise that these personal tales were not the only ones that structured our ideas of urban culture, and that stories of the city by other tellers too were part of the mix.

I ended up with the seemingly rather simple aspiration of bringing together a series of stories about the city – those of the intellectuals (ostensibly abstract and above the battle) with the self-narratives of urban residents and with the tales told in and of a city by its planners, its local groups, and outside commentators in the media and elsewhere. What do these many tellers have to say about urban living? Equally important (or perhaps the same question), what are the narrative processes through which they formulate it?

Bringing together stories 'across the board' like this is a bit unusual. It would be easier to follow the many studies that mainly stay with one type of tale or teller, whether this be autobiographical tales, the theories circulated among academics, or the stories of groups which have somehow been classified as 'other' within our own culture or elsewhere (the 'submerged', perhaps, the 'folk' or the 'oppressed'). Other studies do look at verbal genres across a culture as a whole, but with less interest in the contrasting as well as overlapping tales that are told through them. Insights from these more detailed works and from the current explosion of interest in narrative analysis lie behind the interdisciplinary analysis in this volume – it would have been impossible without them. But none of these approaches are exactly what my study is about. I decided to pursue the rather different endeavour of bringing together a series of stories of the city that are more often kept separate and analysing them within the same narrative framework. Their interaction and overlaps can tell us something about the actualisation of our mythologies of urban life.

The attempt is impossible of course, for there are unending tales of the city. All I could try to do was to include enough to convey something of the multiplicity and range of the stories, anchoring them, in anthropological tradition, to the narrations of one specific locality and one set of local tellers but at the same time – unlike some ethnographic accounts – also relating them to the more abstract story-telling by the culture's theorising intellectuals. I hope that despite the inevitable selectivity, this attempt to analyse a range of different types of stories within the same narrative frame can throw light on our story-telling processes and our storied views of the city.

One practical problem is how to deal with the self-narratives. Referring to the academic stories and even to some of the localised urban tales can be done relatively briefly: many are already in the public domain. But the personal tales cannot be presented so cursorily. I have therefore reproduced some lengthy excerpts in chapters 4–6. This has disadvantages, perhaps explaining why many studies of self-narratives end up dispensing with the narratives themselves. It inevitably lengthens the book and adds to its expense. It probably unbalances it too, for though the self-stories are indeed of the essence, so too are the other tales. And as is now widely recognised, verbal texts on a page can seem quite unilluminating, for they are only a partial representation of orally delivered narrations. But it would be impossible to convey the reality of our multiple urban stories and how they can be analysed as narratives without including examples of some substance rather than just snippets of quotation: hence the six personal tales in the heart of this book.

Throughout I speak of 'our culture' – an elusive term. Consonant with our contemporary suspicion of over-neatly bounded units of analysis, I am fairly unrepentant about leaving it undefined – or, rather, leaving it to my readers to recognise it as and where they may. However, let me add that while the overall coverage ranges much wider, the setting is England and the specific locale that of Milton Keynes, the Buckinghamshire town in southern-central England. This in part makes it a companion volume to my earlier book on music-making in Milton Keynes, providing a second look at the same town and another attempt to bring together activities or genres that other studies tend to keep apart. This second volume is less founded in detailed ethnographic observation than *The Hidden Musicians*, however, and focuses on a different dimension of city life, for I have returned to earlier interests by focusing not on music but on story-telling.

The wider implications of the local tales are relevant throughout, not just their ethnographic uniquenesses. In Britain the image of 'Milton Keynes' has for many people become a kind of epitome of some key urban stories in contemporary culture, a revealing locale therefore to explore our tales of the city. The town's very specificity has come to give it a wider symbolic interest.

The study thus revolves round the multiple ways in which we use narrative to formulate our ideas and experience of urban life. As I have said, the tales are never-ending, both in general and as presented through the stories heard and told in a particular town. Not all are told here, let alone concluded. Other tellers will add yet more stories. But this work does at least endeavour to bring onto the same stage a series of our stories on the subject, from the abstract stories of the theorists, the colourful tales of a particular town, and the often moving narratives told by some of its inhabitants. It tries to analyse them *as* stories, to reveal the conventions behind their construction. And within the story of my work on this study I have also been rediscovering and retelling the plot that is so obvious – even fashionable – in theory but hard to pinpoint in practice: that the opposition between 'ordinary' and 'academic' which is still a familiar starting-point to the tale takes on a different look by its conclusion.

Acknowledgements

It must be obvious that this book could not have been started let alone completed without the help of many others. On a personal as well as intellectual level I am especially grateful to Delia Gray both for her support in general discussion and, more particularly, for contacting the Fishermead dwellers and recording their personal stories; to Dianne Cook for her help every single working day and especially for her assistance with the transcription; to my mother through a lifetime's mischievous telling of tall and not-so-tall tales which continued even through the final months of her life as I started writing this book; and for the long support and interest of my husband, David Murray, in too many ways to list. I am appreciative too of the many friends in Milton Keynes for their co-experience in creating and telling the storied life of this city. I was also greatly helped by discussion with colleagues. This was generously forthcoming both in everyday scholarly interaction (especially within my own institution of the Open University – and special thanks to my helpfully critical colleagues in the 'Culture, media and identities' course team) and at gatherings where I presented some of this material in an earlier form: especially at the Annual Conference of the British Sociological Association's Auto/Biography Group in November 1994 (written up as Finnegan 1996), seminars in the Universities of Joensuu and Helsinki, Finland in March 1996, and the mind-blowing conference on 'Narrative and metaphor across the disciplines' in the University of Auckland in July 1996. I would also express my appreciation for the constructively challenging comments from the anonymous readers for the Press, and for Diane Ilott's perceptive and thorough copy editing: you have all certainly improved the final version. Above all, I and all the readers of this book owe a great debt to the narrators of the moving and unique personal stories recorded and analysed in this volume. Except for George Rowe and Jenny Linn-Cole I cannot thank them by name, for our agreement was that they would appear under pseudonyms. But let me salute and thank them all.

I have sincere thanks to express to many libraries or archives and to their staff, among them the Living Archive in Wolverton, Milton Keynes (thanks especially to Roger Kitchen and Sue Quinn for many kindnesses and encouragement); the City Discovery Centre, Bradwell Abbey, Milton Keynes; the Local Studies section of the Milton Keynes Central Reference Library;

the Commission for the New Towns; and, as always, the Open University Library, especially the ever-smiling assistants on the desk and the wonderfully efficient Inter-Library Loan section. I owe a great debt to John Hunt (Project Officer, Faculty of Social Sciences, Open University) for his expert cartographic assistance with Figures 3.1, 3.2, 4.1 and 6.2 and to Paul Smith (then of the Open University Library) for tracing the poster for Figure 3.5 as well as for his many years' colleagueship. I also gratefully acknowledge the financial assistance in the earlier stages of this work given by both the Faculty Research Committee and the Sociology Research Group in the Faculty of Social Sciences at the Open University.

For permission to reproduce copyright material grateful acknowledgement is due to the following: the Commission for the New Towns, 414–28 Midsummer Boulevard, Central Milton Keynes MK9 2EA, for Figures 3.2, 3.3, 3.8, 4.1, 5.1, 6.1 (street in Fishermead), 6.2, 6.3, 6.4 and the cover photograph, and for the extracts from *The Planning of Milton Keynes* in Chapter 3; Mike Levers, Open University, for Figures 3.6 and 6.1 (terraced houses); Faber and Faber Ltd for Figure 3.4; *Punch* for Figure 3.5; Vera Stone for Figure 3.7; The Living Archive, The Old Bath House, 205 Stratford Road, Wolverton, Milton Keynes MK12 5RL on behalf of the People's Press for permission to reproduce the poem 'The New City'; Bill Billings for his poem 'Old Jacks Dog Died'; Anita Packwood for her poem 'In the Sinking Sunlight'; Norine Redman for her poem 'Early Spring at Peartree Bridge'; and, finally, the narrators of the personal tales in chapters 4–6: they retain the copyright in their own words but gave permission for them to be quoted in this study.

1   Story: 'the orders by which we live our lives'

> We dream in narrative, day-dream in narrative, remember, anticipate, hope, despair, believe, doubt, plan, revise, criticize, construct, gossip, learn, hate, and love by narrative. In order really to live, we make up stories about ourselves and others, about the personal as well as the social past and future. (Barbara Hardy)

We all tell stories and we live in their midst. Barbara Hardy's famous comment (1968 p. 5) well sums up the myriad ways we use narrative to experience and shape our lives. More than just a tool for formulating our autobiographies, story-telling is the frame for our general accounts too, even – as recent commentators now forcefully remind us – for our great meta-theories about the affairs and destiny of humankind.

This view of the major role of narrative in organising our knowledge and our experience underlies the present volume. In one form or another such a perspective is scarcely new. But it has been gathering greater momentum in recent years through the current interests in 'story' within social, cultural and literary theory. In this volume these recent approaches are brought together with the comparative work on myth and story within anthropology, folklore and narrative analysis.

Among the many instances of narrative in our culture are those to do with the concept and experience of urban life. There are many tales of the city (in the large sense of the term 'city', that is, which encompasses 'town', 'urbanism' and 'urban life' generally).[1] It is hardly surprising that much story-telling should focus on this topic or take it as the setting – by the turn of the millennium, after all, more than half of the world's people will live in cities (Sanjek 1990 p. 154). Tales of the city are thus scarcely marginal, but likely to play a significant role in our experience and understanding.

So how do we think about cities? What tales do we use to shape our understanding and our experience of urban life? And how do they work? This volume undertakes the at first sight simple task of telling some of these stories of the city and analysing their nature and significance.

In one way this is indeed a straightforward and familiar task. We are habituated not only to tell stories, but also to compare them, accept or reject them, put them in context. This may be partly an unselfconscious activity, but one we are well accustomed to undertaking. Thus an exploration of the

1

many stories we tell and are told about urban life – an experience likely to be familiar to readers of this volume – can draw on everyday experience of ourselves as story-telling and story-hearing beings.

But taking it further demands some effort at standing back and seeing our stories as strange. It is when we are faced with *un*familiar story-telling that we must work at recognising the conventions that shape it. To see the patterns in what the tellers and hearers experience as 'natural', we need to approach them as both outsider and insider, from the viewpoint, as it were, of the visiting Martian anthropologist.

This dual stance of both familiarity and distancing is a necessary perspective for approaching the tales in this volume. We can listen for example to the local stories about the town(s) we happen to live in, on the surface unproblematic and concerned merely with specificities – but perhaps, seen from a more distant view, also drawing on wider cultural themes and narrative conventions. The personal stories of individual lives can be treated similarly.

My beginnings – well my roots are very firmly working class. My dad was a factory worker all his life, and my mum worked part-time jobs in shops and factories. My first recollection – I can vaguely remember they both came from Southall. But it was a kind of family joke, because my father came from one side of Southall and my mother came from another, and . . . my dad was from the wrong side of the railway track and the railway ran through the middle . . . So that was a sort of family joke. My father's mother and father had a greengrocery shop. And my grandfather who I really don't remember, he died when I was about five I suppose. I only have a vague recollection of him, but he used to go off to Covent Garden to collect the vegetables every morning on his horse and cart. (Brenda Dawson's story; for continuation, see Chapter 4 pp. 60ff.)

That sounds merely individual and personal. But such self-narratives too repay the effort not only to hear their individual voices at all but also to uncover their taken-for-granted narrative conventions and imagery.

The 'Martian anthropologist' figure has become something of a cliché, itself not without narrative overtones. But hackneyed as it is, it conveys the essential idea that there *are* topics which an outsider might wish to ask about in the taken-for-granted ways of our own culture. And what could at first seem more natural than the familiar accounts we hear and tell about the city or than the firsthand experiences of our own lives? In the same spirit, I am also mostly laying aside issues about the 'truth or falsity' of stories to focus instead – as the visiting anthropologist might do – on uncovering the conventions through which tales are formulated and told. This means exploring the sense in which they might indeed be analysed as 'stories' as well as the relations between varying genres of these tales.

Our culturally specific concepts about 'the city' or about 'urban living' and their formulation in stories are approached from the same perspective. To consider what these are and how they are formulated and narrated in 'stories' we need to look not just to the 'obvious' locus of the intellectuals' accounts, but also to tales of specific cities and – a dimension too often overlooked by social theorists – to the narratives through which urban dwellers themselves formulate their experience. These differing types of tales, furthermore, can be illuminated by being analysed within the same narrative framework. They are brought together here in rather the same way that an anthropologist visiting an unfamiliar society might try to consider their varying tales or speech forms within one overview, presenting and comparing those told by local intellectuals, by members of particular groups or localities, and by individuals telling of their own lives.[2]

This volume thus presents and analyses examples of the multiple stories of the city, told by a range of tellers in our culture. Examples from the corpus of personal narratives by dwellers in one particular urban area are given throughout chapters 4–6, six of them at some length. Chapter 4 provides some introduction to the context and performance conventions for these individuals' tales, also taking up the complex issue of how far these formulations of life-experiences can indeed be regarded as 'stories'. Their narrative conventions are considered in chapter 5, while themes of urban living are more directly explored in chapter 6. Chapter 3 meantime recounts a range of stories about the planning, reception and experience of the town in which the personal narrators are living (the 'new city' of Milton Keynes in southern-central England), specific to the locality but also with evocations of wider mythic themes. And these in their turn inter-relate with that other type of narrative which the Martian visitor would also find in circulation: the crystallised and abstract tales of cities told by the scholars, the subject of chapter 2.

Providing some analysis of these tales of the city, both personal and more abstract, is the task of this book. This largely lies in elucidating the narrative themes and conventions that, even if not fully visible to their tellers, lie behind our many narrations of the city. It concludes by broadening the perspective to consider the significance of this multiplicity of stories and story-telling in our culture, of the processes by which they are constructed and told, and their implications for our understanding not only of urban theory but of our own lives and culture.

Before moving to the stories themselves, however, let me say a little more about the background to this study. The rest of this chapter briefly describes how I see my own study relating to the wider work on narrative, and my approach to the delineation and analysis of 'story'.

Perspectives on narrative

There is of course a long literary tradition of studying the arts of narrative, chiefly from cultures of literate and western peoples. This has embraced not only the creativities of individual narrators but also the conventions of style, genre and (though less often) of distribution and reception. Complementing and overlapping this have been studies by anthropologists, socio-linguists and folklorists of the structures and functions of unwritten stories throughout the world, not least of those great myths that arguably underlie and shape our cultural and personal conditions.

These approaches continue relevant. But recent years have also seen an explosion of interest in the concept of narrative. The scope has extended from the original literary context into studies right across the social and human sciences, even more widely. The term 'narrative' has become a fashionable one and now appears in a whole range of sometimes unexpected contexts.

One of the most prominent recent settings for narrative analysis has been in the study of individual lives. Numerous works now revolve round the idea that the self – or life, or personal experience – is essentially constructed by or through narrative, that is, by the stories that we tell ourselves or that others tell about us. The basic concept of 'life as narrative' appears widely in work by psychologists and psychotherapists: the idea that, as Jerome Bruner put it, 'a life as led is inseparable from a life as told ... not "how it was" but how it is interpreted and reinterpreted, told and retold' (Bruner 1987 p. 31). The expanding psychological literature on autobiographical narrative (Neisser and Fivush 1994, Rubin 1996 and a stream of influential works by Jerome Bruner) is now mingling with parallel studies by anthropologists, linguists, folklorists and oral historians on orally delivered life stories and personal narratives, and with studies by sociologists and others interested in auto/biographical texts and processes.[3] Work of this kind forms an important background to the treatment here, not only for the personal stories considered in chapters 4–6 but also for the general idea of narrative as a mode for recounting and experiencing our lives.

The model of narrative as in some sense formulating reality is also now being extensively applied to other contexts in which we interpret or control the world. A huge proliferation of academic work now utilises the concept of 'narrative' or 'story' to examine interpretations and accounts at every level, whether by individuals, groups or institutions, thus extending the idea of narrative well beyond the explicitly 'artistic' works traditionally studied within a literary framework. Studies of organisations, for example, now describe the viewpoints transmitted by managers and their associates as stories: we hear of the 'corporate culture narratives', for example, or of management consultants as story-tellers projecting the 'epic talc' of the manager as hero (Salaman 1997 pp. 253ff., cf. Boje 1991, Clark and Salaman 1996, Roe 1994). A report on industrial urban restructuring is presented as its 'stories of crises' (Metcalfe and Bern 1994), while ideas about tourism or about locality are analysed as 'travellers' tales' and 'stories of places' (Robertson *et al.* 1994, Thrift 1997). Therapists, doctors and nurses are described as interpreting and perhaps shaping their patients' 'stories' of their lives, illnesses or death (Epston and White 1992, Freedman and Combs 1996, Riessman 1990, Sandelowski 1991). It has become commonplace for people's interpretations and assumptions about almost anything – from political events or the nature of government to personal tragedies, ethnic interaction or gender relations – to be labelled and analysed as 'stories'. One succinct summary of this general perspective is Geertz's well-known description of culture as the ensemble of 'stories we tell ourselves about ourselves' (1975 p. 448).

The same terminology is also applied to academic accounts. Scepticism about scholars' claims to 'objectivity' or to 'scientific methodology' is scarcely an innovation. But one outcome of the current fashion of berating the claims of 'positivism' has been a preoccupation with both the relativity of academics' theories and the fluidity and elusiveness of what they study. Postmodernist assessments portray such theorising no longer as authoritative accounts of reality but as merely one set of possible 'stories' among others. Thus the theories and interpretations of anthropologists, for instance, or of philosophers, historians, lawyers or economists have all on occasion been approached as narratives.[4] It has now become not only acceptable but even obligatory in some circles to label such accounts as 'stories' or 'narratives', signalling their crafted, contingent and in a sense fictional nature and reacting against a 'realist' or correspondence theory of truth.

The grand theories that sanction wide-reaching philosophical or disciplinary paradigms are not exempt from this critique – the foundational 'meta-narratives' as Lyotard has it (1984 p. xxiv). Clegg writes of the 'good story' told by the key theorists of modernity like Marx, Durkheim, Weber and Simmel, each 'a grand master of narrative' who gave his theory 'a narrative structure in which a central idea of capitalism, differentiation, Protestantism, individuation, played an ambivalent heroic role' (1993 p. 15). Landau (1991) similarly regards the great 'narratives of human evolution' as essentially versions of the widespread hero tale, while Schafer pinpoints the basic narrations in psychoanalytic theory (1992). The contending meta-narratives underpinning historical study can be seen the same way: stories about deeds of personal actors as contrasted to plots driven by class-based causes or by epochal historical stages which move the action forward; or as stories exemplifying what Tonkin calls the 'myth of realism' (1990, cf. also White 1973, 1987). General theories across the social science and human-istic disciplines are now commonly analysed not as something of a higher order, but as themselves constructed – like stories – to convey the tellers' position and deploy the conventions of a recognised genre.[5]

These recent approaches point up questions about the (often hidden) conventions and themes through which these accounts are formulated – about the interest not just of their overt content but also of their poetics. There is a lot more narrative around, it seems, than we realised! They also have the merit of focusing attention onto the processes by which theories are constructed and disseminated, interesting parallels to literary creation, and of encouraging the sceptical analysis of dogmatic would-be 'above-the-battle' pronouncements. They thus form an illuminating background to the present study's aim of treating a series of differing 'stories of the city' rather than recommending one 'true' or permanent interpretation. They feed too into the more general view, cited at the start, which envisages story-telling as crucial to our existence and realisation as human beings.

Some positions taken up in current studies are controversial, or at any rate have been less utilised in the present study. Recent approaches to narrative have sometimes been closely associated with, or colonised by, scholars publishing under the banner of postmodernism and/or cultural studies. These highly visible if sometimes elusive clusters of writing are often taken to represent a new and distinctive approach to culture. In some senses this is a misleading claim. The basic ideas are shared among writers of many different backgrounds, as scholars deploy a new vocabulary to re-convey the essentially interpretative and socially constructed – rather than 'objective' – nature of accounts given by individuals or organisations. But there is also a special push in many 'cultural studies' publications to produce a distinctive critical perspective on the political or self-interested nature of the 'stories' under study, giving the term connotations not so dissimilar to those of the once much-used 'ideology'. Publications in this vein invoke writers like Gramsci (1971) and Foucault (e.g. 1972, 1980) to highlight issues about hegemony and power, sometimes taken as near-obligatory models in any analysis of story-telling, as of cultural life in general. The concept of story has become a dominant theme in cultural studies, where 'narratives and their interwoven textures are the stuff of life' and 'a theory is a story with a plot whose ending is satisfactory explanation' (Inglis 1993 pp. 244–5). But their analysis is sometimes so tightly directed to the critical dissection of power, consumption and the storied inequalities of race or gender that it screens out other issues.

The concept of 'text' is another frequently recurring image in recent work on story, especially in cultural studies where it is often associated with the semiotic and structuralist analyses of writers such as Saussure and Barthes. Human beings are here essentially 'signifying' animals and the underlying model of communication tends to be a linguistic one, drawing liberally on such metaphors as ('en-' and 'de-') 'coding', 'signification', 'reading' or 'inscribing' (enunciated for example in Hall 1997). These may not be the most effective metaphors for indicating the *telling* and contexted perform-ance of stories.

Criticisms of the limited scope of a cognitively based model of human culture bring us back to some earlier and still continuing perspectives on narrative, predominantly from anthropology and folklore. These suggest that focusing on a narrow concept of 'text' can inhibit a full account of story-telling. Earlier critiques questioned the practice of taking 'the verbal story-text' as *the* unit for analysis (for example in Labov's seminal work, 1972) on the grounds that this drew attention away from the equally consti-tutive aspects of performance, circulation or enactment. Similar queries could be raised about the recent predilection for taking 'text' as the key term for analysing cultural processes. The concept is no doubt broader than some previous usages, but it still turns the spotlight more on somewhat decontextualised cognitive signification (and general political import) than on the kinds of issues that are now increasingly uncovered by scholars working on performance, artistic conventions and the ethnographic set-tings of speaking.[6] My own perspective, as in earlier works, accords more with this latter approach. Although the overview nature of my project here has precluded the kind of detailed study of performances and stylistics practised so successfully by linguistic anthropologists and others writing in the ethnography-of-speaking and performance traditions, I would agree that any analysis of stories should also include some attention to story-*telling* and to questions of context, delivery and active participants.

The implicit tone of many narrative analyses circulating under the 'post-modernist' head is that of demolishing pretension and undermining unwarranted authority-claims. Critical scrutiny of scholars' statements continues, of course, to be pertinent. So too does the inclusion of other voices than those of the scholars or the establishment. But I am more doubtful about the position that since final truth is impossible, there is no point in aspiring to a reasoned detached judgement of the evidence, or about a form of relativism that suggests that every story, every theory, is equally acceptable (issues to be returned to in chapter 7). In this respect criticisms of the postmodern turn in 'literary anthropology' are well taken (e.g. Reyna 1994, Spencer 1989 esp. pp. 159ff.). The more extreme postmodernist positions also run the risk of blurring *any* distinctions between differing types of accounts. All are 'constructed' – true enough perhaps, but we hear less of the actual ways in which they *are* so constructed as narrative. The term 'story' can be just another fashionable kneejerk label unless there is also some explanation of how far and in what sense this notion is really appropriate for examining specific cases.

My own scope is more limited. While my study certainly draws on some aspects of this recent work, it is concerned neither to demonstrate some all-embracing relativist model, nor to classify *all* theories and descriptions of 'reality' equally as stories. Rather it focuses down on certain features of story and applies these to the cluster of accounts that I refer to as the tales of the city – those multiple narratives in our culture formulating the ideas and experiences of urban living. I will be exploring the sense in which these accounts can indeed be analysed as forms of 'story', how they are structured as narrative, and how this can illuminate their nature and their cultural roles.

I would thus take issue with certain current positions or wish to go beyond them. But in a more general sense this volume necessarily builds on both earlier and more recent work on narrative. It draws on the view of story as art-ful communication – a view consonant with traditional literary analysis but no longer confined just to that; on the role of myth as elucidated in anthropology and folklore; on the idea of self-as-narrative that now appears across so many disciplines, most notably in psychology; on the relevance of contexting, performance and process from folklore, sociology and, above all, from anthropology; on structured conventions of plot, style and protagonists from literary, anthropological and narratological studies; and on issues about relativism, the multiplicity of our storied views of 'reality' and the construction of narratives now being debated among postmodern writers and their critics. It also draws on that in one sense outmoded, but in another still vital, anthropological aspiration to a holistic rather than separated view of culture. Here that evinces itself not in the impossible project of covering 'everything' but in the more modest aim of bringing together multiple narrations relative to one key topic in our culture rather than – as so often – treating them separately.

What's in a 'story'?

Against that general background of approaches to narrative, let me briefly sketch my own view of 'story' and its key features.

Understanding the term is in one way easy. 'Story' is no technical concept but a familiar and readily used word in everyday speech, a shared understanding that I will be drawing on. But its very centrality in everyday language also – as so often – carries a wealth of meanings and unspoken assumptions. There is a vast literature on definitions of 'story' or 'narrative', and on the approaches and controversies that relate to these definitions. I will not enter into the details of these debates (handily summed up in Riessman 1993 pp. 17ff.), but for the purposes of this volume I must begin with my own somewhat simple characterisation of what features I consider are significant in 'story' – not so much a definition as an indication of the main areas I will be focusing on in my analysis.

I take 'story' to be essentially a presentation of events or experiences which is *told*, typically through written or spoken words. This brash statement immediately needs further elaboration. The main dimensions to which I will be drawing attention throughout – not exactly definitional criteria, but significant for the view I take of the key properties of story – are: first, a temporal or sequential framework; second, some element of explanation or coherence; third, some potential for generalisability – something of the universal in the particular; and finally the existence of recognised generic conventions, varying for different types of story-telling or tellers, which relate to the expected framework, protagonists and modes of performance/circulation. In the stories presented in this volume I take it not only that most or all of the above will be detectable, though perhaps to different degrees and in differing forms, but that these are also salient features for analysis.

These features broadly recur in one form or another in the now-vast literature on narrative analysis and are not so far, either, from the conventional wisdom about what we mean by 'story' in everyday conversation. Indeed our general understanding of the term 'story' – and certainly mine in this study – emerges from this complex and continuing interplay between our everyday usage and the more theoretical debates of the scholars. However, the particular approach is specific to this study, developed not as a contribution to general issues of definition but merely as the working basis for analysing the stories in this volume.[7]

Each of these features needs further comment.

A series of past tenses depicting events set within some kind of temporal framework is what we normally expect of a 'story'. We readily accept the tales of Adam and Eve, of Cinderella or of an individual's life experiences as stories in that they present a sequence of events (whether 'fictional' or 'true' is not an issue) in contrast to, say, a synchronic description of a landscape or the Sermon on the Mount. Despite some complexities and controversies, this temporal element is a widely accepted view of story in conventional wisdom – the presentation of events taking place in the past.

Temporal framing is not limited just to the literal use of grammatical past tenses however, or to strict chronological sequence in some 'objective' sense. Our main expectation of a story may be its presentation of *past* events, but a narration can also include present and future references, and its sequential element can be deployed in varying ways. And while the events may all in one sense be depicted as in the past, from the standpoint of the story's main timescale they may still be to come (like the then-future sequel in the Garden of Eden narrative, the 'lived happily ever after' closure in many tales, or the 'what happened to the main characters later' ending to some novels). Events are not necessarily presented in exact chronological sequence either, but also through flashbacks and previews, and a story can be cyclical or circumlocutory as well as linear. Some kind of temporal ordering is of the essence, but the route is not always a linear one and can also wander through byways, diversions and circularities.

But a mere listing of past events with no connecting thread does not make a story. We expect something more than just temporal sequence, something to give it an intelligible plot. This 'something more' takes various forms. The story may communicate to audiences in a familiar and thus satisfying framework through recreating one of the widely recognised plots identified by literary analysts and folklorists (notably Propp 1968, also Burke 1945, Lüthi 1987, Paulme 1976, Prince 1989, Scholes and Kellogg 1966). It is more often possible than we might at first imagine to detect the patterns of the hero-tale, the rags-to-riches plot, the growth to maturity, the effects of villainy, or the fall from grace: the Golden Age lost. Or it may take the form of some underlying evaluative theme which – unlike a chronicle merely recounting a series of unrelated events – conveys a unifying moral ordering to listeners sharing this viewpoint. Such elements are matters of degree. They may not appear explicitly nor be equally convincing to all auditors. But some kind of explanatory framework or sense of intelligible causality is part of what we normally assume when we call some account neither just a description nor a chronicle but a story.

A third feature is closely allied to the second, but important enough to be noted separately. This is the element of generalisability that is in one way or another inherent in what we call a story, the sense of the universal somehow embedded in the particular. This feature is even more elusive and relative than the first two. In some stories it does come through explicitly. But in many it is to be found beneath the surface, with the more 'universal' and reflective aspects conveyed not just in verbal text but through the context of narration (whether in written form or live delivery to an audience) and the often-unspoken imagery shared by the listeners or readers. This partly overlaps the second feature, but the prime emphasis here is on shared understandings about the *kinds* of causes that are significant, so that the story can be heard as one example of a more general pattern. Or it may draw on resonating themes or images which for its specific teller and audience communicate something beyond the here and now of contingent events. Awareness of the universal in the particular is not confined to the traditional literary canon but can be sought in all story-telling, spoken no less than written.

Finally, and again partly overlapping with the previous features, there are the recognised generic conventions about content and delivery. To find effective expression and to communicate to an audience, story-telling must build on shared expectations about structure, style, protagonists, mode of distribution and content. It is true that we are increasingly aware that generic conventions can intermix, are seldom cast in concrete and can be manipulated and contested, not just blindly followed (Abrahams 1985a, Bakhtin 1986, Finnegan 1992 pp. 137ff.). But stories worthy of that term are not told without *some* conventions – emergent perhaps rather than fixed – which help to shape their telling and reception.

As will become clear in later chapters our stories of the city come in a variety of genres, overlapping but distinctive enough to manifest their own conventions, fit subjects for the analyst's exploration. Established story forms have their expected roll call of protagonists, for example. These are often more than just actors that appear frequently in quantitative terms; they are 'symbolic types' (as Turner puts it, 1982 p. 74) which give a deeper import to the individual characters portrayed in the tale, chiming in with the understandings of both teller and audience. In the academic urban stories these protagonists are impersonal and not infrequently evil – quickly recognised by their readers even from a brief allusion. In the Utopian tales of building new cities the heroes are different: the developers and their organisations, working in combination with the 'people'. These contrast yet again with the acting and narrating 'I' and the friends and family portrayed – and expected to be portrayed – in the personal narratives.

Conventions about performance and distribution are also among the key differentiating features between different genres. They play an important formative role in the actualisation of the story. For though in this study 'story' is envisaged as primarily presented through *words* (I am mostly excluding narratives in other media such as pictures), nevertheless a story is not just a self-standing verbal text. It communicates through more than just words. Since modes of delivery and circulation are still often overlooked in text-based narrative analyses, their significance is worth particular emphasis. Recent work in literary theory and media studies as well as in performance studies has often looked beyond older models of the autonomous narrative text to the constitutive role of all those involved. Studies of oral story-telling demonstrate the importance not just of the contexts and media through which the story is delivered, but also of *all* the participants in the communicative activity as a whole – readers as well as writers, listeners and bystanders as well as speakers (see for example Bauman 1986 esp. chapter 6, Finnegan 1992 pp. 94ff., Smith 1981 and (for work in media studies) Morley 1993). This provides a backdrop to the perspective of the present analysis, which encompasses not just the texts of stories (the products) but also the processes by which they are formulated and communicated.

This may seem obvious enough for *oral* story-telling. But conventions about the expected modes of delivery and circulation can also be explored for written forms. The genre of academic writing exemplified in the theoretical stories of the city is a case in point. It is easy to overlook the narrative conventions deployed in scholarly story-making, socialised as many of us have been into the idea of academic theory as neutral and 'scientific'. But postmodernist writers have successfully drawn our attention to the way that scholarly accounts are in practice formulated through their accepted poetics – the rhetorical conventions which shape the author's account of findings and conclusions (Clifford and Marcus 1986, echoed by many later writers). Such critiques of academic genres usually confine themselves to style and structure. These are important elements, certainly. But if we take the issues of delivery and performance seriously, other dimensions also deserve consideration. The medium, occasion, mode of presentation, intended or actual audience(s) and their understandings, typical uses, participants in the communication process – all these, and not just the properties of the verbal text, make up the conventions of the genre(s). Taking such aspects into account provides a fuller perspective on our story-telling.

The central point I am making in this opening discussion is the rather obvious one that any form of story-telling has its accepted conventions about structure, style and communication. These may be flexible rather than fixed and perhaps multiple more than singular. Often they are not the subject of self-conscious reflection by either their tellers or their readers/hearers. But we would scarcely label just any unmarked sequence of words as a 'story' or a 'narrative'. Story-telling, that is, is not an automatic or a random form of verbalisation but follows local cultural conventions. These deserve empirical study in actual settings, not just theoretical assertion.

Exploring these narrative conventions and the complex ways the varied tellings interact takes us beyond a set of trivial tales told by a few idiosyncratic individuals and their at first sight minor stylistic attributes. It can also bring us into touch with some of the profounder orders of our culture, expressed as they are through the deeply human activity of story-telling. As W. J. T. Mitchell introduced his classic collection *On Narrative*:

The study of narrative is no longer the province of literary specialists or folklorists borrowing their terms from psychology and linguistics but has now become a positive source of insight for all the branches of human and natural science. The idea of narrative seems . . . to be repossessing its archaic sense as *gnarus* and *gnosis*, a mode of knowledge emerging from action, a knowledge which is embedded not just in the stories we tell our children or to while away our leisure but in the orders by which we live our lives. (Mitchell 1981 pp. ix–x)

2   Abstract tales of cities: the narrative in urban theory

Academic urban theories make up one influential set of stories about the city. They tell of the nature of cities in general and of how these more abstract themes unfold in the specificities of urban experience. The narratives they recount, interacting with the other tales told in later chapters, powerfully shape and reflect the ways we see and experience city life and envisage its development.

In this chapter I am focusing on the main theories in current circulation to illustrate the ways in which they can indeed be regarded as forms of narrative. They comprise the 'classic' models based on nineteenth-century social theory and further developed in the writings of the 'Chicago school', together with those more recently enunciated under the labels of urban ecology, political economy, world system and cultural studies. Since that is only a simplified selection, let me make clear I am not offering a comprehensive account of urban theories, let alone presenting their complexities and variations or fully referencing their many appearances.[1] My aim is to highlight the narrative features of some currently influential theories rather than retell the stories.

The term 'story' may at first sight seem unjustified when used of academic theory. Most of us have been brought up to picture 'theory' as some kind of analytic and abstract meta-formulation, of a higher order than contingent description or passing anecdote; more akin to revealed quasi-oracular truth than characterised by the fictitious or art-ful associations of 'story'. Further, we might reasonably take urban theories as representing a logical rather than a narrative mode of knowledge.

But as explained in the previous chapter, it has become increasingly acceptable to refer to academic theories and interpretations as 'stories' (or as 'tales' or 'narratives' – terms mostly used interchangeably here). Clegg's reference to the 'good stories' told by Marx, Durkheim, Weber and Simmel, for example, prefaces his fuller analysis of the narrative structure of social theories more generally, among them the tales told by the Chicago urban theorists (Clegg 1993 p. 15 and *passim*). Indeed a view of theory as narrative has by now become near-standard terminology for many writers in the

14

social sciences, especially (but not exclusively) those writing in the so-called postmodern and cultural-studies styles. It is less common however to combine this terminology with an explication of the sense in which 'story' can indeed be aptly used of the theories, or to turn the spotlight primarily onto their narrative features.

So in what sense can these urban theories be analysed as 'stories'? This chapter focuses on how far the features of 'story' picked out in the last chapter can indeed be found in our abstract academic theories of urban life.

Temporal ordering and urban theories

Our first narrative feature may at first seem absent from academic urban theory: that is, a temporal framework or set of past tenses. For the overt model of social theory explicated among academics and transmitted to students is commonly still of something timeless, not about unique events but a distilled account that is in some sense applicable to all cases.

But a second look quickly reveals a temporal dimension to most urban theory. Cities are depicted as arriving late in the story of humankind, at least in the form that we now recognise them. As one version of a widely accepted narrative recounts it, 'the coming of the industrial revolution [and] modernity' brought 'a fundamental break with the way human communities were organised in the past . . . [and] created new types of cities' (Kasinitz 1995 p. 1), while in another archaeologists have told of the 'urban revolution' moving us from prehistory to history. Though the details vary, some temporal sequencing is detectable in most of the generalised accounts of the nature of town life. Sometimes the tale tells of major historic stages or leaps between different eras ('modern', 'premodern', 'postmodern'), as in Kasinitz's retelling above. Sometimes it is of gradual changes through time, portrayed through metaphors like 'progress', 'evolution' or 'deterioration'. Sometimes it is through projections into the future as a story started in the past moves towards its completion.

A temporal frame is one dimension in the theories recounted in the well-known 'Chicago school', exemplified on the one side by the ecological writings of Burgess and others, on the other in urban analyses by Wirth and his followers. The classic social theories of the nineteenth century too are essentially rooted in stories about change over time. These are the grand narratives told out in the Marxian evolutionary tales or implied through Durkheim's contrasting stages of mechanical and organic solidarity or Tönnies' *Gemeinschaft* as against *Gesellschaft*. These influential theories, formulated alongside the experiences of industrialisation and urbanisation, represent a major narrative resource through which social scientists provide shape and explanation for these historical processes.

These great narratives underlie the classic urban stories which, in their turn, still mould many contemporary analyses. Their central concepts do not perhaps *necessitate* a predetermined sequence over time. Nevertheless their basic plots unquestionably invoke a temporal perspective. In fact it is in part due to their temporal ordering that the stories are ultimately convincing and satisfying for their tellers and hearers. The natural order of events, runs the tale, is for 'community' to come before 'association', for complex forms of integration to follow the simpler arrangements, for feudalism to be the stage before capitalism, tradition to precede modernity, the structured foundations of social bonding to be superseded by fragmentation. And if 'community', say, or close-knit urban 'villages' still remain within a town, the story weaves these in as survivals persisting from an earlier stage of the plot. The evolutionary paradigms of the nineteenth century – another hero tale (Landau 1991) – still provide an impelling framework for our ideas about urban life and about the nature of society. In these classic tales the essential plot, then and now, is of historic change.

More recently developed theories might seem less likely to have a chronological frame. But here too, if less prominently, their expression assumes a temporal setting.

This is partly due to the continuing influence of the classic formulations, even in at first sight highly different approaches. The evocative plot of community superseded by alienation, rural by urban, tradition by modernity, still moves both tellers and listeners. Newer theoretical approaches sometimes construct their own chronological sequences. The urban ecology stories portray waves of ecological processes over time. Others tell variously of older forms of local urban neighbourhoods being replaced by postmodern transitional space (Zukin 1992), or of the colourful changes brought by the new 'postmodern era' (Bird *et al.* 1993, Watson and Gibson 1995). There is the tale too of the old order fracturing as new forms of information obliterate 'the sense of collective memory and tradition of the locality' (Featherstone 1993 p. 177).

One appeal of the many political economy analyses again lies in their temporal framing. Dramatic narratives portray the development of urban forms as both result and condition of the advent of the capitalist mode of production, surplus and the class struggle (for example Castells 1977, 1983), or narrate the struggles and changes in which cities play their part over time. Alternatively they develop variant tellings of the basic plot to explain how 'the narrative structure predicted in the classic texts of Marx had not occurred' (Clegg 1993 pp. 16ff.). Cultural geographers tell of the new geometries of social power now arising from the unequal reorganisation of global economic space, or extend the timespan by portraying the 'postmodern' condition replacing the earlier phases of modernity (Massey 1993, 1995, Harvey 1988, 1989).

Behind the more specific episodes, an underlying plot often gives the Marxian-rooted tales a longer temporal span. This is the shadowy but powerful storyline of an earlier and happier stage in human affairs before the spread of international capitalism and its dire effects in modern towns – the prelude to the rest of the tale. That lost era is seldom explicitly recounted, but the tales hint at the local autonomy of the past with its greater freedom from the world-wide economic forces constraining us today. The tale of a transition from older and more natural freedoms to the imprisonment and oppressions of the present is the more effective for its evocation of the evolutionary narratives which quietly lie in the background. It draws too on those well-known plots which have moved people through the ages: battles between contending protagonists, or the move from fortune to misfortune.

Temporal themes also appear in the partly overlapping 'world-system' approaches, with their portrayal of the 'global' context within which local experience must be analysed. Here too the implied background to the story is of earlier rural freedom being undermined as the processes of urbanisation and colonialism and, more recently, of accelerating globalisation draw urban centres into becoming both cause and effect of world-wide economic–political trends. A few narratives foretell a possible happy ending. Mostly they are bleaker. The bad fairy of political and economic exploitation triumphs in one or other of her various garbs, often as 'capitalism' or as multinational companies with their scope 'to roam the globe' (Massey 1995 p. 201).

Other versions of the academic urban stories return to the plot of sequential eras in social development. Most build on ideas of 'modernity' (with its 'pre-' and 'post-' stages) to evoke fables of the past, present and future, setting current situations within a longer temporal perspective. Influential analyses of the 'crisis of identity' and 'decentring of the self' in the present era (Sennett 1973, Lasch 1984, Hall 1992), 'the old order fracturing' (Chambers 1993), or 'the fragmenting tendencies of modern institutions' (Giddens 1991 p. 186) are episodes in the story of successive stages of human history and their outcomes in the city.

There are also the tales about transcending space and the 'new information age', told by writers such as Meyrowitz (1985), or Harvey's accounts of 'the informational city' (1989). Some of these retell the pessimistic stories.

They recount the erosion of earlier locally based urbanism by global markets, transitional space or 'postmodern urban landscapes' (Zukin 1992). Others lead towards a happier ending. In the now-vanishing 'modern' era, goes the tale, people were constrained by locality, congregating perforce in industrialised urban settlements to satisfy their need for physical contiguity. But in the knowledge-based era now dawning, new technology releases them from these local bonds. The age of the 'information city' will replace the industrial city – if indeed, in that Utopian stage, urban settlements are needed at all. The story turns ultimately on the familiar cyclical plot of mankind retracing its steps back to that older freer state destroyed by the cruel incoming forces of industrialisation and urbanisation – the classic tale retold. The same narrated sequence unwinds: from premodern to modern-industrial, and, finally, to the postmodern Information Age.

The currently influential stories of urban theory thus do turn out in one way or another to manifest that basic element of story-telling: the presentation, implied or explicit, of temporal sequence. The temporal frame, furthermore, is continually brought to our attention through the clear before-and-after referencing of constantly used terms like 'postmodern', 'postcolonial' or 'postindustrial'. In their temporal dimension at least, the abstract theories can indeed be treated as 'stories'.

Plot and coherence in the academic tales

The urban theories also embody our second story-telling feature, for they are always expected to convey some element of explanation, something more than a mere chronicle of unordered events. In so doing, their tellings surprisingly often recall basic narrative plots familiar from other contexts.

Temporal structure itself sometimes provides the coherence. *Post hoc* is readily acceptable as *propter hoc* when tellers and audiences can relax into the seemingly logical and well-ordered sequence of a familiar plot. The motivating causes invoked by urban narratives also represent shared understandings about how such stories should unfold. Heroic (or devilish) tales of modernity, of progress, capitalism or technological development portray, it seems, precisely the kinds of events and sequences that can be expected to happen, carrying their own conviction.

The plots exemplify widespread narrative themes. Some retell the transition from misery to happiness either in particular circumstances – like the triumphs of shanty-dwellers transforming their surroundings – or in more wide-ranging terms. Abstract social theories recounting the move upwards from the primitive state of nature into the civilised life of modernity are buttressed further through tales based in the 'Whig theory of history', the notion of 'progress', the hero-story of evolution or the Information-Age tale's teleological invocation of the happy future. Here we have – almost literally – a tale of rags to riches.

In most urban theories, however, the plot remarkably often leads towards an unhappy rather than happy conclusion – from good to bad fortune. It depicts the troubles on the way and their continuance into the present. Occasionally it concludes on a high note, recounting how the freedom and civilisation brought by urban life vanquishes the earlier tyranny of tribal and communal tradition. More often it tells of the fall, depicting the original free state of nature yielding to new oppressions of alienation and the constrictions of town living, or, as Harvey ends his tale, to the 'plainly sick and troubled' state of present capitalism (1989 p. 278). The rags-to-riches plot sometimes seeps through in these harsher tales, but only as lament for the rags in the midst of guilt-laden riches.

Such plots are intelligible to both tellers and audiences: familiar in our own culture and perhaps resonating more widely too. They also go with a moral ordering, that telling device for conveying a shared sense of coherence. This partly works through the emotive and evaluative overtones of the key terms: 'modernisation', 'community', 'progress', 'exploitation', 'alienation'. In a sense practically all urban theories are in one way or another about the struggle of good and evil. The stories' moral conclusions on the actual result of that battle vary of course. As Flanagan points out, 'Where ecologists speculate that the changes simply indicate the progression of the metropolitan form through a similar sequence of stages along the path to greater functional efficiency, political economy focuses attention on the negative consequences and social costs' (1993 p. 77). Similarly the happy conclusion in stories of the liberalising role of cities ('city air makes free') contrasts with the pessimistic narrations of the artificiality, alienation or oppressions of city life. The latter are in the majority, for urban theorists mostly have bleak and anti-urban tales to tell. The use of these recognised evaluative endings, whether happy or, as more often, sad, gives each story a potent source of coherence, of moving towards an end which is often both foreordained and value-drenched.

The theoretical accounts often convey an extra impression of depth and conviction by evoking some deeply entrenched symbolic classifications. These are the powerful oppositions of community/association, nature/culture, rural community/artificial town, belonging opposed to alienation, tradition versus industrialisation and modernity, communal unchanging continuities set against the rupture of urbanisation. These themes still come through in theoretical stories about urban life, not just in the 'classic' theories but also in tales told in political economy, world-systems and cultural studies contexts.

Despite the rise and fall of differing approaches in urban theory, these familiar binary oppositions and their associated romanticism still have a remarkable influence (see Flanagan 1993 pp. 4, 13ff., 149–50; Savage and Warde 1993 p. 33 and Chapter 2). The overall plot, not always narrated explicitly but surprisingly often detectable in the background, is a retelling of that far-reaching Golden Age myth: of the prior state of rural and communal nature destroyed by the artificial culture of the town.

The universal in the particular

The urban theories recounted by academics also imply something of the universal – a third feature of story-telling. They are not without some concrete referents, of course. Indeed such tales are expected to be transferable, at least in principle, into stories about particularities, providing templates through which the stories of specific events or situations can be told and interpreted. But the academics' tales, far more than other story-telling genres, are explicitly concerned with the general, with somehow highlighting the universal even when analysing the particular. This indeed is almost the definition of academic theories: intellectual, crystallised statements specifically formulated as abstract representations and carrying some absolute applicability which transcends the merely contingent. It is the accepted role of those recognised as intellectuals in our culture – and above all of card-carrying academics – to tell us that kind of story.

The degree of abstraction varies. Some academic stories move closer to the unique end of the continuum – though go too far in that direction and they may be chided as not proper 'theories' at all (Flanagan 1993 p. 156). But most utilise a vocabulary of abstract concepts. Even the concrete referents are often generalised: 'the modern city', 'the urban environment', 'the community'. And when references to specifics *are* made (groups, localities, individuals), these come through as somehow less real than the abstract figures which transcend them. Individual human actors may be alluded to but are usually off-stage.

The same is true of the protagonists in academic stories – those symbolic or emblematic types that give depth to otherwise apparently particularistic tales. In keeping with the stories' typical plots and style the dramatis personae are usually impersonal powers and abstractions. They more often embody the forces of evil than of hope. These protagonists set the plot in motion, sometimes controlling the action, sometimes working in alliance or struggle with others. They link to the moral dramas depicted in the tale, above all the resounding battles between good and evil, fortune and misfortune.

It is these abstractions, not human personalities, that drive the action or experience its consequences. Personal agents are brought into the scene in a few theoretical stories and there are some exceptions to the general trends (notably Cohen and Fukui 1993, also parts of Hannerz 1980, Pahl 1970a, b, 1995, Sanjek 1990). But even in accounts by tellers who like Giddens (1984) aspire to veer away from more deterministic perspectives, people enter more as general constructs than as individual persons. The dramatis personae are figures like 'the consumer', 'the worker', 'the commuter', 'member of the elite', 'urban man', 'the metropolitan type', or are presented as representatives of class, ethnic, religious or gender categories. In so far as individuals appear at all, their role is more often as victims, not heroes. The stories bring forward instead those evocative heroes and anti-heroes of 'industrialisation', 'urbanisation', 'economic forces', 'urban environment', 'modernity' or 'globalisation'; of 'resistance', 'consumption' and 'power'; or, most menacing of all, the witch figure of 'international capitalism'. There is also 'progress', that two-faced fairy, and the insubstantial and ambiguous trickster called 'postmodernity'. Central to many of the stories, and as we shall see a recurrent theme in urban tales, is that constantly hovering but ever-vanishing figure of the darling love, long lost but in some stories found again – 'community'.

Conventions of academic story-telling

For their effective expression and communication these academic tales must draw on recognised patterns of form, context and delivery. Those who tell and those who hear or read them have expectations about how they should be circulated, expectations which must by and large be met for the tales to count as the specific genre of academic theory. It is a matter not just of stories, but of story-telling.

As with other narrative forms in active circulation, the generic boundaries are not permanently fixed. New variants and crossovers arise, as do challenges to all or any of the conventional expectations. But the genre is clearly enough recognised for such challenges to make sense. Telling this genre of tale has conventions which have to be learned, arts into which new participants must be inducted.

Many of these generic features will be evident from the earlier discussion. It will be no surprise, for example, that the verbal style is characterised by a high proportion of abstract and general words. There is no definitive list of terms, for the genre is not a closed one, but some recur often enough to serve as clear generic signals. Indeed one of the tasks of the acolyte social theorist is to learn to present accounts which deploy key words like 'urbanism', 'identity', 'alienation', 'ecology', 'sociation', 'urbanisation', 'suburbanisation', 'gentrification' or 'counter-urbanisation'. Explicit generalisability is expected, or, at the least, allusions through which participants can evoke the larger stories which they jointly share. For this reason retellings based on the recurrent plots are welcomed and acclaimed in academic story-telling. One notable stylistic element is the reference to tradition: story-tellers invoke the authority of previous tellers in the same genre, whether in agreement or rebuttal of specific episodes in their narrations.

As for their presentation, academic story-telling typically uses words rather than pictorial, auditory or material forms (though with some limited use of diagrams). Print, typescript and written manuscript are the expected media. Spoken presentation based on a notional prior or ultimate written form is sometimes acceptable, particularly within the rituals of university lecturing or academic conferencing. But *the* prototypical story-telling channel is assumed to be an academic book or an article in a publication classified as 'learned'. A somewhat ponderous style is also expected. Ken Plummer neatly characterises academic story-telling as 'almost ugly in its stark, clichéd, monotone manner'. He continues, 'much sociology . . . tells the dullest stories in the most dreary ways – and often deliberately so, for this is the mantle of scientific story telling: it is supposed to be dull' (Plummer 1995 p. 171; see also Becker 1986 esp. pp. 40ff.).

There are also recognised conventions about context and audience. Academic urban stories are typically directed to initiated or initiand members of the specialist academic in-group, communicated in the appropriate style and atmosphere. Group identity is partly defined through its members' shared participation in the due dissemination of these tales. The participants are academic peers, students within a higher education context and potential publishers, editors or reviewers – the other actual and would-be initiates.

The uses of these academic tales are manifold. As with other story-telling genres, their tellers can recount the tales to serve such diverse purposes as to attack others, show off, advance group or individual interests, teach, mock, bore, earn their salary, fulfil the required rituals, maintain continuity, impress interviewers, push a political viewpoint, examine, woo, establish themselves as members of an elite – and a host of other uses. The ideal purposes of particular genres as overtly represented by their tellers seldom permanently constrain human ingenuity.

Among the recurrent and typical roles of the genre, however, are also those of providing a vehicle through which participants can and do formulate an understanding of the human condition, not least the urban human condition. Despite their abstract garb, rehearsing these stories is not a purely cognitive matter, for they are imbued with shared emotive and evaluative associations. As with the myths of other cultures, they function as sanction and justification for the current order as well as a launching ground for counter-versions. By telling and retelling versions of the immensely powerful plot rooted in long-enduring notions of evolution and romanticism, they shape their participants' understanding and experience of what it means to live in cities, and thus, ultimately, of themselves and their condition.

Unpacking the narrative features of urban theories and classifying them as stories may seem irreverent, even anti-intellectual! It is true that I share the view that the dogmatic and elitist style in which some academic theories have been presented can be challenged, and that none need be considered as *the* revealed truth about the world, urban or otherwise. This position is nothing new, indeed it is familiar in social scientific literature. My point, however, is the more neutral one that we can apply narrative analysis to the abstract theoretical tales told by academics in just the same way that we can – and do – to those by other tellers. This can illuminate both their conventional form and their hold on us, revealing how they play on accepted plots and themes. Taking an outsider's view on them, as it were, we can see them neither as merely 'natural' phenomena nor as conclusions based on essentially rational or empirical scrutiny. Rather, they are created, disseminated and understood by people drawing on recognised conventions about genre, theme and plot. And far from such an analysis undermining their significance it in fact brings out the profound influence of long-enduring plots and imagery in formulating our thinking and actions. The mythic symbolism communicated through the continual telling and retelling of these stories is neither an accidental nor an incidental dimension of our culture.

3   Storying a concrete city: cows, gardens and other urban tales

The tales of the last chapter are not the only stories we tell about cities nor the only voices we listen to. They are influential ones, certainly. But it would be a narrow view of our storied culture which looked for our tales of the city *only* in abstract narrations by the accredited intellectuals.

To move to other stories of the city current in our culture we have to anchor them in a specific urban locality. It is important to consider these more concrete tales, for it is only in a local setting that their role in formulating lived urban experience can be understood. So the next step is to turn to a set of stories told in the urban framework of a specific English town.

Our example is that of Milton Keynes. This is the so-called 'new city' in Buckinghamshire in southern-central England that was planned in the late 1960s and had by the mid-1990s grown to a population of around 150,000. Partly grafted onto older settlements, partly built on green fields in the north Buckinghamshire countryside, it has attracted a great deal of national publicity, both favourable and harsh. So much must suffice as a description for the moment – for as will become clear, even that much already picks on some more than others of the many themes in the town's tales. More of the city and its people will emerge as its varying stories are told in this and the following chapters.

So what of the stories of this particular town? Some themes of the academic tales will reappear, if in more concrete form. But there also prove to be local narratives whose plots and viewpoints sometimes contrast sharply with the theorists' tales. There is, first, the planners' story, interesting among other reasons for the background it gives to the building of Milton Keynes. There are the 'garden city' and Utopian stories, partly overlapping and partly diverging from the planners' version. And then there is the central role in the mythology of Milton Keynes played by the infamous 'concrete cows' – among external commentators *the* dominant image of the new city – and the stories that turn a rather different light on these famous concrete sculptures.

This chapter recounts these stories and comments on their narrative features and wider associations. Unlike the theorists' tales of the last chapter, these locally anchored stories will be unfamiliar to many readers. They are thus presented at greater length, sometimes with extensive quotation from their tellers' own words.

The planners' tale: a story of destiny fulfilled

Our intention is that the Plan shall lay the foundation upon which an organic process of development will grow and become a living reality as the people who come after us plan and build for the future . . . Our purpose is . . . in the end, to build a good city. (Lord Campbell, first Chairman of Milton Keynes Development Corporation, in Foreword to *The Plan for Milton Keynes* 1970 pp. xi, xiii)

For many people *the* story of Milton Keynes is that of its planners, in the wide sense of that term which includes architects, administrators and builders. To put it more concretely, it is the story of the Milton Keynes Development Corporation. This story starts in 1967 with the plan for a new city in north Buckinghamshire for London's overspill, and the appointment of a Development Corporation to oversee it. During the next twenty-five years the Corporation superintended the largest urban development project undertaken in the United Kingdom, and by 1992 had 'substantially completed the task' (MKDC 1992a p. 35), having established a city with a population of 150,000 and still growing. The development was complex and involved many agencies, but the basic story is told as a simple and glorious one. It has a definitive start, successful conclusion and accepted lead player in the action – MKDC, the Milton Keynes Development Corporation.

The tale can be told in the words of representatives of MKDC itself. They are quoted at length for they give a succinct account not only of the planners' story itself but also of many of the city's structural features, providing some context for the alternative stories which follow.

Among the many essentially similar versions of the tale here are, first, some extracts from MKDC *Press Briefing Papers* issued in 1990. These recount the start of the story and the formation of the guiding 'Master Plan'.

In January 1967, the then Minister for Housing and Local Government, Mr Richard Crossman, designated under the New Towns Act 22,000 acres (9,000 hectares) to include Bletchley, Stony Stratford, and Wolverton, as a site for the new city.

He decided it should be called Milton Keynes, the name of one of the 13 small villages within the Designated Area.

In March 1967 Milton Keynes Development Corporation was established, its brief being to secure the laying out and development of the new city . . . In December 1967, the planning consultants selected by the Development Corporation, together with their own co-consultants, began their task by preparing the Master Plan for the new city.

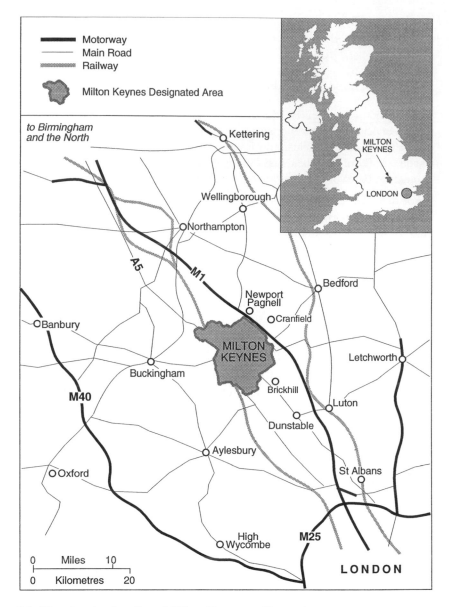

3.1 Map showing location of Milton Keynes and its environs

During 1968 they prepared an Interim Report, in close collaboration with the Corporation, BCC [Bucks County Council], the local authorities in the area and central government. This was published in February 1969 and formed the basis for further work by the consultants on the Plan for Milton Keynes.

The new city of Milton Keynes was to provide initially houses and jobs for a total of 250,000 people by the 1990s. Though the planning of the new city began in the late 1960s, it was crucial that Milton Keynes should provide the kind of environment people would both want and need when it reached maturity more than 20 years hence.

Thus Milton Keynes was conceived and born into an age when the fabric of society and its institutions were set to face considerable change and review. The new city was to meet those changes with unprecedented success.

The tale dwells on the creation of the great 'Master Plan' which was to play such a key role in the development of the city:

When the planning process for the new city began, Milton Keynes Development Corporation talked to those concerned with all aspects of modern life, both locally and nationally . . . For the first time in the building of a major new urban area, planners looked not only at physical and economic development but at social and community development as well.

As the consultation process proceeded . . . the Corporation identified six inter-related goals still as relevant today, as the city enters a new phase of development, as they were when it was in its infancy.

These goals are:

- Opportunity and freedom of choice
- Easy movement and access, good communications
- Balance and variety
- An attractive city
- Public awareness and participation
- Efficient and imaginative use of resources.

(MKDC 1990, 2, pp. 2–3; 3, p. 1)

These six 'goals' are prominent throughout the planners' story. From the original Master Plan in 1970 to the retrospective *Milton Keynes Planning Manual* prepared in 1992 as a record of MKDC's achievements, and in near-identical words, they are ritually recited across the years as the mythical charter at the heart of the unfolding story.

There were differing interpretations of these goals over the years but also some striking consistency in the basic narration. In contrast to the single-class image of earlier new towns, the culmination of the planners' story was to be a 'balanced' population, both over the city as a whole and within each new estate. From the start 'the market' was depicted as one key actor, the ultimate goal being a mix of rented and owner-occupied housing. The plan laid down the road system to divide the city into its 'grid squares', providing for the interspersing of employment, residential and activity areas rather than the concentration of other cities. Similarly the city was to be multi-centred, though with a special 'focus' on Central Milton Keynes. Finally it was planned as a low-density settlement in a landscaped attractive environment.

The Development Corporation account went on to elaborate this sixfold charter from the perspective of 1990, looking both back and forward:

1. Opportunity and freedom of choice
The city should offer, both to its newcomers and existing residents, the greatest possible range of opportunities in all areas of life, such as education, housing, employment and leisure. For instance: there should be housing across a wide range of types, price, size and character, for sale and for rent; journeys should be equally convenient in all directions from every home; bus stops, schools, shops, pubs and sometimes local employment areas should be grouped at the edge of residential areas bounded by main roads so that each family should have a local centre within walking distance. As a consequence to the provision of freedom of choice, the Corporation proposed that extensive information services be established so that people in the city were kept fully informed of the choices open to them.

2. Easy movement and access, good communications
An early decision was that there should be a high degree of accessibility between all the areas and activities which constitute a city – health, education, industry, recreation etc. Milton Keynes was to be multi-centred, with land use dispersed evenly throughout the city, but with a strong focus in Central Milton Keynes for certain citywide and sub-regional facilities, and for commercial office development, thus avoiding peak-time 'pressure points' common in older, 'radial' type cities. To this end, a grid system of roads was proposed, which should combine good general accessibility with flexibility to allow for growth and change. The system should then provide a city of grid squares, with all intersections at ground level, approximately one kilometre apart. The plan stipulated the need for free and safe movement for pedestrians and cyclists, and on the public transport side, that buses should run at frequent intervals with stops within easy walking distance. . . . The Corporation attached . . . great importance to good communications both within and outside the city, whether by road or rail, or by use of telecommunications and post services.

3. Balance and variety
Milton Keynes was to be a city with a wide range of age, social and racial groups . . . an attractive place in which to live and work for people with a wide range of incomes . . . no large scale segregation of kinds of people e.g. a west end for the rich,

an east end for the poor. There should be a general distribution of housing types across the city, although the Plan recognised that the mix of housing types, for social and practical reasons, could not be taken beyond a reasonable point. It was crucial to the city's success that the existing communities in the north and south of the city should be integrated with the newcomers, so the first phase of development was to concentrate on drawing these two together to give them a common meeting point in the new city's geographical centre . . .

4. An attractive city

Set in undulating North Buckinghamshire countryside and blessed with two rivers, a canal, streams and a cluster of small villages brought together by a network of old lanes and historic highways, the Designated Area provided a rich foundation on which to build a city to which people would respond with pleasure. The Corporation aimed to provide a multi-centred city – so that existing centres like Bletchley, Stony Stratford and Wolverton did not lose their identity – which was open, mobile and accessible, with a central area planned to give richness and variety with none of the noise, pollution, traffic congestion and inconvenience common in older cities and towns. The main road system should be attractively landscaped to present various changes of scene while off the main roads local character should be maintained by sympathetic blending of the new with the old.

5. Public awareness and participation

The Corporation recognised that a city planned to accommodate change should encourage the citizen to understand the changes and to be able to voice an opinion at all times. To this end, MKDC provided then, and still does today, information through a wide range of channels, so that citizens may take full advantage of this opportunity . . .

6. Efficient and imaginative use of resources

The Corporation, responsible for ensuring that all resources available to it were used effectively and efficiently, should enable investment by all other public bodies, and from private sources, to contribute towards the city's growth in the most economic way . . .

Though laid down nearly 20 years ago, these six goals have lost none of their relevance, priority or sense . . . Their fulfilment is partially completed and remains the driving force of the Corporation's work. (MKDC 1990, 3, pp. 2–5)

In these tales of the city's growth, the MKDC's Master Plan is presented not as a rigid blueprint but as a flexible process adaptable to changing needs and conditions. It was to 'evolve continuously during the life of the Corporation, in the light of experience and in response to changes in government policy and the economic climate' (MKDC 1992b p. 187). Nevertheless, in the planners' tale it was this plan that foreordained the structure of the city, its form for the future.

The tale of this destiny-laden plan is told in many MKDC publications. A glossy booklet, *The Planning of Milton Keynes* (MKDC 1992a), produced

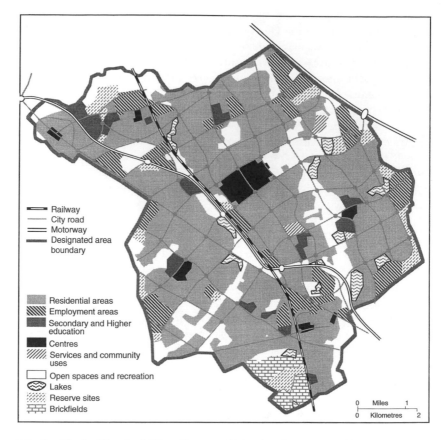

3.2 The Master Plan for Milton Keynes, 1970. The plan prepared by the Milton Keynes Development Corporation which guided the building of the city (used by courtesy of the Commission for the New Towns, adapted by John Hunt from the original colour version in Fig. 1.4 of the Milton Keynes Development Corporation's *The Milton Keynes Planning Manual* (1992))

shortly before the Corporation came to its end, retells the tale for a wider audience. It recounts the 'structuring principles' that achieved the six sanctified goals and defined 'the character of the city':

A 'grid' pattern of main roads serving dispersed land uses
The dispersal of homes and jobs allowed for an even distribution of traffic, and the road system was designed to avoid the rush hour congestion associated with towns with a radial road system . . . Through traffic could be kept out of the 'gridsquares' formed by the city roads.

A city centre
Designation of Central Milton Keynes (CMK) was an exception to the general principle of dispersed land uses. Located close to the geographical centre of the city, CMK would contain a substantial shopping centre, cultural and leisure activities, housing and offices to serve the population of the new city and the surrounding area . . .

Linear parks
A system of linear parks was based on the valleys of rivers and streams. The linear parks were to be a major structuring element.

Overlapping catchments
Homes were not to be grouped as discrete, inward looking neighbourhood units, but were to be part of overlapping catchment areas, according to the different requirements of each household. Thus no area would be exclusive or self contained and maximum choice would be available to residents.

Activity centres
Local facilities, including shops, pubs, schools and bus stops, were grouped at 'activity centres', located where main pedestrian routes crossed the mid-points of each length of city road so that they were easy for residents to reach by car or on foot. This principle has been extended subsequently so that local roads as well as pedestrian routes often connect adjacent gridsquares through grade-separated crossings providing access to local centres from both sides.

Pedestrian routes segregated from city roads
A safe and convenient movement system for pedestrians was a fundamental requirement . . . The needs of cyclists, as well as pedestrians, were taken into account by making the continuous system of 'redways' wide enough to be shared by both.

Incorporation of existing settlements
The Master Plan aimed to incorporate existing towns and villages into the new city, whilst seeking to maintain their individual identity as far as possible. The role of the existing towns has been strengthened and all thirteen villages within the Designated Area have undergone some enlargement including some infill development where appropriate . . .

The character of the city
Milton Keynes was to be a low density city in a predominantly green setting. There were to be no buildings higher than three storeys except in CMK where up to six storeys might be acceptable.

The Master Plan emphasised, however, that the goal of variety and choice would only be met if, within the low density as a whole, there were some areas with a more urban character. (MKDC 1992a pp. 7–8)

The storyline is strong and confident: 'the structure of the city as built incorporates all the basic elements of the Master Plan' (MKDC 1992b p. 20). It tells of the happy ending as the leadership of MKDC brings the city to the fulfilment of its pre-ordered destiny.

That gives the essential planners' story. There are also more complex versions, with further elaborations on the pre-Plan birth pangs, the turnings over time, the internal politics or the tribulations on the journey toward the successful conclusion. Additional episodes were recounted in public MKDC documents at the time. Others became part of the story later as further accounts of Milton Keynes' development were published by both MKDC and others.

This is not the place to chronicle the detailed course of events or to trace the arguments and modifications in policy (for an informative overview see Bendixson and Platt 1992). However, the evolving story was not without controversy, and a brief look at some of its twists and turns can put both this and other stories in perspective.

The 'multi-centred' ideal proved elusive. Official accounts retained the 'multi-centred' vocabulary, but the 'focus' on Central Milton Keynes turned into its acceptance as *the* city centre – not that that stopped people complaining about its deficiencies. Many residents felt that the 'existing communities' of Bletchley, Wolverton and Stony Stratford, about whose continuing identity much was said in the original plan, were left out in the cold. Transport proved contentious too, with heated debate at the start and continual complaints since. Early mono-rail proposals were rejected in favour of a combined pedestrian, bicycle, private car and public bus system. Many praised the city's 'redways' for walkers and cyclists, but dissatisfaction gathered about their upkeep and limitations. And while car drivers flourished, the bus system drew especially vigorous criticism from residents (perhaps tacitly accepted by the downplaying of 'good communications' in recent versions of the story – MKDC 1992a, 1992b).

Changing circumstances influenced the detailed unfolding of the plot. The target of 200,000 population by the 1990s was reduced, due partly to falling household size, partly to external political and economic pressures. The recession reduced employment, left office blocks vacant and slowed planned developments. Governmental policies in the 1980s and early 1990s affected the balance between rented and owned housing, and forced a reduction in public controls, increasing privatisation and the sale of city assets; the central shopping complex was sold to a Japanese company in 1989. In 1992 MKDC was wound up and its responsibilities divided among other agencies.

Other elaborations of the story portray the tribulations as well as benefits encountered by incomers to the new city. An MKDC booklet, for example, circulated for both local and external reading in 1975, tells of 300 families moving into Milton Keynes per month – success for the Plan – but also of the difficulties they faced: 'mud, a minimum of amenities in the early days, and inadequate public transport' (MKDC 1975 p. 2). There were plans in place to meet such problems, continued the account, amenities being expanded, a Community House set aside as an initial meeting place, community workers helping new arrivals, 'Dial-a-bus' service in some areas and temporary corner shops. But there was another unforeseen trial for newcomers:

'The financial stress can be considerable' says the Rev. John Dean, a Methodist minister, whose parish includes several new developments. 'Many people have just not been educated into coping with the problems facing them. They take on too much in trying to make a nice home' . . . There is a great temptation to try to rival the showhouse, which can cause financial problems as can the running expenses of the house. For instance those who are used to paying for their gas and electricity on a coin meter, can discover that the arrival of a large quarterly bill can come as a nasty shock. (MKDC 1975 pp. 4–5; for other accounts see Kitchen 1974, 1975)

Despite these more complicated versions, the basic plot was straightforward: a success story that started off with the designation of the new city area and the MKDC's formation in 1967, continued through the trials and successes of the intervening period, and reached its happy fulfilment many years later. The ending was not fully closed. But it was a conclusion of a sort, recognised in the twenty-fifth anniversary in 1992 as the city having reached 'maturity'. The account by MKDC's partial successor, the Commission for New Towns, eulogised the triumphant conclusion: 'The planning and development of Milton Keynes and the quality and character of the environment created have all been exceptional. It is a major success in British planning' (Llewelyn-Davies *et al.* 1992 p. 67).

The tale manifests the various characteristics we expect of story-telling. It has, first, a clear temporal frame, with a known date for its start and – if less precisely stated – for its end. It has a teleological flavour too. For as well as narrating the successive implementations of the plan through a series of past tenses, it casts the eye forward from the first formulation of the Master Plan, the prophetic pronouncement that already held the seeds of the future.

It also has a coherent and persuasive plot. There is beginning, middle and (relatively completed) end, presented in terms which make sense not only to the tellers but also to those other colleagues, agencies, patrons, potential incomers and Milton Keynes residents to whom it is directed. It tells an uplifting tale of the exploits of planners and administrators, of the 'Master Plan', of the new 'city' and its 'citizens', and of its business initiatives and innovations – a story of destiny fulfilled. The underlying evaluations add to the tale's persuasiveness through emotive words like 'community', 'choice', 'an attractive city', 'quality of life', 'participation' and the development of 'a good city' (Lord Campbell in MKDC 1970 p. xiii).

The Development Corporation is unquestionably the story's glorious hero. The 1992 *Planning Manual*, produced to record its achievements, states uncompromisingly:

Since 1967, Milton Keynes Development Corporation has had responsibility for all aspects of the planning and development of the city. Many other agencies have been involved but the Corporation's role as landowner, planning authority and developer has been central to the enterprise. (MKDC 1992b p. 9)

The tale shows MKDC as cooperating with other parties and processes. And of course it was not a monolithic entity but in practice contained many differing interests, from members of the Board to outside architects and advisers or the many administrators and other employees associated with it. Nevertheless, in the story as a whole, MKDC's heroic role is clear – the central character, wielding its weapon of 'the Plan' and making the destiny come true.

Another player sometimes lurks behind the scenes, aspiring to a share in the lead role: 'the people' or 'the citizens' of Milton Keynes. Even before the full plan is enunciated, the prelude foreshadows this, for 'the final form of the city should be an expression of its people's wishes, hopes and tastes, and it is a first principle in our planning to make this possible' (*Interim Report*, Llewelyn-Davies *et al.* 1968 p. 13). Lord Campbell identifies those same actors in his foreword to the Master Plan. 'We want the citizens of the new city to be involved actively in its creation', he writes, adding that the translation of the plan into homes and jobs and leisure will be 'a continuing process of research and consultation between the Corporation and the citizens of Milton Keynes' (MKDC 1970 p. xi).

The story thus includes the Plan's responsiveness to the city's people who are joined in the action. Two of the six sacrosanct goals are linked to encouraging both newcomers and existing residents 'to take part in the development of the city' (MKDC 1970 p. 17). 'Master-planning by consultation' was expressed as 'the special hallmark of the new Milton Keynes' (Board minutes, Bendixson and Platt 1992 p. 37). Similar aims are expressed for MKDC's information documents and 'Household surveys'.

Though not explicitly featuring in all versions, the 'people' and their changing needs and wishes thus also play a role in many tellings.

Other protagonists enter the story as well. Though less prominent than
MKDC, the journey is also peopled by architects and consultants, the
government, Borough of Milton Keynes, Buckinghamshire County Council,
local and national interest groups, investors and sponsors. More impersonal
agencies also sometimes assist or hinder, like 'the economic climate', 'social
change' and 'the market'.

MKDC is sometimes portrayed as invoking the aid of more shadowy
bodies still. Hidden natural forces figure in some stories, working alongside
the planners to bring cities or communities into being. Thus the Master Plan
seeks 'to anticipate the forces which create cities and facilitate their healthy
development' (MKDC 1992b p. 17). Similarly, 'stable communities' can be
accelerated through MKDC's neighbourhood development procedures but
otherwise take 'a minimum of 10–20 years, left to natural forces' (MKDC
1988 p. 3). Lord Campbell contrasts Milton Keynes with those 'other cities
of this size [that] had grown over generations and centuries' (MKDC 1975
p. 8), going on:

I always have this acute consciousness that one is . . . simply the yeast starting a
process. I always believed that the people who came to live in the city, including
the people here, would gradually take over, and it would become an organic
process. (MKDC 1975 p. 10)

A later Chairman, Lord Chilver, used an analogous metaphor: 'What you
want to do is give such momentum that evolution doesn't stop. You then
allow other forces to come in to continue the evolution' (*Business Insight*
March 1991, quoted in Bendixson and Platt 1992 p. 259). The unfolding of
the plot is envisaged as akin to that of an organism with its own natural
growth span. The 'birth' and 'infancy' of the city are frequent images, with the
city destined to reach its 'maturity' some twenty years after its birth or, alternatively, at the turn of the century (MKDC 1970 p. 10; MKDC 1990, 2 p. 3).

The story has its established conventions about its contexts and audiences. It was told mainly under the control and at the wish of MKDC and its
supporters. The principal audiences to whom they directed it were government, potential investors and its existing and future residents, both business-
es and individuals.

The Development Corporation made great efforts to tell its tale, for its
brief included publicising its work and selling its wares. Its efforts are
reminiscent of the city-making 'boosters' of the nineteenth-century frontier
(Hamer 1990) as they similarly worked to attract new residents, build up

their settlements and, like MKDC, claim the appellation of 'city' to validate their aspirations. MKDC's boosterism deployed all the means at its disposal, which meant going far beyond print and the muted style of the academic stories. There were press briefings; formal reports; personal representations; coloured photographs and artwork; exhibitions in and outside Milton Keynes; eye-catching advertisements at the London railway terminals; brochures, booklets and pamphlets; serial publications; talks; posters; television programmes; and glamorous public events. The detailed tellings varied – like all effective stories it was adaptable to audience and occasion – so that the narrators could variously emphasise the attractive countryside-like setting of Milton Keynes life, as depicted in Figure 3.3, or its business opportunities. The central plot never varied: the success story of the new city of Milton Keynes.

This tale and its tellings are of one city at one finite period of time. But the terms in which it is told also carry more universal overtones. Evocative concepts like 'community', 'city', 'citizens' and 'environment' run through the narrative. It draws on memorable imagery like the power of human planning to affect people's lives and places; individuals as participants in the process of city creation; the appealing organic metaphor by which a city grows and matures in part through natural forces; and a great destiny worked out over time. The ending is a direct contrast to the bleak one of most academic tales. But it provides an equally recognisable plot as it portrays the glorious hero and his helpers jointly winning through to the story's happy and predestined ending.

Tales of Utopias and garden cities

A further set of stories both underlies and diverges from the planners' tale. This lies in the tales told in the context of the garden city movement. A brief summary of the plot is relevant for the Milton Keynes stories.[1]

The 'garden city story' is widely attributed to the Londoner Ebenezer Howard. His account at the turn of the century looked forward to cities of a new kind, planned to combine the apparent benefits of both country and town and avoid the disadvantages of each (summarised in his famous diagram in Figure 3.4). Their planned layout and surroundings would be crucial, with a population, limited to about 30,000, dense enough for urban compactness and ready circulation by its residents but sufficiently dispersed for spacious gardens, recreation and individual diversity. A radial layout would combine amenities in the centre with dispersal of industries round the edge and mainly agricultural countryside surrounding it on the outside.

"IN MILTON KEYNES WE ARE OUT NUMBERED BY TREES 15 TO 1."

3.3 The good life in Milton Keynes. One of the many advertisements by the Milton Keynes Development Corporation stressing the attractions of the new city (by courtesy of the Commission for the New Towns)

The land would be vested in a quasi-public trust, facilitating municipal planning but securing the rising value of the land not for private investors but for the residents. Control would be local not central, giving scope to the free enterprise of the town's citizens.

Though Ebenezer Howard played a part in developing the towns of Letchworth and Welwyn Garden City, his vision was never fully realised. His portrayal of small and compact cities surrounded by countryside was superseded by the low-density, suburban 'garden city', with the 'country' element *within* the city. Nevertheless his basic story was extremely influential. It linked both to nineteenth-century concerns with greenery, air and light in cities (Weber 1989 pp. 88ff.) and to longer Utopian images of the perfect town, as in Thomas More's sixteenth-century tale of the gorgeous buildings, fine gardens and vineyards of the fabled city of Amaurote (*Utopia* Book II chapter 2).

Howard's vision – his story – has both a temporal framework and a developing plot. The city is first planned, then its building and peopling lead on to a successful conclusion as the economic benefits and individual freedoms destined in the original plan come to fruition. The city itself sets the timescale, for once it reaches its optimum population it is complete. To be true to itself it will not encroach on the surrounding country and as with

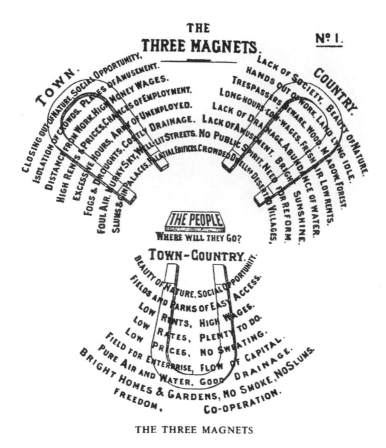

THE THREE MAGNETS

3.4 'The three magnets': Ebenezer Howard's vision of town–country relations

other living organisms reaches maturity and then stops growing – like 'a flower or a tree or an animal' (Munzer and Vogel 1974 p. 17). The plot is an intelligible one, drawing on and combining the familiar values of individualism and of public responsibility. Howard's new cities were to give, on the one hand, both 'fuller and freer opportunity for [the society's] members to do and produce what they will, and to form free associations, of the most varied kinds' and, on the other, 'a condition of life in which the well-being of the community is safeguarded' (Howard 1946 [1902] p. 131). The evaluative impact of terms like 'communities', 'healthy living', 'the good life', 'freedom' and 'social opportunity' is further reinforced by the choice of protagonists: not central government but local authorities; neither elite nor landlords but a 'community' of local groups and institutions and, above all, of the individual people of the town. The story is not of passive reaction to industrial conditions but of the ordered intentional exercise of human will.

The story was partly circulated through published books and pamphlets, embellished by vivid illustrations like that reproduced in Figure 3.4. Ebenezer Howard's publications reached a wide range of readers through his *Garden Cities of To-morrow* (the 1902 revision of his *To-morrow: Peaceful Path to Real Reform*, 1898). But another main channel was personal communication: lectures; individual approaches; committees and pressure groups, among them the Garden Cities Association (later the Town and Country Planning Association); and the many people living in Letchworth and Welwyn Garden City. The tone is more practical than theoretical and the story recounted in popular rather than technical language – perhaps one reason, together with Howard's lack of formal education, for its relative absence from the main academic stories.

There is something of the universal in the story. It is presented as potentially generalisable to many different places, and evokes powerful and recognisable themes. The familiar antagonists of town and country appear again but are in this story eventually reconciled. The tale deploys moral themes of both individualism and public control for the benefit of its citizens, Utopian visions of the good town and, perhaps most basic of all, human beings' ability to create their own lives, leading ultimately to the happier ending.

While not following Howard's specific blueprint, elements of the same story lay behind such philanthropic attempts to produce better living conditions as Bournville (Cadbury) or Port Sunlight (Lever). It also partly shaped British enthusiasms for new towns, and, in turn, for Milton Keynes. The garden city story overlaps with the planners' tale in its stress on spacious, airy living conditions, access to the countryside, the combination of a planned framework with diversity and flexibility for the city's people, and the final happy conclusion. However, though referred to in a few MKDC narrations, it is not regularly presented as a prominent part of that story. There are significant differences too. Unlike Howard's original concept, the Milton Keynes story is of a low-density city, dispersed rather than radial, and with the 'country' *in* the city rather than surrounding it. And Howard's portrayal of local enterprise and responsibility by local authorities is in the Milton Keynes tale replaced by an agency responsible to central government.

Nevertheless, for some tellers and audiences Milton Keynes can be classed as among these Utopian and garden city tales. Milton Keynes thus becomes one episode in a story of universal significance, recounting the ability of human creativity and planning to bring about not just the good life

3.5 The garden city story: a 1920s poster for Welwyn Garden City

but the good life *in cities*. Unlike the pessimistic academic stories, the planners' and the garden city stories share a storyline that leads to a happy ending for both city and individual.

Milton Keynes: realm of the dreadful dragon and the concrete cows?

The planners' tale and, to a lesser extent, the garden city vision are evocative stories about Milton Keynes. But there is another very different story about what the city is like and how it developed.

This story recounts how the planners and bureaucrats built Milton Keynes as an artificial and unnatural settlement. A version of this tale is told of many new towns; but it takes a particularly sharp form when applied to Milton Keynes. It tells of a settlement without soul, lacking the centre and traditions which give older towns their identity. Milton Keynes is a maze of disconnected roads, brash new constructions without human memories, a cultural desert. It was imposed by concreting over the villages and the country – the famed lost 'Buckinghamshire countryside' – and remorselessly ferrying in countless unrelated and uprooted newcomers. At best it might be modern and utilitarian, but without roots grown over the generations it only masquerades as a 'community'.

This story is constantly told and retold of Milton Keynes. Even sympathetic tellers depict it as 'bold, new, shiny, rational, progressive and materialist. (Is that why the Japanese like it?) It symbolises a society that is, as Kathleen Raine puts it, "still in the power of its machines"' (Bendixson and Platt 1992 p. viii). Other narrators put it more dramatically. The *Mail on Sunday* features John Osborne's account of this 'deranged planners' Utopia . . . a gleaming gum-boil plonked in the middle of England' (Osborne 1994 p. 10), while comedians mock its 'rabbit hutch housing' and 'lunatic architects' (White 1980 p. 95). On its twenty-fifth anniversary, *The Times* leader expatiates on 'Paradise mislaid', the language more solemn but with the same underlying narrative:

Some congratulation must be in order for those who have striven to coat the Buckinghamshire countryside with grids and plazas. Of all this century's attempts at Utopian settlement, Milton Keynes is perhaps the least arrogant and the most flexible. But the anniversary is none the less a memorial to a tradition of social engineering that must be seen as dead and buried. Hardly, however, to be mourned.

Milton Keynes was the last desperate throw of a generation of British planners who were distasteful of the traditional British towns and cities and had the political power and public money to fashion the environment to their will. Humans, they believed, would be more contented in settlements designed as architectural unities rather than by developing and enlarging existing villages, towns and cities . . .

An eagerness to force large numbers of people out of city centres, shared with authoritarians in less democratic societies, led to the desertion and dereliction of many of Britain's inner cities and the spoliation of millions of acres of countryside . . . The architect was god and history was the devil. (*The Times* 24 January 1992)

The recurrent theme of authoritarian new towns imposed upon the traditional rural countryside comes out clearly in *The Times'* concluding plea to 'protect the rolling acres of rural Britain from another Milton Keynes'.

Dave Rimmer's depiction of Milton Keynes as 'The non-place urban realm' tells the same tale to readers of *Harpers & Queen*, but in even more pessimistic tones. He dwells on Milton Keynes' rootless, unhuman character:

A featureless roundabout on an empty road. Through a clump of skinny trees you glimpse the ribbed flank of an anonymous high-tech industrial unit. A supermarket trolley lies abandoned by a sign indicating the way to the centre of the town. But even now, at rush-hour, there is no pull in that direction . . . There are few cars. No people. Just another roundabout. And another. And still another, from which two of the roads trail directly into an unsettling, undeveloped void . . .

Everything seems at once both unbearably new and depressingly desolate. The lack of pedestrians anywhere but in the shopping mall lends the impression – true or false – that there is absolutely nothing happening . . . [a] sense of lifelessness . . . Nor is Milton Keynes for you if, like me, you are a lifelong Old City-dweller who is accustomed to a rambling patchwork of history gone wild. The patchwork of development is no substitute. (Rimmer 1986 pp. 78, 80)

This is an extreme version. But some such 'kernel story' (to use Kalcik's (1975) term) is the basis of many popular images of Milton Keynes. A columnist uses it to depict the then leader of the Opposition as faceless and nondescript: 'if Tony Blair was a place, he'd be Milton Keynes' (*Independent* 4 July 1996 p. 5). It is joked about as the place you'd like to send your mother-in-law to (Bendixson and Platt 1992 p. 115), or attacked because its children 'uniformly speak with a previously unidentified and hideously glottal accent' (Osborne 1994 p. 10).

Milton Keynes has managed to become a modern myth . . . Its name has become a convenient shorthand for a whole herd of contemporary bêtes noires: insensitive public planning, vapid corporate culture, rootless suburbia, hick provincialism, ugly modern architecture, faddish new technology, car-mobile life-styles, horrid modern housing and so on. (Rimmer 1986 pp. 78–9)

The local poet and artist Bill Billings is thus tapping into familiar themes about planners and bureaucrats in his poem ostensibly about the destruction of his dinosaur sculpture. For his ironic complaint about 'Wavendon Towerology' is also about the red-tape ogres of the Development Corporation (then based at Wavendon Tower):

> Old Jacks dog died
> It died in Milton Keynes.
> It's not the only animal to die in Milton Keynes,
> My Dinosaur died in Milton Keynes,
> It did not have a birth certificate,
> In fact it had no certification –
> It didn't have its:
> Existology certificate,
> Its Do-ology,
> Canology,
> Rantology,
> Pigology,
> Kidology,
> Wavendon Towerology
> Certificates.
> That's why it died in Milton Keynes, along with Jacks dog
> With no apology.   (Billings *c.* 1981)

Similar tales were told during the early planning too. Existing residents concerned about the proposed changes drew on the same kernel tale of faceless planning opposed to the richnesses of human history. Speakers at a meeting in Stony Stratford invoked their town's 400-year-old traditions to highlight their 'horror when people start planning human beings' (*Wolverton and North Bucks Express* 3 April 1970), while others warned of the advancing 'concrete jungle', of 'social indigestion', and a 'patchwork quilt across north Buckinghamshire' (*Wolverton and North Bucks Express* 18 October 1968).

Milton Keynes was like the worst horrors of science fiction. A local newspaper column recalls 'the Thing from outer space', but insists that 'the real threat to-day' comes from 'the planners of the "Brave New World" and the Thing in North Bucks – the M.K.D.C.' (*Bucks Standard* 30 April 1970). Later the same columnist writes of the planners' view of 'Humanity as calculable' as they create 'urban eyesores filled with the rootless victims of their extrapolated population graphs' (4 June 1970). In the story reported in the *Wolverton and North Bucks Express* (3 April 1970) Milton Keynes and its advent were the 'dreadful dragon'.

Some news stories were less hostile to the city plans. But even they drew on contrasts between the old order of thatched cottages, old churches, timbered houses or rural fields and that of the coming city. Constantly juxtaposed with articles about the city plans there were photographs of historical churches or – the favourite – of the centuries-old inn in the old village of Milton Keynes, after which the city was named (see Fig. 3.8 on p. 53). They were able to play on deeply held images of the English countryside contrasted with the artificiality of planned urban life.

Residents within the city, once established, less often tell this kind of story. But the images are still there to be called on. They appear evocatively in 'The New City', printed in a local anthology by Milton Keynes writers:

> They're building a New City
> Around the place where I was born,
> Trees and hedgerows
> From the ground are slowly being torn,
> Roads are snaking from here and every place
> Building many houses for a cosmopolitan race,
> The colour of many peoples
> We see along the street,
> And tongues we've never heard before
> In the City of hide and seek.
> We're losing all the old folk
> People we knew so well,
> Who spoke to us in our language
> With so many tales to tell.
> I find it hard to remember
> Where the old landmarks used to be,
> Guess it doesn't matter much
> Only to folks like you and me.   (E. Wells in Davis 1980 p. 23)

The images are the more stirring for the underlying story they implicitly invoke. It is a story of how through time the earlier rural life of Buckinghamshire, the traditional forms and the diversities of historical experience have been destroyed – literally concreted over – by the heartless products of the planners. The integrating plot is a coherent and intelligible one, making sense to its many tellers and listeners. It draws on the familiar – and generalisable – theme of the opposing forces of artificial planning and human tradition. The bureaucrats' dragon defeats the human spirit and the age-tuned communities.

Enter the 'concrete cows', to give the story additional bite through a single memorable image. This group of six black-and-white sculptures (Figure 3.6) was given to the city in 1978 by Liz Leyh, then artist-in-residence. They are now displayed in a Milton Keynes park near the railway line. These concrete

3.6 The famous concrete cows of Milton Keynes (photograph by Mike Levers, Open University)

cows are referred to over and over again when people picture Milton Keynes, whether in speech, in writing or visually. They feature constantly in local and national newspapers, in the broadcast media, and, indeed, almost every time outsiders mention Milton Keynes.

They are particularly prominent in the press and broadcast media. 'Milton Keynes' and 'concrete cows' become near-synonymous, usually in the context of a derogatory joke. One ingredient may be the snobbish metropolitan contempt for the provincial upstart's pretensions. But if so the vocabulary and imagery are readily at hand to use. News broadcasts on Milton Keynes use film of the concrete cows as background (perhaps lingering on a shot of a dog cheekily raising its leg against one) or sign off with a jokey reference to them. Journalists start from the familiar image even when going on to criticise it. Milton Keynes is the place with 'concrete cows, 15m trees three feet high, and roundabouts with one entry and one exit' (Stewart Dalby in the *Financial Times* survey, 3 April 1992). 'Although you have never been there, you know all about it. It is the place with the concrete cows . . . laid out like a printed circuit board' (Dalby in *Financial Times* 18 January 1990). The *Observer*'s twenty-fifth anniversary coverage pictures Milton Keynes as built by 'social engineers . . . a community where even nature is reduced to concrete' (Laurence Marks, 19 January 1992) and John Grigsby in the *Daily*

Telegraph's account of Milton Keynes succinctly expresses the widespread view that 'The cows are a reminder that offices, roads, shopping centres and factories have swamped a piece of Buckinghamshire countryside. The counterfeit, in the form of a piece of social engineering, has replaced real cows in real fields' (23 January 1992).

The story is also widely distributed through informal channels. An inhabitant of Welwyn Garden City invited to talk about his town on the radio interposes quickly with 'Well we're not the Concrete Cows place anyhow' (*Anderson's Country*, August 1994). Phone up to give your address for the gas bill and get the response – 'And how near are you to the cows then?' Again and again people laugh when Milton Keynes is mentioned and allude to the concrete cows. Milton Keynes residents, well acquainted with this pessimistic story of their town, brace themselves when asked where they live and wait for the mention of the cows.

This Milton Keynes story has wide resonances, one reason why it circulates so successfully. 'Cows' are redolent of all that is rural and 'traditional': the countryside, rhythms of nature, age-old villages, thatched cottages, cows grazing in green fields, the natural untrammelled community of the past, the world we have lost. Set against this is the artificial imposition of the town, faceless anonymity, alienation and the dead hand of authoritarian bureaucracy – 'the concrete jungle'. Trying to unite the two opposed concepts is more than just an oxymoron, it is a kind of disruption of the natural order. So a story of concrete cows implies a kind of self-contradiction within the image itself. The effectiveness of the concrete cow version feeds on a deeply rooted opposition between rural traditional nature and planned artificial town.

This story of man-made town opposed to natural country is a long-told one, encapsulated in William Cowper's famous line 'God made the country, and man made the town' (from 'The Task' 1783). It can seem particularly apt for any new town's story. The same view renders 'garden cities' incongruous as well, elegantly expressed in Ronald Hine's poem early this century about the attempted garden city of Letchworth:

> God the first garden made,
> And the first city Cain,
> Deep in a proverb thus 'twas laid,
> Profound, precise and plain.
> But garden-cities, garden-cities!
> Who the deuce makes garden-cities?
> Will someone please explain? . . .
> For then we'd know, for weal or woe,

Where all these mad mixed-blessings flow,
And folk would be no more perplext,
With that dark thought they are now vext,
Is God or Man to blame?

(Ronald Hine quoted in Munzer and Vogel 1974 p. 37)

The implicit binary opposition recalls the classic pessimistic tales of academic urban theory recounted in the last chapter. They too are rooted in those same profound classifications: natural countryside contrasted to imposed artificial town; belonging opposed to alienation; tradition and community versus modern bureaucracy; historical continuities against the rootlessness of urbanisation. Here again we have the Golden Age myth, not always narrated explicitly but clearly detectable in the background. Its unhappy ending in imposed new cities or concrete cows again retells the loss of age-old traditional forms, superseded by the artificial and heartless products of the modern bureaucrats.

'Not just the concrete cows': stories of history and humanity

There is also a contrasting tale. Narrated through local books, pamphlets, advertisements and verbal statements, this tells of a place with its own history and traditions, some predating the 'new city', others created over the last twenty-five years. The narrative is presented through accounts of the long history of the area and its colourful local variety. Milton Keynes is no rootless standardised piece of collective engineering, goes this story, but is characterised by rich human memories, diversity and its own established and emerging cultural traditions – a place with a heart.

One example is Jonathan Flie's local publication _Not the Concrete Cows: a Kaleidoscope through the City of Milton Keynes_ (1994). This is presented as a 'warts-and-all' picture of 'the good, the bad and the ugly parts of this city of ours ... fortunately not Utopia', reprinted from his local press columns (Flie 1994 p. 5). The collection recounts historical events and landmarks: local legends of the Romans and of Boadicea, wartime memories, the Grand Union canal and the history behind the road and place names in the city. More recent episodes include 'Dial-a-bus', the Milton Keynes Hospital Action Group and the story of Queensway in Bletchley. Such tales evoke a wide local response and Flie found that his 'historical researches in Milton Keynes [have] generated the greatest interest of all I have published in _The Citizen_' (1994 p. 39).

Local groups similarly celebrate the history and diversity of the area. There are the local archaeological societies, the campaign for a museum of the wartime code-breaking history of Bletchley ('Enigma'), the People's Press of Milton Keynes, anthologies by local writers and the many collections of old photographs from the locality (like Birch 1987, 1992, Croft 1984, Mynard and Hunt 1984, Wright *et al.* 1979). Colin Whitmore's *Exploring Milton Keynes* dwells on the tale of 'Domesday Milton Keynes 1986 AD', tracing localities to their Domesday origins (*c.* 1989 p. 82), while Fisk's *Milton Keynes* (1981) rejects outsiders' 'revulsion to the place' to portray instead its 'original settlements, the ancient villages and towns . . . The irreplaceable historical qualities . . . [are] not being swept away . . . but included [in the new city]' (Fisk 1981, Introduction).

The local Living Archive Project, founded in 1984, has taken a particularly prominent role in formulating and narrating this story of a rich and varied history. With the aim of engaging residents of all ages and backgrounds 'in celebrating and creatively sharing the history of lives and events that have shaped Milton Keynes and continue to shape it' (Living Archive strategy document, May 1996), its high profile 'documentary arts' activities are conducted through a combination of oral history interviewing, researching, plays, creating songs and music, sewing textiles, editing books and arranging exhibitions. Nine large-scale musical documentary plays based on local sources have attracted large numbers of volunteers and enthusiastic audiences over the years. *Days of Pride*, for example, tells the story of Hawtin Mundy from New Bradwell (now part of Milton Keynes), portraying his first world war experiences as a soldier and the events on the home front while he and his companions are away (also in Mundy 1984). The Living Archive also encourages the collection of local reminiscences and their publication in books with both text and photographs. Its recent leaflet (1994) hits a familiar theme:

> So you thought
> **Milton Keynes**
> was just
> **concrete cows**
> in a
> **concrete jungle?**

> New towns have an unjustified reputation for being soulless,
> cultureless concrete jungles. The Living Archive Project
> in Milton Keynes is actively dispelling this myth.

In this set of stories the development of Milton Keynes is no longer a disruption of the natural order but part of the wider history of Buckinghamshire, merely one episode in a longer plot. The Wolverton and District

Archaeological Society's *Victorian and Edwardian Milton Keynes: a Photographic Collection* (Croft 1984) follows the same line. It tells how Milton Keynes is dependent on history, not just on 'man', and places recent events within the diversities of a longer timescale:

Each town or village has its own particular story to tell and it is this diversity of historical circumstances and surviving features which gives Milton Keynes its own unique image . . . The recent changes in Milton Keynes have been rapid and in some people's minds total. But in their own small way, the survival of these old photographs has ensured that some memories and images of the earlier landscapes and villages will be preserved for posterity. (Croft 1984, Introduction (no pagination))

It also puts the twentieth-century city into historical perspective by comparing it to the nineteenth-century 'new town' of Wolverton (now part of Milton Keynes), quoting the then Rector of Wolverton:

How marvellous is all this, especially when we remember that only twenty years ago the fox was hunted and the pheasant shot; the ploughman whistled and the nightingale sang where now we have a mighty Factory, a spacious Church, noble Schools, and convenient reading and Lecture Rooms. (quoted in Croft 1984)

Similar themes of humanity and a wealth of history are prominent in publications by the Milton Keynes People's Press and other local writers. The Milton Keynes writers' group 'Speakeasy' launched its *Words Worth* magazine for 'writers with vision at the heart of Milton Keynes' (1996). A common approach is to take the story back before the founding of the new city through the lives of people brought up in the area. Greta Barker's *Buckinghamshire Born* (1980) does this, as does Rice's compilation (1982) of 'Village memories' from Woughton-on-the-Green (now incorporated into Milton Keynes but still with some village character). There are some nostalgic touches about the loss of innocence and 'the rural bliss of yesteryear' (West 1992 p. 156) but the main story in such publications is of historic continuities and human experiences, rather than of a heartless new city. The continuing centres of Bletchley, Stony Stratford and Wolverton have their own lengthy – and equally fascinating – historical tales, and so too do the long-established villages. The overall story is a panegyric of historical roots and local lives within the variegated and unique areas that now continue within Milton Keynes.

Other narrations tell of more recent times. As the last twenty-five years become history, so they too take their place in the past as historical tales worth telling. The framework is again of historical diversity and human creation. Many narratives centre on experiences of residents and newcomers in Milton Keynes in the period since the beginning of the new city. *Pioneer Tales* (Turner and Jardine 1985) documents the lives of people coming to 'a new life in Milton Keynes', as did the 1995 'When I arrived in Milton Keynes . . .' exhibition in the city centre. A local mythology is crystallising about the pioneering years, picking out particular episodes among the emergent shared tales. They tell above all of the 'mud' of the early building days, the roads that went nowhere and the short-lived but much-celebrated 'Dial-a-bus', and dwell on people's efforts to build up a home from nothing, the lack of local shops before the central shopping precinct opened, the 'Milton Keynes is dying for a hospital' campaign and the building of the city centre church.

The concrete cows sometimes appear again. But this time they are human-ised or gently laughed about, related to the diversity and history of the area. An illustrated children's booklet, for example, tells the tale of Millie Moo, a little concrete cow who lives happily with her family in Milton Keynes in a field close to the historic Bradwell Abbey; curiosity gets the better of her, and she sets off on various visits within and beyond the area (Stone, 1981, 1985). Locally produced postcards, calendars and emblems reproduce the cows, they appear in advertisements, local publications, band names and church sermons. The literary magazine *Upstart!* for writing from Milton Keynes opened its publicity with a leaflet prominently decorated with witty pictures of electronic cows under the headline 'Do electronic cows dream of Milton Keynes?', and the invitation 'If you're bored by dreary jokes about the city of roundabouts then subscribe now to a magazine that will really give people something to talk about.' On the same lines the Living Archive calls for young participants to help create the new play *Big Bill Campbell Rides Again* which 'tells the story of a grass cutting gang who live on a roundabout and fancy themselves as cowboys, go rustling and steal the concrete cows from that dastardly rancher Milton Keynes' (*Living Archive Project News-letter* February 1995). The concrete cows are no longer the symbols of faceless concrete jungle or the incongruity of a 'city in the country', but interact with its history and its diverse people, subject to human control.

They also merge into another, related, story. This recounts how, far from soulless concrete, Milton Keynes has now emerged as a notably 'green' city. Letters in local newspapers laud its parks and trees, often in rebuttal of some 'concrete cow' account they have seen reported elsewhere. Local writing about Milton Keynes townscapes celebrates their wildlife, light, the sky or the uniquely pointed beauties of particular localities. Norine Redman's 'Early Spring at Peartree Bridge' (one of the new city estates) presents a notably contrasting view to the story of an engineered concrete jungle:

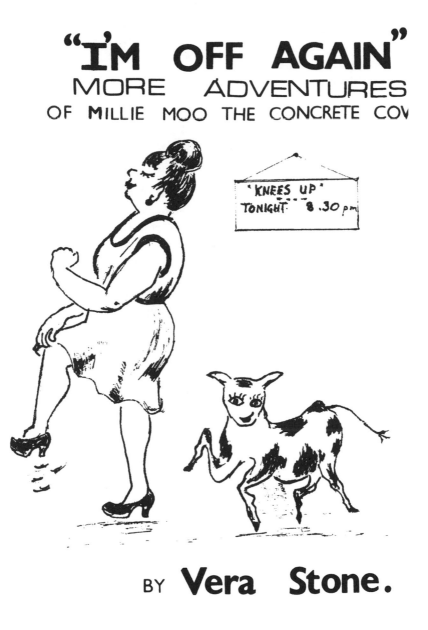

3.7 An alternative view of the cows: Millie Moo goes visiting. The more light-hearted approach to the concrete cows in the local children's book by Vera Stone

Whipped by chill March winds
The trees dressed in
Varying shades of new green
Bow and bend, back and forth.
White horses skim the canal
A moorhen paddles furiously.
The hostile meeting of stormy winds
And scudding grey clouds,
Release the cold, cold rain
Of early Spring. (Karen, Norine, John 1985 p. 25)

This 'green' story is similarly alluded to in the products of the various writing groups and poets' meetings held in Milton Keynes, another example being Anita Packwood's 'In the Sinking Sunlight', reproduced in chapter 6 (p. 163).

These more humanistic accounts imply the temporal framework characteristic of story, for they convey the chronological past lying behind Milton Keynes and its people. The overall plot allies the town and its experiences with the long history of Buckinghamshire, its villages and its rural traditions, and presents a sympathetic account of the recent episodes in this longer story.

The recurrent theme in this set of stories is the rich history and diversity of the area and of its inhabitants. The tales are thus able to tap into another widely known narrative framework used in our culture for presenting the unfolding of history. This depicts unique human lives and histories, developed in different directions – both good and bad – rather than predetermined by some external programme. The specific stories often find the roots of their episodes in earlier traditions and landscapes and thus appear with differing content, conveying diversities rather than uniformity. But they are based in an essentially similar plot, one conveying a coherent and intelligible story. It tells of human beings as moulding history, not just being moulded by it, and of themselves as an active and constitutive part of that history. Its rejection of the opposed story of standardised pre-packaged plan or 'history as the devil' could not be clearer.

These stories are mostly told by residents of Milton Keynes rather than by outsiders. Not everyone in Milton Keynes actively tells them, and, like other stories, their telling is more explicit among some participants than others – local organisations and activists play a prominent part. However, such stories are not just the creation of a small body of interest groups. They circulate through illustrated books, pamphlets, textiles, collections of photographs of the locality, appreciative recognition of features of the local

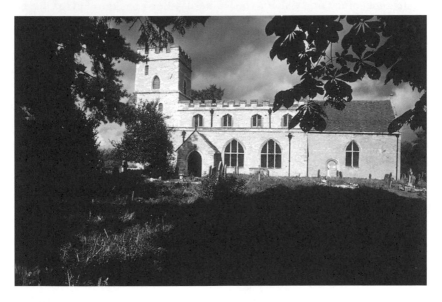

3.8 Valued images of a lost rural age or of a still-present history? The Swan Inn in Milton Keynes village and St Andrew's Church, Great Linford. These two buildings are much reproduced in publications in or about Milton Keynes, sometimes symbolising opposition to the new 'concrete jungle', sometimes in celebration of the wealth of history still continuing within the city (by courtesy of the Commission for the New Towns)

landscape, personal reminiscences and local newspapers. Their telling is intertwined with the active participation of a wide range of residents in a whole series of contexts: local exhibitions, plays, songs, local associations, school projects, local radio documentaries, sermons, letters and poems.

They also surface in some official sources. Despite its 'dreadful dragon' image in the pessimistic version, MKDC was not always the enemy of local historical interests. The Master Plan anticipated a city with 'strong local character' and 'rich variety' (MKDC 1970 pp. 15–16) and took some interest in the preservation of historical buildings and sites (MKDC 1970 p. 332). Place names were often taken from historical antecedents, some with echoes from Saxon times, others from existing field or farm names. The 1994 *Official City Atlas* asserts that 'though [Milton Keynes] is constantly looking to the future, its past is not forgotten'. The Milton Keynes tourist brochure exploits the same theme in its focus on the 'wealth of history and tradition', highlighting the old coaching town of Newport Pagnell, Stony Stratford with its 'Georgian High Street . . . [and] the inns which reputedly gave their names to the expression "Cock and Bull story"', Bletchley's 'Enigma' decoding in the second world war and the Domesday Book background to villages within Milton Keynes (Southern Tourist Board and the Milton Keynes Borough Council, 1994). And for the future, the CD-ROM being produced by the Commission for New Towns will surely depict episodes from the later parts of this Milton Keynes story, further crystallising them for posterity.

This story is not unchallenged and the others remain in circulation. But it has been strongly emerging in recent years, recounting and in a sense creating Milton Keynes as a locale with a history, partly its own, partly related to the longer continuities of the area. Often presented in terms of a counter to the 'concrete cow' image, it is more than just its negation, for it also affirms a long-existing alternative narrative. Unlike the artificial rootlessness depicted in tales of a heartless new city, this is a narrative framework for the widespread concern with the past and with the role of human memory and historical continuity in people's sense of their own reality. Such accounts show the area and its inhabitants as possessing a rich, diverse and memorable past and future.

On the face of it the contrasting stories in this chapter contradict. Nevertheless they are all stories which people can and do utilise in their tales of Milton Keynes. They are not always kept separate, nor are they the exclusive property of particular groups. The essential point, however, is that people can retell and, as they wish, embroider them in the full expectation that their narrations will be recognised and found familiar by their listeners and readers.

The focus here has been on the stories of Milton Keynes. But all four sets of stories also represent widely told tales of our culture. The upbeat tale of the fulfilment of the city's foreordained destiny under the heroic leadership of the planners, and the partly overlapping garden city stories with their focus on long-dreamed Utopias and local action, have many parallels elsewhere. So too has that other story, recounted in tellings throughout the land, which endeavours to create and recreate the local human history of an area in all its rich diversities, part of the human search for roots and identity as well as faith in a human meaning within the unfolding of the years. And then there is that enormously influential pessimistic tale of how the artificial and alienated city superseded the traditional harmony of the countryside. It is told in Milton Keynes through the figure of the concrete cows but also expresses a set of images long held in both the popular imagination and the intellectuals' theories.

The point is not the literal truth or falsity of all or any of these narrations. They ultimately draw on mythic tales which are told not just of one particular city but of other towns and other experiences throughout our culture. They are currently narrated in particularly vivid and extreme ways of Milton Keynes. There is something about the concept of a 'new city' which seems to attract the extreme versions of the tales (especially the pessimistic ones) and for some tellers Milton Keynes has been quintessentially cast in that role. Perhaps Milton Keynes' significance thus lies not just in its concrete reality but also in its symbolic role as the current focus for the creative retelling of some deep myths of our culture. But these fundamental themes are deployed in stories elsewhere too, as tellers and listeners draw on the store of known plots, imagery and conventions to interpret, shape and, in this sense, create their experiences of the city.

4   Storied lives: the tales of individual urban dwellers

We turn now to the *personal* stories of individuals who came to Milton Keynes and lived there. They too play a part in the portrayal of urban life. For though the more general stories treated so far are clearly relevant for our narratives of urban life, any serious investigator must surely also include the narrated experiences of individual tellers – stories pinned down to a specific urban locality and narrating the specificities of time, place, and person.

Chapters 4–6 focus on this genre of personal tales, referring in particular to the accounts of their lives told by thirty-five individuals living in one of the Milton Keynes housing estates. We will need to consider the ways in which these personal utterances can indeed be justly described as 'stories' and their tellers as 'narrators' (terms which I will be using throughout but which I hope will be acquiring greater conviction and meaning as we progress). What narrative conventions can their tellers deploy for temporal ordering, for expressing generality, for constructing their plots? What, if any, are their key themes and images? And through what accepted conventions are they told and heard? Of equal interest, what themes emerge in the stories and their tellings which can be set alongside the multiple themes of city tales treated so far?

I also give a large place to substantial extracts from the stories themselves, told in their narrators' own terms. This should bring home that these tales are indeed those of individuals, each recounting personal experiences unique to their tellers. Tempting though it always is for the analyst to move quickly to generalisations, it should be clear from these extensive tales that there is no single 'message' or definitive list of 'themes' to be automatically read out from them. Personal narratives are less often told and heard in the academic literature than are the more general stories. And yet they exist, and these creations of unique individuals are surely of some significance not only for their tellers but also for our understanding both of how stories in practice interact in urban contexts and of our visions of urban life.

Six tales are thus recounted in this and the following two chapters, interspersed with the analysis and with shorter quotations from the remaining twenty-nine narrations. Each is introduced at a particular point in the argument, giving concrete illustration of how the more general patterns can work out in a particular tale. It also needs to be remembered however that each tale is complex, embodying a multiplicity of features beyond those currently under scrutiny and, further, that while many other tales in the corpus may exemplify similar points each does so in its own individual way.

Unfortunately only a small selection can be reproduced here in any substance (for brief notes on the other tales, see appendix 2). But it seems only fair to let at least *some* speakers present their accounts at some length – even if only in the limited medium of printed transcript – rather than appear just in short quotations selected by the researcher. It is only, too, on the basis of some substantial extracts that the complexity and the generic conventions of this form of story-telling can be appreciated.

The personal narratives

The personal stories which form the main focus in chapters 4–6 were told by thirty-five individuals who at the time of their narrations (1994) were living in the Milton Keynes estate of Fishermead. This housing estate, started in 1974, was one of the first to be developed as part of the 'new city'. It shared many of the features of the planners' aims of a 'balanced' population with both pleasant local conditions and easy access to other parts of the city, and its development had gone alongside that of other new estates and facilities in the new city as a whole. It had its own characteristics too: near the city centre, more dense than the peripheral estates and with a high proportion of terraced housing. At first highly praised by architects and planners and, as one narrator put it, 'one of their plum estates', by 1994 it had acquired a less savoury reputation – not totally accepted by its residents – as one of the lower class and less prestigious areas of Milton Keynes. Its inhabitants however remained articulate and active, coming from many backgrounds in social, economic, occupational, geographical and educational terms.

Beyond the fact that all these thirty-five narrators were in 1994 living in Fishermead, their stories otherwise recount a range of unique and contrasting experiences (further illustrated in the brief notes on each narrator in appendix 2). Their tellers differ in background, outlook and the proportion of their lives spent in Milton Keynes. Even among those who had spent years in the city, many had not come directly to Fishermead nor would necessarily remain there permanently. Several had first come to Bletchley – one of three main settlements predating the foundation of the new city although now within it – or to one of the other new estates. Many had successively moved between several localities, an accepted Milton Keynes pattern. For some narrators their time in Milton Keynes represented most of their lives, for others only a relatively small proportion. But, short or long, they between them brought their experiences – and their stories – to the creation and maintenance of the city.

Once solidified into transcripts on a page, as here, the stories give the impression of being fixed and bounded products, printed texts like any other. But the status of such 'texts' is by no means transparent, and their analysis needs to be preluded by some explanation of their selection and processing.

First, then, the narrators of these stories were selected as individuals. Though there was some attempt to seek a range of ages and backgrounds, individuals were found not by 'sampling' but mainly by 'snowball methods' – the various contacts leading on to others. In other words neither the specific estate of Fishermead nor the individual narrators within it were chosen for their 'typicality'. This term in any case makes little sense in studies of personal narrative or perhaps of urban life generally where an interest in variety and personal difference is as reasonable as a search for 'the typical' (whatever that might be). Ultimately, these stories were recorded in the knowledge that they were likely to be heterogeneous rather than representative of any collective trend – except that perhaps each *was* characteristic of urban life, and of personal narration, precisely in being unique.

This is a point worth making. As Cohen and Fukui (1993) point out, the stock figures into which individuals are often typecast in academic urban stories miss their essential multiplicity. Variegated individuals, being recalcitrant to quantification and generalisation, are often projected in the scientific literature as somehow not quite real and thus best omitted unless under some general category like 'the consumer', 'the urbanite', 'the rural dweller' – or whatever the current academics' metaphor happens to be. But although it will be only too obvious that the thirty-five narrations cited here are an infinitely small selection of the story-telling of Milton Keynes people, their narrators are at any rate unquestionably real and individual dwellers in a real town, not speculative generalisations, and they are telling their own stories in person.

Second, in order to appreciate the stories' generic conventions, it is necessary to understand something of the processes through which they were told. This is more fully discussed in the final section of this chapter. Briefly, the narrators were recorded in the setting of their own homes, where they were invited to tell the story of their lives informally to a friendly interlocutor from the same general area of Milton Keynes during a recording lasting about one hour. Although some tellers needed some encouragement and narrations differed in both content and fluency, none of the speakers found the idea of telling their own story an unfamiliar one.

A third issue concerns how to present stories of this kind. There is always an editorial not just authorial hand. This is especially so in the case of tales that, like those here, have been recorded within particular constraints and transcribed from an oral to a written mode. As an immediate prelude to the narrative that follows, suffice it to say that, like the others, it has been edited in various ways (to be described later) before reaching the format of printed text. In the text below, as in the others, interviewer comments or queries are italicised and in brackets, editorial explanations enclosed by square brackets, and omissions of any significance indicated by dots within square brackets. In accordance with the narrators' own wishes most personal names have been changed.

We will be returning to these issues, but after that brief clarification let us move to a specific example of the genre. This is the story of Brenda Dawson (not her real name) who in 1994 was living in Fishermead but also had many journeys behind her, storied experiences which she brought with her to her life in Milton Keynes and in Fishermead. Her story, like all those quoted, is fully individual and unparalleled – and yet at the same time, in its unique way, illustrates several of the themes and narrative conventions which will be the focus of the later discussion. As with the other tales, the text is introduced by a brief note to assist the unfamiliar reader: in printed format the main lines of the narrative are sometimes obscure not just through the reduction of the oral performance to the limits of a unilinear text but also because of flashbacks and unspoken understandings, known to interviewer and speaker but not immediately evident in the written tran-script.

Brenda Dawson's tale

About forty-nine in 1994, Brenda Dawson starts her story with her growing up in Southall and her 'firmly working-class roots'. The narration lingers on this early history, then shows her leaving home to join the WRAC, meeting her husband in the army, then moving round as an army wife. It vividly recounts her arrival in the then-new Tinkers Bridge estate in Milton Keynes in 1976 (fairly early in the new city's development) after her husband left the army, then her move to Fishermead in 1980, again following her husband's job, and her reflections on the nature of the city and the estate she was then living on. As her three children got older, she started work herself, at first unqualified, but after a series of more demanding jobs and a diploma in social work she was now in more satisfying work, and finally, as her story puts it, recovering something of her own 'identity'.

* * *

Well my beginnings, yeh, well my roots are very firmly working class, my dad was a factory worker all his life, and my mum worked part-time jobs in shops and factories. My first recollection, I can vaguely remember they both came from Southall, but it was a kind of family joke, because my father came from one side of Southall and my mother came from another, and it was like my dad was from the wrong side of the railway track and the railway ran through the middle sort of thing, so that was a sort of family joke. My father's mother and father had a greengrocery shop, and my grandfather who I really don't remember, he died when I was about five I suppose, I only have a vague recollection of him, but he used to go off to Covent Garden to collect the vegetables every morning on his horse and cart.

When they first started, so I don't really recall the shop, but when he was dead and my grandmother used to run it on her own, and we used to go on Saturdays and you could go down and help yourself down to the grapes or whatever favourite fruit of mine was in season at the time, and it was just paradise really you could go down and help yourself. So that was nice, and so my father sort of grew up in that kind of em . . . – in that both his parents had come from rural areas. They came from Chalfont St Giles and my grand-father had come from Devon. On the other side of the family, my mother, her father had actually worked as a factory worker, he was a cabinetmaker, so he was a skilled worker, and my grandmother was a dressmaker at one time. And again – I only vaguely remember my grandfather, he died when I was four, but I remember he was a really lovely man, very tall over six foot, and had this wonderful bushy moustache, which tickled when you kissed him. I always liked their garden and it was a wonderful garden. And they had this sweeping staircase in the house, so that you could sort of come down there in long dresses and things and perhaps my imagining ran riot, and my grandmother had this wonderful dressing table with three mirrors on and I used to perform in front of this mirror, I would be the Beverley Sisters [well-known popular singers of the time] or whatever all in one. So that was great fun. She had lots of clothes which she would let me dress up in, it was lovely that. So after my grandfather died then we actually moved in with her.

We always lived in Southall in those early years. The first house I can remember is we had the ground floor of a two-storey house and they had been made into two separate flats, and we had the ground floor, and my mother was very friendly with the lady upstairs who had a daughter called Gloria who was a bit older than me, and then we moved to the Beehive Cottage, which was a row of ten cottages. Called the Beehive Cottage because of the pub on the corner. And we lived there until my brother was born, so we lived there until my brother was about seven I suppose, and we started school. I went to North Road Primary School, which wasn't my nearest school, but it was the one that my grandfather had gone to, and had a very good reputation, and so I got sent off to North Road school. I used to go to my grandmother's for lunch, because I didn't like school dinners, and sometimes she liked the cinema my grandmother – she would meet me after school sometimes with some sandwiches and a flask and we would go off to the pictures which wasn't far away from the school, and we saw films like 'The Al Jolson Story', and 'Richard III', which my mother wouldn't have gone to see with her. But she took me along and I loved all of it. I loved the pictures always, and with her.

So when she became ill, she had had bronchitis every winter very badly, and when it became a lot worse then we moved from Beehive Cottage and actually moved in with her [. . .] It had an outside loo, and no bathroom at all. And I can remember the tin bath coming in, from the nail it hung on outside, coming in every Friday and filled up from the copper. And my grandmother used to do her washing with this big copper and it would all be done on a Monday and hung out, then she would stay up until it was dried and ironed, and it was for the week. So it was very kind of traditional. She kept chickens at one time, but that was sort of before I moved there.

It was quite a big garden and my father he changed what had originally been the hen coop, he changed that into like what was a garden house really, for me to play in, and then also my brother when he got older. So that was nice because I could have my own space and disappear off down the garden to my house [. . .]

An enormous landing and it had four great big cupboards, and my grandmother was well into preserves, I mean she had loganberries, rhubarb, blackcurrant, gooseberries in the garden and this woman next door had this massive Victoria plum tree, so the arrangement was that any of the plums on the branches that over-hung my grandmother's garden were hers to do whatever she wanted with. So there was always masses and masses of Kilner jars in these cupboards with preserved fruit in, and she used to also bottle vegetables, because she grew a lot of vegetables, and gallons of marmalade, and it was always like this treasure trove [. . .]

So we lived in Southall, I suppose I grew up when things were rapidly changing really, I mean I can remember the first supermar-ket opening at the top of the road which was quite an astounding thing, like you went in and took the things off the shelves, and took them to pay at the end and you didn't have somebody asking you what you wanted [. . .] – totally different and quite bizarre it seemed. We had a lot of small – I mean there was one particular bakery which my grandmother bought her bread from, when she stopped making it herself, and I used to get sent off to get the bread some-times and the greengrocers, and the fishmongers and it was all sort of very locally and everybody knew each other and my grand-mother. And of course when I first became aware of shopping, ration books hadn't been phased out totally, so I can still remember ration books, and family doctors, who had been the family doctor for donkey's years and she actually delivered me, and all of those kind of things. My photograph was on her mantelpiece, which was where she kept all her 'specials' as she called them.

It was all very traditional. And it was the time in the fifties when there was – more jobs than people to do them, so a lot of people, a lot of men came across from India and Pakistan and worked in Wolf Rubber Works which was the big factory up on the station bridge, and then later their families joined them. And so that was really the changing face of Southall, which initially wasn't met with any great hostility, but I suppose like everything else people felt threatened, as they saw more and more black people coming in. Gerard's the greengrocers became a sari shop and all that sort of thing [. . .] And this assumption, and I suppose it was an assumption that I had, until I got older and listened to them talking, but because they shared houses and you had three or four Asian families in one house, you thought that was how they lived. And it wasn't like that at all because a lot of them had come from quite big houses in India and hated that bit just as much as anything else. The assumption was that that was the way they lived, and it wasn't our way of living.

I went to school locally. Then when I was thirteen we moved to Hayes, which was the next town. So I was in secondary school by then, when we moved to Hayes, my grandmother had died when I was thirteen, and my mum just had tremendous difficulty in that house, and she just wanted out [. . .]

And my father's mother as well at that time she had a fall down her stairs and she was getting on a bit, and she never regained her sight after the fall [. . .] so she went to live with my father's eldest sister, he was the youngest of a family of three and he had two older sisters, and so she went to live there with my Auntie Molly. I used to go over one evening a week and just make sure she had something to eat after school and get her tea and she went to bed about nine, and make sure she got into bed safely, that sort of thing, and then come home, so I used to do that when I came out of school, I was only about fourteen, fifteen. That was, well she was fascinating, and I used to listen to stories of her childhood, and how she had to walk four miles to school and back in all weathers, and what they used to get up to. It was wonderful, it was like living history, I liked that.

We still lived in my grandmother's house at that time – no, we must have moved to Hayes [. . .] So I used to cycle back from Hayes to Guides meetings and I still carried on going to the same church as well, the church my parents had been married in at Holy Trinity, and the family had gone to for years. A couple of my cousins were married there, and I wasn't actually confirmed at Holy Trinity, it should have been, but the churches in the area used to take it in turns, it should have been Holy Trinity's year, but St George's were having their centenary so they asked if they could have it there instead. So it was quite funny really, like breaking the chain, because my parents had been married there, I had been baptised there, and I had assumed I would be confirmed there, and probably end up getting married there. And the chain was broken, and it was like oh right. And all the time thereafter I never thought in terms of marriage there, or those kind of things, it kind of really broke it and got away from that sort of mould, a bit strange really.

So that made me really think and so we lived in Hayes, and then when I left school I had done shorthand and typing at school and got a job in Westminster County Council at their head office, and worked for the education department in the section that looked at university grants for students, which was quite interesting, because I got to meet some of them sometimes [. . .]

My mother didn't approve. My mother very rarely seemed to approve of anything I did, so I guess I gave up on her approval. She didn't approve of the fact that I had to go to London to work, because there were a number of offices around Hayes, and then we had got large factories, there was EMI, there was Fairey Aviation, and the Nestlé Company and Quaker Oats and a number of them. So that while I was getting on the train and going up to Westminster every day, it totally mystified her. And in fact a friend of mine worked in Westminster as well, and she worked on the floor above me, so there was the two of us. And then there were three girls who had got jobs in banks in London, that I was at school with, and so it was quite good on the train, and we used to meet up. I always had liked trains, I liked it. But whether it was mother didn't like the idea of my going into London, I don't know what she thought I was going to get up to. She was probably right, whatever she thought!

I suppose it was out of sight, out of mind, really, what was I getting up to while I was there; and she couldn't keep the finger on me as much as she would have done if I had worked around there, and she would have got feedback from various people, and of course it didn't happen. I think I was quite a secretive child in a way, with her. Even now I don't share everything in my life with her, and I'm careful about the bits I share and the bits I don't. And I have always been that way with her.

My dad was always there, whether you needed him or not, he was like the solid bit, and I always knew he was there if I needed him and that is how it felt when I was growing up, he was OK, and he was the one who would stop up and wait for me to get in when I was older, enough to go out and went to parties and things and he would be sitting there, which I always would think was a total waste of time, bless him, because I just walked in and say goodnight and go to bed [. . .] They weren't hard and fast parents by any means, I think I had not as much freedom as young people have these days, but I had quite a bit in comparative terms.

Yeh, then what did I do? I worked in London, and my cousin – and I had grown up with the extended family, which was really nice, my mother's brother lived in Hayes anyway when we were living in Southall, and I had got Victor and Derek and Marie, and Marie was twelve years older than me but we were quite close and I used to stay there some weekends, and my other cousins who lived not far from where my grandmother had the greengrocery shop and they were two girls and I was the younger one there, and we used to stay at each other's houses quite a lot. When my grandmother was alive, I suppose it was the matriarchal thing really, everybody used to descend on grandmother, especially at the weekend, so if you hadn't seen them in the week, Saturday mornings it was a real gathering, and then Sunday was family tea and people popped in at various other times and it was almost ritualistic that you gravitated to grandmother's.

So that was a big change when she died, and all that stopped and then there was no focal point any more and then I didn't seem to see so much of relatives in quite the same way. But Daphne and I kept in touch and Marie and I still do now.

So Daphne decided to join the Wrens and I thought this a really good idea. (*To your mother's dismay I suppose?*) Yes, oh dear, dear. But having said that, it was an acceptable way of leaving home. I had run out of things like looking for a bed-sit in London, that was frowned on, or sharing a flat with a friend, no, that was out. And sort of joining the WRAC, although she didn't really want me to, at least it was a way she felt I could leave home but still have that safety.

So I joined the WRAC in I think '67, January '67, I was seventeen and a half, and off I went and did that. And strangely enough, though I trained down in Surrey, I actually got posted back to the Ministry of Defence, so I was back living in barracks at Mill Hill and travelling into Westminster every day, just down the road from where I had started off work, rather strange. I quite enjoyed that, I met all sorts of interesting people, that was the bit I liked about it [. . .]

Then I went to Germany, and I was over there, as PA to one of the generals over there. And that is where I met my husband and came back and came out of the army, and we got married, because at that time married couples couldn't work on the same station anyway. They weren't really geared up to sort of coupledom. So, my three and a half years were up and so I came out of the army and got married. He stayed in, he didn't come out of the army until '74.

So I became an army wife, that is an experience and a half I can tell you. It is really degrading in a way, you are not a person in your own right [. . .] Of course I was never very good at sort of lying quietly down like a doormat and so I used to complain about things sometimes and that didn't go down very well. You weren't supposed to do that as an army wife, you weren't supposed to have any opinions and you definitely didn't state them, so I wasn't a very good army wife I don't think. I wasn't at all. So we then moved around a little bit, Jim went off to Aden, after Stuart was born, he was about, I don't know, he was born in the October and Jim went off to Aden in January on another company posting, there was a crisis then in Aden.

So I moved back to my mum and dad's and stayed there with them, I had moved back before Stuart was born, he was born in Amersham, and by this time my parents had moved down to Chesham, they had done that just after I joined the WRAC. That was quite difficult too, because it meant I went back home but it was back to Chesham which had no roots there, and that was odd and I lost contact with a few people, well you didn't sort of bump into people you had been at school with. There were one or two who I kept in touch with and still do now, but like everything else you mean to keep in touch but it never happens does it? [. . .]

Then when he came back Stuart was just turned the year and he then got a posting down to Okehampton down in Devon and we had quarters down there, and I disliked it. I had wanted to buy a house not far from where my parents lived, not to live in it but just as an investment. Because at that time, it was just prior to the first gazumping, so this particular house that I had seen, was only about £3,500 [. . .] and it was really nice, but I couldn't talk Jim into it. I do regret that, that I didn't have the money or anything to go off and do it myself, and so it had to be a joint thing, but not that many years later it was sort of £16,500. By the time we came out of the army it would have been about £27,000/£29,000, so it would have been a good investment [. . .]

So we toiled around various army quarters, we moved from Devon to Taunton, and both Guy and Susan were born in Taunton. And then when Susan was six weeks old we went up to Glasgow and we stayed up there for about five years, Jim was up there, and he finished off his army service up in Glasgow. And we put down our name on the Chiltern Council list [for rented housing], just as a safety thing, so at least when he did come out of the army at least he was on a council list somewhere. As far as I was concerned it really was just a safety thing, and we moved from Glasgow to Airdrie, and I quite liked Airdrie and the kids were quite happy in school there, so it seemed quite good. And I actually looked for properties all around the Airdrie area, and I mean at that time you were looking at £7,500/£8,000, but Jim decided he didn't want to buy, and then he had trouble finding work when he came out. He was, well as far as the employment people were concerned, he was in this peculiar sort of bit, he had done clerical work in the army, and he was a Warrant Officer 1 when he came out. So they considered that his qualifications were too good for a lot of jobs, but they weren't anything special or outstanding, and he didn't want to go into the Civil Service, which would have been a natural follow-on [. . .] so he ended up being a postman, and that didn't suit him because he discovered that it played up on his back to do that.

So I said well perhaps we ought to look at coming back down south [. . .] And so we decided to contact Chiltern and say look we have had our name on the list for ages and what have you got to offer us? So what they had to offer us was – Milton Keynes!

That's how we came to Milton Keynes. It wasn't planned, it was just a name on the list. Jim came down, and Milton Keynes, at that stage, there was nothing here really. So he came down to look at it in '75 and they offered him Tinkers Bridge, Beanhill or Galley Hill, I think it was, either Galley Hill, or Fullers Slade, I can't remember which one of those [new city housing estates: for locations see Fig. 4.1]. And he decided that in terms of housing and what he saw as the surroundings, that Beanhill was the better of the three.

And so we arrived – and I mean I hadn't seen any of them – with furniture in tow, and stood outside this biscuit box and thought 'My God what has this man brought me to!' It was just horrendous. I thought 'I'm not living in a biscuit tin.' I just thought, 'He is telling me this is the best, he has got to be mad, I'm not living in one of these.' However, I didn't have any choice at that time.

Inside they were quite comfortable, and we got into the sort of swing of being here. And the kids settled into school without any problems, and I then started to look around for work that I could go to. It had been a decision that I wouldn't work while the children were small, but once they had gone to school and were rooted, then there wasn't any reason why I couldn't. I started off doing some factory work [. . .]

So that was us at Beanhill. It wasn't a place where I wanted to stay for too long, but I looked around for jobs which were more amenable really with the kids being at school. I worked as a welfare assistant at [a local school], looking after a little girl who was

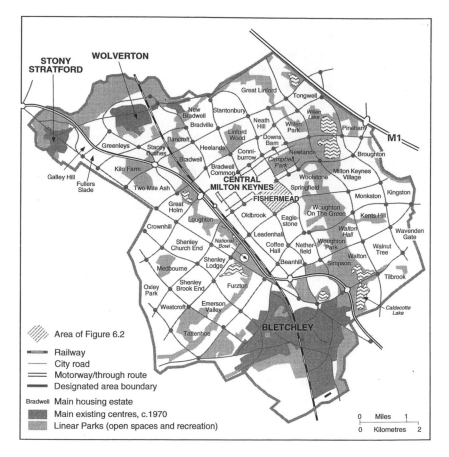

4.1 Map showing the main areas of Milton Keynes. The map shows the main
housing estates and other areas to and among which the narrators moved, the
location of Fishermead (where the personal narrators lived), the linear parks, the
older-established towns and the main road patterns in the 1990s (by courtesy of
the Commission for the New Towns, revised by John Hunt)

waiting for a place within special education. So they had a welfare
assistant just for two terms to supervise her. That, I really enjoyed, I
liked that and that was handy because it was practically at the top
of the road, and all those sorts of things.

It gave me a chance, and it was something totally different from
shorthand typing that I had done before, working with people, and
I liked the kids and the staff there were very good, and I was in all
sorts of things. I became secretary of the PTA [Parent–Teacher

Association] so we did various fund-raising events, so it felt like getting back into the main stream of things. Having kind of lost your identity, I think which you did then more so than now, you were somebody's wife, somebody's mother, and of course when you went anywhere it would be 'Oh this is Jim's wife', you know, and I would say, 'I'm Brenda.' They would sort of look at me a bit, and think, 'What sort of woman is this?' but you lose your identity if you are not careful. So it was very good because you know, I was sort of earning some money. It was just getting things sort of back for me – a life which wasn't just totally involved with children and looking after husband.

That was part-time, so that was OK. Then because more and more estates were being built, so I got a form and put down that I would like to go to Great Linford or Downs Barn, or – I can't remember what the third one was, but I know Fishermead wasn't on the list. Then Jim was fed up with the job he was doing, and he decided that he thought he would quite like a shot at being a school caretaker, and [. . .] what they had done was to earmark a property on Fishermead so that is how we ended up here. So again no choice, and by this time I was sick to the back teeth of not actually having a choice of where I was going to live. Because, obviously living with parents you don't have a choice, and the army tells me where I go, and then it just seemed, you know, so I took an instant dislike to this house actually. But it is not a bad house actually, it has a lot of potential, but I just took an instant dislike to it, and we have been here ever since [. . .] Yes it is an improvement on Beanhill, but it still was that I had no choice in the matter, and I would have liked that [. . .]

The first time I had ever lived on my own [was during her diploma course in Bedford]. Because I went straight from home into the WRAC, then got married, had the kids, and I had never ever lived on my own . . . And so I really enjoyed that and it was a totally different experience and I quite liked that I discovered. A diploma in social work. [She recounts her successive jobs as welfare assistant at a school, then a tutorial unit welfare assistant, followed by residential work with adolescents with social services from 1983 to 1989.] I had a break for a bit while I decided what I wanted to do, and then did some temporary work, again in social work with adolescents, and then worked for the rehabilitation scheme with adults with learning disabilities. And so I really enjoyed that, and went off to qualify. I am working with adults with learning and physical disabilities. (. . . *So you have got the job you want, at long last.*) Yeh, yeh. It has been worthwhile.

Well, I've actually liked living in Milton Keynes. I think it has been interesting watching it grow. We came here when there was no city centre, no nothing. It was just mud everywhere [. . .] And then the 'Dial-a-ride' [special bus service] started, and I thought that was brilliant. They would stagger home with your shopping trolley from Bletchley and they would drop you off at your door, and I thought you can't beat this and this is really good.

But yeh, I have seen it grow and it has been nice, and the city centre opening up and, yeh, it is a bit now like it has been interesting and exciting seeing it grow. And now in doing that the city has got much smaller, everything now seems nearer. Before there were sort of oceans of open land in between. And I had learned to drive so everything seemed so much nearer now, whereas before even doing something like going to Stony Stratford seemed like a major thing, because you had to get on one bus and change at the city centre and get another, and it seemed like a major thing. And now it doesn't seem anything to Stony Stratford. We used to go, I used to take the kids on the bus to Emberton Park in the summer, but the boys got then that they would cycle there and up to Brickhill and stuff like that. I mean they've really enjoyed Milton Keynes growing up, they've liked that [. . .]

Yeh, I think Milton Keynes has still got a lot to offer. When my kids were starting school here, there were a lot of families which had moved up from London for places because they wanted better accommodation for their kids, and they wanted them to grow up in somewhere where the air was a bit fresher and they had gardens to play in. And I mean we had sort of arrived here for different reasons, and I had been quite lucky with army quarters in terms of always having a nice house and garden, but I could see why so many people did move in here. For some things, like I liked the idea of the little play areas, that were very close, we had one at the bottom of our particular little road in Beanhill. We have one here at the end of the court, and so it meant that you could have this letting your kids out and they weren't very far away, and you could look out the front door and see them, and so that was quite nice, and my kids liked it. They were able then to go to their primary schools totally on the redways [the pedestrian/cycle routes] [. . .]

And there were always things going on, even on Beanhill itself. I can remember we had a street party, it must have been the Queen's Jubilee, and there always seemed to be bits and pieces going on that the kids could get involved in. Then of course over the last few years, with the advent of the Bowl [outdoor arena] as the city has grown. And yes, you didn't have to go too far, I mean I went to a couple of plays and that which was on at a hall in Bletchley, and to events at the Leisure Centre, and I liked the pool, because they were all at different ages and stages and it was nice and safe for them. Or we went and played bowls, or table tennis or stuff, always seems to be plenty to do [. . .] We would go off to Simpson, or to Woughton-on-the-Green, or up to Brickhill [villages in or near Milton Keynes] and there was always somewhere at the weekends where you could get out to the open and take the dog, take the kids and a picnic. We had quite a few picnics at Willen Lake and stuff like that, and they sort of would cycle as they got older and I would meet them there or whatever. So, I think they have grown up with perhaps more freedom than they might have had, more fresh air and space to run around in [. . .]

(*What about Fishermead itself?*) It's got noisier over the years. Yes, it has got noisier. I find it a nightmare when I am driving into the estate, because of the design with the houses on either side, and the parking areas in the middle and then the trees and bushes, it is a nightmare, and you just wait for a child or animal to run out, and I crawl along, and I think perhaps that the greenery is a bit over the top from a safety point of view. I know, you can use the other argument that it does slow people down, but it doesn't slow every-body down, and even if you are crawling along at 10 miles an hour. So that I think needs looking at. I quite like, I think, I don't know, the straight grid lines. I mean that is all over the city centre, I don't think it has particularly induced to begin with, a kind of community feeling, whereas nooks and crannies do, don't they.

I suppose for me, since coming to Milton Keynes, although I was involved with the PTA and everything while we were at Beanhill, certainly since I have been on Fishermead I have worked full-time [. . .] so I mean for the first time I suppose I don't feel I know my neighbours very well at all, I mean I say hello and how are you, but I don't really know them.

I am in a nook and cranny here, with six houses in a courtyard, which could be, but I'm not here in the daytime, and when I was doing shifts, I think my neighbours found that a bit weird. I used to go out in the afternoon and not reappear until the next day, strange woman! And certainly doing my course and moving out, they didn't have a clue what was going on. So I have not got really friendly with any of the neighbours around here, we are on nodding terms, hello and things like that. So that is the first time when it has been my experience where I have not, but then I have other friends that live in the area so . . . I mean as far as friends go, I mean I liked actually living in Bedford, and I have some other friends who moved from Milton Keynes to Bedford, and another friend of mine, the one I phoned just now, she has moved to Newport Pagnell, so people are beginning to . . .

But I still think it has got a lot going for it, events like 'Folk on the green', and the weekends at Campbell Park, previous years when the Development Corporation that was then, put on these events in Campbell Park, I can't think of anywhere else where you would get that sort of entertainment totally free. I mean where would you have a musical event on the Friday, an opera on the Saturday and then the 'Folk' on the Sunday? You just kept pinching yourself, and then the different events at Willen as well. The other year when the Indians were doing there, it was a beautiful weekend, wasn't it? I can't think of anywhere else where you would have this on offer really. I think it has got a lot going for it. I have been to various productions that they have done at Stantonbury, and, yeh there is a lot going on, I know people knock it and say they want to get out of it, but that doesn't seem to happen so much now, people seem to have settled.

There is a lot of different housing around, which breaks up the monotony [. . .] and I quite like how they have mixed the council properties with the private property. I mean they are not that mixed in terms – but you haven't got all the same on the one estate. I quite like the original idea of Milton Keynes, was that you didn't sort of have your inner city areas you know the average area, these sort of suburbs but you had these pockets of housing, industry, commerce, all around. So that all the major estates were linked into an industrial area and a commercial area, and I think that works better, because the city centre is light and airy, and the shops, and it is not this horrible dark place, crammed full of industry and stuff like that. So I think those kind of ideas have been really good and have worked for Milton Keynes.

Performance and text: story-telling as well as story

Brenda Dawson tells a tale that vividly depicts her adventures and experiences as well as her reflections on that tale as narrator. There are also comments on Milton Keynes and on the teller's views about cities. We will be returning to both these aspects: the narrative patterning in chapter 5 and the related topic of urban images in chapter 6. Before considering these however, we must first face some of the issues about the processes of telling and communicating such tales.

The story printed here gives the clear impression of a well-ordered and bounded text, the individual product of its unique and reflective author. It can readily be seen as falling within the broad category of 'personal narratives' and/or of 'life stories' as these terms are used by – among others – folklorists, anthropologists, psychologists and narrative scholars.[1] The category is a well-recognised one even if its precise definition carries some controversies (see e.g. Langellier 1989), and many such tales have been collected, published and analysed. The Milton Keynes stories by tellers like Brenda Dawson and her fellow narrators thus have many parallels.

However, allocating this and the other Milton Keynes tales to this broader category does not tell us everything about them. Indeed, jumping too hastily to conclusions on the basis either of the general comparative literature or of transcripts like the one just reproduced can conceal some of their complexity and genesis. Some further discussion of these aspects will also provide the opportunity to explore the conventions by which the personal tales are circulated and the manner in which they are constructed and used.

The picture commonly evoked by the overlapping terms 'personal narrative' and 'life story' is of a text: not necessarily a fully ordered account of someone's life or experiences, perhaps, but in essence a sustained single-voice text produced by one author, the narrator. This is further reinforced by the standard convention (also followed here) of publishing and analysing these narratives in the form of printed transcriptions.

This picture gives a false impression or, at best, simplifies a more complex process. Most published personal stories are represented in the form of linear texts. But they actually arose from an interactive or dialogue situation where a second participant (and maybe others too) played a significant part in framing, eliciting and recording the story. It is true that some interviewers succeed in evoking a relatively uninterrupted flow from the narrator – 'succeed' because capturing something which can be presented as a sustained text is often assumed to be the aim. But a more common basis for published self-narrations – and certainly for those here – is an interchange in which a second participant actively contributes by, at the least, implicitly defining the situation, initiating the proceedings, and keeping it going by facial cues, polite responses, verbal rejoinders and queries. As Briggs (1986) among others rightly argues, interviews carry their own problematics as communicative events. And our accepted conventions about behaviour between two people when one is answering an invitation from the other to talk about some aspect of their life actually prescribe that the 'listener' takes an active role in the exchange, at the very minimum showing interest and curiosity.

This 'dialogue' quality in story-telling is more or less eliminated in most published texts. Such transcripts seldom, one assumes, deliberately falsify the original. But they inevitably transform it by the very process of translating the multi-channel medium of spoken communication into the narrower medium of print. Other participants in the occasion all but disappear; the visual, auditory and other paralinguistic communicating is omitted; and the multi-faceted performance reduced to linear, one-voice monologue. Expressions that look 'ungrammatical' or 'uneducated' in a written (unlike oral) medium are tactfully smoothed out to suit written conventions of punctuation and paragraphing, the repetitions of live interaction are compressed, and the interviewer's contributions mostly omitted. Many analysts come to feel committed to 'their' narrations and – consciously or not – present them in a form likely to communicate effectively and with dignity in writing. So while most transcripts of personal stories appear on the surface to be written forms, they do so through creative, and usually tacit, editorial moulding.

The issue cannot be wished away. If spoken tales are to be conveyed through written communication at all, some degree of transformation is ultimately unavoidable, the only question being of how much and in what directions (my own procedures are described on pp. 75–8 below; for further comment on these issues see Fine 1984, Finnegan 1992 pp. 186ff., Oring 1987 pp. 252ff., Riessman 1993 esp. pp. 11ff., Watson and Watson-Franke 1985 pp. 16ff.).

The problem alerts us to important aspects of personal stories – at any rate of those studied here – that we might otherwise misunderstand. For though the printed narratives do indeed originate from the voice and tale of the prime teller, their first form was oral utterance not ready-made linear text. These utterances have been processed to turn them into a univocal and permanent print format, removing us from their original genesis in an interchange between two people, and on a specific occasion.

We should not fall into the opposite trap, either, of presupposing some alternative, more natural way in which people 'normally' tell life stories which is somehow 'falsified' by the practice of recording and transcribing personal narratives. For individuals do in practice converse in situations that are in part shaped by other people, and telling a personal story is commonly a response to someone's else's questions. The questioner, furthermore, is often – as here – not part of the narrator's everyday routine but a new acquaintance, someone in a newly developing friendship, an interviewer from outside (a familiar concept nowadays after all) or someone slightly removed from the usual domestic round such as a grandchild. It is over-romantic to search for the 'authentic' asocial telling. Some kind of interactive setting is indeed precisely our established convention for telling stories of the kind treated here – *spoken*, not written down, by their narrators.

Some awareness of these issues – insoluble in one sense, but also illuminating about real-life processes – is a necessary background to appreciating the nature of the stories printed and studied in this volume. The one-voice linear transcripts printed or quoted here do not have a one-to-one correspondence with the original live delivery. Nor was that performance itself enacted in some impersonal setting, free from human interaction.

A brief description of the situation and processing of the 'texts' analysed here should make these points clearer.[2] Brenda Dawson's tale, like those of the other narrators, was tape-recorded in a session of about an hour. This session was arranged and the recording conducted by Delia Gray, an experienced interviewer assisting on the project who lived in the same general area of Milton Keynes as the narrators (though not in Fishermead itself) and was clearly a fellow member of the city who shared its stories and its background. In most cases she spent some time beforehand getting to know the speakers and making sure they wished to participate. She provided a brief written statement which explained that the research concerned 'people's memories of their lives and how these affect their experience, specially in Milton Keynes', and that they were being asked to spend an hour or so 'talking informally about your own life and memories'.

For the recordings Delia Gray encouraged the speakers to talk generally about their lives, in their own way. In the setting of personal interaction in a speaker's own home she responded with the conventionally expected courtesies of acknowledgements, expressions of interest, and in some cases queries to keep the narration going. In Brenda Dawson's tale, for example, she responds with a murmured expression of fellow-feeling to the dramatic points in the narration and shows how well she had heard the account of the mother's disapproving attitude and appreciated a crucial stage of the tale by interjecting 'To your mother's dismay I suppose?' during the episode recounting the teller's break from the parental home. She generally included a few unpressing open questions about reactions to Fishermead or Milton Keynes if these did not come up anyway; in Brenda Dawson's case these led into some, though not all, of her comments on Milton Keynes and on Fishermead. But in general the sessions were undirective and the tellers left to take their own route. The narrators varied in fluency and some were more eager or available than others to talk about their experiences (perhaps one reason, besides the interviewer's gender, for the larger number of women). However, the concept of producing a personal account of their lives seemed to be a familiar enough one in all cases. This applied even to those who struggled to keep going or for whom this was the first time they had presented a sustained, relatively lengthy narration of their story.

Spoken interviews or oral performances can only be translated into written words through being partially transformed. Transcription presents real problems, for not only is there no one correct way to complete it, but the choice of textual presentation should ideally match the intended readership of the final transcript. Some versions attempt to convey performance qualities through special print techniques (as in Tedlock 1972 or the journal *Alcheringa*; see also Fine 1984 and Finnegan 1992 pp. 203ff.), sophisticated strategies which play an essential role for some research purposes but in other contexts may be a hindrance. As Linde points out: 'It takes time to learn to use elaborately notated transcription systems, and . . . readers confronted with extensive unfamiliar transcription conventions tend to skip the examples, which is the worst possible outcome of a choice of transcription system' (1993 p. xi). Since my own purpose was, broadly, to present the personal stories in an accessible form for an interdisciplinary readership I decided to use a simple linear version which can be readily read, whilst knowing well that this means losses as well as gains.

The recordings of the Milton Keynes story-tellings therefore had to be subjected to this further processing. The tapes were first roughly transcribed, reproducing in typescript the words of both participants, including most of the interviewer's courteous acknowledgements etc. as well as most so-called 'false starts' of more than a word or two, but without any attempt to represent paralinguistic features like volume, pace or heightened emotion. A copy of this transcript was sent to the speaker.

Then, after some further checks against the original tapes and any corrections from the authors, I transformed this into a written and mainly univocal version. This was partly done through paragraphing and punctuation, designed as far as possible to match the original delivery and make the sense clear for readers not present at the original interview nor able to hear the tape's auditory clues. I did not try to 'correct' sentences or grammar which in written form can appear somewhat rambling or even 'incorrect' (though perfectly appropriate to the interactive situation of oral exchange), but I did occasionally add short explanations in square brackets to aid the reader.

More radically, I mostly cut out the interviewer's polite or encouraging responses which to the reading eye can disrupt the flow, and, for the same reason, many of her queries (if necessary clarifying the speaker's referent in square brackets). Other passages were omitted when there was a great deal of repetition, or comments from third parties which the speakers themselves clearly regarded as interruptions. Omissions were also made when it was advisable to retain confidentiality or, more often, to contain the length of this volume – a limitation imposed on many reproducers of personal narratives by the constraints of print and publishers' conventions (often not explicitly acknowledged).

Again this was not easy. I have, for example, cut a certain amount of Brenda Dawson's lengthy account of her childhood, mainly because it was over-long for the space available but also because (perhaps?) some of the detail might be uninteresting or off-putting to general readers. But should I really have done so? or chosen those particular passages? or should I have cut more? Whatever the answer, in these (and no doubt other) transcripts there are in practice many omissions, those of any substance indicated by dots. Given the purpose of the transcripts I was not over-literal about marking minor omissions like repeated words or hesitations suitable in oral delivery but awkward in print, unless these seemed to have some emotive significance. Apart from the square-bracketed material mentioned above, additions were not made: that is, the transcripts represent the story told on the one specific occasion of the recording, they are not compilations incorporating material collected in other contexts.

The proceeding described above may sound well organised, but in fact posed continual questions. For example, many oral narrations in one sense flow on seamlessly. In oral interaction this may be a matter of effective, dramatic or subtle stylistics but appear 'poorly expressed' in a written format. How should this be punctuated and paragraphed in print? How far, for example, should the rapid flow in (what has been printed as) the first two paragraphs of Brenda Dawson's narrative be split up into 'sentences'? In one way there *are* divisions in both her delivery and her logic, and punctuating certainly makes it easier for the reading eye. On the other hand, these divisions are relative not absolute and there is a sense in which the oral flow is the more effective in its original utterance for *not* being split up by full stops. In such cases, ultimately the transcriber exercises fairly arbitrary judgements (indeed the alert reader may have noticed the slightly different format of the 'same' excerpt in chapter 1, p. 2). In both Brenda Dawson's and the other narratives the final punctuation could equally well have been inserted differently.

The same applies in the case of reported speech and reported thought. Brenda Dawson recounts her reaction 'Oh right' to the break in the chain of the family's church tradition, and 'Oh dear, dear' to her mother's dismay about her leaving home. She also verbalises her reaction to the dramatic moment of facing the 'biscuit box' of her imposed new home when she saw it for the first time. Whether or not to present these and similar examples within inverted commas in the printed text is always a moot point. It is not necessarily a trivial one however, for the effectiveness and wider implications of the narration sometimes lie in the way it slips among differing dimensions of direct/indirect reportage, linked into the narrator's degree of narrative distancing from the events being recounted (see chapter 5).

Similarly the retention or otherwise of (on the surface) repetitive or time-gaining verbal tricks like 'you know', 'I mean', 'well', 'sort of' or (common in Brenda Dawson's narrative) 'yeh' seems innocuous at one level. And yet at another they can carry wider implications for the universalising and distancing elements of the narrator's art (again further discussed in chapter 5). Here too I have ultimately made fairly arbitrary judgements.

The delivery arts and interactions do not come across in the printed transcript – pauses, non-verbal exchanges with the interlocutor, facial expressions, atmosphere, tone. Brenda Dawson's comment on her mother's exaggerated fears about what she was up to while she was in London – that 'she was probably right, whatever she thought!' – was uttered as a humorous aside. Similarly in Shirley Lambert's story (below, pp. 106ff.) she remarks, not with literal meaning but with humour and self-mockery, that she gave up stealing 'because it just wasn't paying'. In print such remarks, sometimes originally produced as a kind of ironic reflection on the action, can be misread. It is near-impossible to reproduce this in print, but it does need to be remembered that key facets in many narratives' complexity may be lost in transcription.

In general, then, the texts as printed here do certainly convey something of their narrators' art and storied experiences. But much is either 'missing' or transformed. The transcripts cannot give a definitive or neutral representation nor fully match the original occasion, subtlety and form of the original delivery.

The published literature sometimes gives the impression that people are constantly telling their life stories or, at least, waiting for the chance to do so, with a worked-out monologue somewhere lurking in their minds; and, further, that capturing that kind of text is a necessary condition for studying personal narrative. But this model may again be misleading. It is true that some tellers may have up to a point rehearsed elements in their stories before, even in a sense added certain episodes to their repertoire of tellings. But their stories may lie less in bounded and sustained texts than in continuing smaller dialogues, variable tellings, bitty interchanges, responses to questions: a narrative *potentiality* or ability which can then be verbalised, more or less coherently and lengthily, in response to a particular situation.

The concept of talking about their lives turned out not to be at all an unfamiliar notion to the tellers recorded here. But few if any had actively narrated their personal stories in the forum of a concentrated one-hour session (the centenarian Timothy Hopkins was a partial exception in having previously written a story of his life). On the occasion of recording, some tellers formulated a relatively sustained and fluent story with little prompting. They had doubtless told parts of it before in other situations, having perhaps formed the habit (or the need) of formulating some articulate rationale of their lives or attitudes, or reached a life-stage when reflecting back on one's life story is an expected activity. Other speakers were less fluent overall, though sometimes eloquent on particular episodes. Some tellers engaged in more conversation with the interviewer, resulting in more divergence between oral performance and edited written transcript than where authors had in some sense rehearsed aspects of their tales before. Some were surprised by their capacity to tell their story, commenting that they had never done it that way before. But all had the resources to do so. All responded to the occasion by formulating their personal story in a form which – fluent or not – both told of their life and was specific to the situation.

The stories printed and quoted here were thus each delivered on that one particular occasion. Narrations produced on other occasions would not necessarily be identical and, depending on the purpose or the listener, could cover just some of the episodes narrated here, or different ones again. In that sense the transcripts here are 'fragments' – except that the term 'fragment' suggests some existent continuing whole from which these are torn off. In fact the narrations need to be pictured less as closed written texts than as a personally accessible resource – a store of accepted narrative patterns interacting with their own unique experiences and perspectives. Speakers had the capacity to draw on this resource to fashion a story – long or short – appropriate to the situation and the audience.

We thus need to reassess the models in many published studies in order to appreciate the nature of these personal tales from Milton Keynes. In practice, the genre as actually practised is probably messier, more plural and less textually sustained than we often assume. This is certainly the case with the stories here. Despite the texted impression given by the transcripts, we should avoid imposing an implicit model by which only the 'best', in the loaded sense of coherent bounded texts in the written style, qualify as full examples. On the contrary, their conventional themes, plots and protagonists are no less significant for being activated in fluid personal performance rather than in written text. Indeed, the oral setting lays all the more onus on the individual teller's skills of drawing on both conventional pattern and personal originality on the live occasion of performance.

Understanding the relatively fluid nature of the personal stories – potential resource as much as a fixed text – is also relevant for the *use* of these stories.

In one sense the Milton Keynes examples resemble other story-telling in their potential for being used for almost anything that the teller and listener(s) choose. They can be told to comfort, amuse, attack, complain, show off, protest, overbear, scandalise, woo, bore, satisfy an interviewer – and a thousand other things. There can be no definitive list of uses any more than of individual people or their situations.

The comparative literature reminds us that narrative does more than just reflect or report experience. It also shapes it. There are many analyses of how people set their own lives in perspective and give them depth through linking their own stories to wider symbolic images and myths, a relevant perspective on the tales here (Myerhoff 1980, Abrahams 1985b). The very fact, too, of narrating one's life to another person can somehow give it a greater sense of 'reality', an aspect particularly stressed in gerontological contexts (e.g. Bornat 1989) but equally applicable to all ages. Narrative creates order out of chaos and gives meaning to what otherwise might seem anarchic or fragmented (Bruner 1987, Abrahams 1985b, Shotter and Gergen 1989, Hall 1992). It can use the 'consoling plot' to aid our comprehension of a plight 'that, by being made interpretable, becomes bearable' (Bruner 1991 p. 16, citing Kermode). The telling of self-stories above all can formulate and realise personal experience through narrating the continuity and actions of the individual self. Bruner sums up his influential view of 'life as narrative':

The ways of telling and the ways of conceptualizing that go with them [in self-narratives] become so habitual that they finally become recipes for structuring experience itself, for laying down routes into memory, for not only guiding the life narrative up to the present but directing it into the future. (Bruner 1987 p. 31)

And if in a way *all* the stories we hear and tell, of whatever kind, help to shape our world, it can still be claimed that this is true in an especially poignant way for the stories we tell of our own lives where 'story' and 'experience' in some sense coincide. The 'experiencing' itself is cast in narrative form, made meaningful through the vocabulary and conventions of the personal story.

It might be unwise to assume that all these claims could be applied literally, and equally, to every single life story, particularly given the flexible and open-ended nature of the personal story genre studied here. The Milton Keynes stories – like, I surmise, those told by many people – were mostly not carefully meditated or sustained narrative texts. Nor were they deliberately worked up and 'improved' between a series of recording sessions (as were some of the stories analysed in the literature). They are shaped, indeed, in accordance with the accepted conventions for such tellings, but had probably not been told in *that* particular form before, nor would be again.

Nevertheless it seems that these personal narrations did function as a form for organising and not just 'reflecting' their authors' experience. Both at the time of the recording and from follow-up discussion later, it became clear that the tellers found having told their stories satisfying, sometimes surprising and illuminating. They found the enactment a kind of proof of the reality and significance of their lives and of their capacity to – in a sense – control and give weight and meaning to their experience through the action of verbalised narration.

The narrations recorded here were produced for a specific occasion. But it emerged at the same time that the narrators did indeed have the cultural arts to draw on narrative themes and conventions for narrating their lives, realising these in a truly personal story of their own individual and unique experiences. This potentiality for personal narrative is actualised through the range of conventions discussed in this and the following two chapters. This rich resource for personal creativity and control is no less significant for eventuating not always as a 'full' sequential text but also through smaller episodes, shared understandings, dialogues and verbalised interpretations. The processes of 'making the world' and of formulating, ordering and validating personal experience through self-storying can be found not just in lengthy texted narratives, but also in the flexible self-narrating resource recognised in our culture and activated by individual narrators like those represented in this volume.

5 'That's my story': narrative conventions in personal tales

Personal narratives of the kind discussed in the last chapter form one notable category among the manifold tales of the city. These are the tales, after all, of the current urban residents, the people who between them experience and create the city. At first sight these personal and idiosyncratic tales may appear to have little about them that could reward detailed examination. But as Barbara Johnstone puts it in her analysis of American Midwest stories, 'It is in our nature not to notice things that happen routinely' (1990 p. 2). The 'artless' impression given by these personal narrations in fact conceals cultural conventions of structure, content or delivery that are no less significant for being mainly below the level of consciousness.

This chapter discusses some narrative features of these personal narrations of Milton Keynes dwellers, both those tales quoted at some length in this and other chapters, and the corpus of (in all) thirty-five narratives recorded in the housing estate of Fishermead in 1994. We will be exploring the conventions through which the narrators shape their stories' temporal ordering, the dramatis personae expected to figure in their recounting, and the explanatory themes which give unity and satisfaction to their plots.

Though no story is 'typical' or fully exemplifies any one of these conventions, a lengthy extract from a second tale can give a helpful backdrop to the discussion here. Once again it is prefaced by a brief note and additions/omissions are marked by square brackets.

George Rowe's tale

72-year-old George Rowe (his real name) was brought up in Cranfield, a village not far from the present Milton Keynes, where his parents had also been born. He started work in the local brickfields when he was fourteen. After war service in the RAF, he worked in London until he and his wife decided to move to Milton Keynes. They considered the various estates available at that relatively early stage of the development of Milton Keynes, and decided on Fishermead, moving into his present rented house in 1976, at the same time as his wife's sister and her husband moved into the house opposite. George Rowe had been a widower since 1984 and lived alone with his devoted dog.

* * *

Well I was born at Cranfield, which is not that far from here, is it? [. . .] My sister lived at Cranfield, and my parents, well as far as I know they were born in Cranfield [. . .] Going back to the early days, I can really remember when we had a fairly large garden and so forth, we used to keep pigs, three fattening pigs. Chickens. And we always had cats around, because they produce mice don't they having livestock around, and the cats used to keep them down, well and we never had a dog those days.

Really I just went to the elementary school, and that was it, it was brilliant. One of my earliest memories was being pushed in a push-chair to go blackberrying which was coming down towards Moul-soe and that way, because my father worked on a farm between Cranfield and Moulsoe and so forth. I can remember that, and can remember going into Bedford hospital when I was I think four, and can even remember the bed I was in and so forth. A kitten scratched my eye [. . .] and it produced an abscess and so forth and I was in hospital three weeks. I can still remember clinging onto my mother, didn't want to be taken away, anyway, it is amazing, but I don't expect you want to hear about those days, I'm sure.

Another thing I can remember as a small child is being in the school concert and having to learn the alphabet backwards, and to make it more simple the whole class had to do it, probably the only school in Britain who knew the alphabet backwards. I think it is my party piece today, in actual fact. My son, I taught him, because funnily enough it all rhymes [he demonstrates]. It takes me longer to say it forward.

I had two brothers, older than me, my sister the eldest was eighteen years older than me, and I understand that between my brother and myself, who there was nine years between, there was a daughter who died, but I don't know the details of it. I just don't know. Anyway I arrived in 1922.

I went and worked in the brickfields when I was fourteen, at Stewartby. And those days you had to cycle, if you never cycled you never got to work, you know. About five and a half miles, something like that. Well if it snowed too heavy you didn't go. It was a pound a week including three shillings time-keeping bonus. If you were late by one minute – they gave you three minutes to clock on in the morning, whatever time you were supposed to be there, whether it was 7.30 a.m. or 6.30 a.m. or even 7 a.m. – they gave you one minute, if you had on your card four minutes past, you lost your three shilling time-keeping bonus for the week. I never lost it once, I have always been a time-keeper [. . .]

I can remember playing a lot of cricket, there were only two sports I really enjoyed, football especially. My brothers being older than me used to take me up to watch the Arsenal from Bedford station. We were then taken to the Palladium in the evening and the tickets then in those days were six shillings, that was the days of, you have probably heard of Flanagan and Allen, 'The Crazy Gang'. They would take me horse racing at Alexandra Park. They were much older than me, and I was lucky. I think it still goes, there was a News of the World fashion competition and my mother shared the top prize of that in the thirties. You had to pick out of nine, whether they were hats or skirts, or what, you had to choose which was in order of merit, which was best, and she shared it with someone else who came from Bristol. The odd thing is that my wife and I was down near Torquay, and we had been racing that particular day and [. . . met a couple] and in the conversation we talked about her winning the fashion competition, and it was his parents who had shared it with my mother. Now, it doesn't seem possible! [. . .]

Well the war came along and we went into ammunitions, and from there onwards was working in the ammunitions and me working in there stopped me going in the RAF straightaway type of thing. Although I had got my number and so forth in 1941, I didn't go until 1942. Getting on for nineteen, twenty I think. Well, everyone else was in, I suppose, that was what you had to do.

I basically just did clerical work, orderly rooms and that type of thing, because I had worked in the brickfields and so forth. But one of the best things that came out of that, I worked in that specific section where parachutes weren't actually made, but they were packed for the fliers and goodness knows what, and we were drop-testing parachutes. Drop-testing yeh, as it was special ex-type parachutes they were for the people who had to drop into other countries. Yes, we used to pack all the things for agents, that used to be flown over and dropped in, wherever, and they would come to see what was going into their packs, radios, and goodness knows what. I was lucky and was selected to drop-test with the para-troopers, not physically but they were attached to dummies which were thrown out of the aircraft, and you had to lift them out and drop them out of a hole, about as big as this table that they used to drop out of [. . .]

[In 1943] they whisked me off to Blackpool, in the first place, and then I missed the draft from there, and I didn't go until 1944 to West Africa. As far as I was concerned it was a doddle, well it was because I was working in the orderly room, no, they had lights on and goodness knows what in West Africa [. . .] I came back in April 1945. I will say I was playing football five nights a week, in West Africa, what with various inter-sections and various navy teams and whatever.

Well I enjoyed it. I had already got married in between. I got married on the 1st December, 1943, when I got embarkation leave and had twenty-four hours to go to Blackpool. So we went out and got married, we had a special licence. We were going to get married in the following January, and then seeing I got a recall notice and I was going to go overseas, and we then brought it forward to the Saturday before recall sort of thing. And on the day we was sup-posed to get married I was back in Blackpool. I got married on the Wednesday, by owing to the vicar getting a special licence and someone to marry us with two witnesses, I haven't got a photo. One of the funniest things was the wife stayed with her mother, and I went down to the clergy anyway, to get the special licence and he said to me 'Who is going to marry you?', and I said 'Well, Mr Shaun King', he said 'I have got a funeral on of an RAF boy, would you like to come back and rehearse with me?' So can you imagine, I was in a hearse!

We went out and got married, and bought her the ring after-wards. I have a photo upstairs of us together at a very early age, but no wedding photo. I just stayed the night because I should have been back in Henlow, stayed the night and the police came for me the following day and said why wasn't I back at Henlow. My father-in-law said 'Well he is going back tonight, he got mar-ried', so they said 'Oh all right we will let them know', and I went back, no problems and I arrived in Blackpool on the Saturday and on the Sunday morning I came home again because I hadn't had time to have leave, they said I had to be back within four days.

Then I had trouble at home and I stayed longer, nothing happened, you have to talk your way out of these things, don't you? I enjoyed the life.

Well, when I came back from West Africa I was stationed at a place called Little Staughton, that is in Bedfordshire as well. [I stayed in the RAF] until October 1946 in actual fact, I came out. I moved on from Little Staughton into Northolt, I got a posting to there, and I moved out to Clapton in London. [East London] is my old stomping ground [. . .]

My sister-in-law and her husband didn't really like the flat they were living in, in Clapton. And then all of a sudden my wife's sister said to her about they were going to go to Hackney Town Hall and saw about Milton Keynes being born, because that was what it was called, 'being born'.

She told my wife about it, and my wife said 'What is keeping us here?', and I said 'Well it is my job, isn't it?' She said, 'Well, Joe is going to actually commute, why can't you do it?' So I said, 'Well I can do, nothing really keeping us here', and Hackney was getting worse by that time, in 1976, and we had a flat in a high rise block of flats in Hackney, on the sixth floor. But my son was away by then, he had studied with night school and so forth to be a quantity surveyor [. . .] He met his wife down in Butlin's, and next year, well, they will be twenty-four years married come the 23rd of this month, I've got a card for him, ha, ha. You don't know what lies in store for you really, do you?

And then we came down ourselves [to Milton Keynes] because we had a car and so forth, with my brother and sister-in-law, drove around, there wasn't much around at that particular time, in 1976. They arranged for us to come down, our tickets were bought, I don't know who bought them for us, but you had a travel voucher, anyway, and, as I recall, it was a matter of then they picked us up from the station [. . .] and they took us round the sites which had been built, because they had started so many years earlier [for location of the various estates named see Fig. 4.1]. We went to Netherfield, and to Coffee Hall, I don't know in the city, I can't remember the names. (*Conniburrow?*) Conniburrow wasn't built until after, it came with this lot because they are all of the same design, they found out what a mess they had made. (*Stantonbury?*) Yeh. (*New Bradwell?*) Oh it has a bit of a bad reputation up there, oh. (*Fullers Slade?*) Fullers Slade, yeh there was only one house up there and we all trooped into this house type of thing and had a look round, and we went to Eaglestone as well, that's right, and at the end of going around, because Springfield they hadn't really started to build that at all. Oldbrook, I mean near the roundabout just down the bottom here, there wasn't anything beyond there at all, they used to walk down to the railway lines with all the overhead electricity pylons down there as well, and it was all fields all the way down, apart from in some instances. There was a road going nowhere, that is what they used to say about Milton Keynes, all the roads lead nowhere [. . .]

Well when I was working in London I used to have the other old dog, and from 1976, that was a very hot summer, and we had this other labrador and we used to take him out. [After moving to Fishermead] we used to be up at 4.15 a.m. in the morning and out with the dog at 5 a.m. and jump in my car and go to Bletchley at 6 a.m. in the morning to catch the two minutes past six train to London which gets into London about seven minutes past, having stopped at practically every station all the way through down to Euston [station]. And then from Euston I used to get on the underground at Old Street, from Old Street walk down to Commercial Street, to the factory. Rushing back was the worst thing. I used to get away a bit early, we were supposed to finish at 5 p.m. but we used to get away a few minutes earlier, a big rush, to get back to Old Street, and then from Old Street to Euston, and get into the main station [. . .] I was fit as a fiddle in those days, running up the steps together.

I took on an allotment, and I was doing that then, from 1976 and we actually started in 1977, and until my wife died. And then I thought what the heck am I working like this for, for nothing to give your produce away, frankly, so that was that [. . .] I would go straight down to the allotment [from the train] and then get home here about nine o'clock and have dinner. I had to go out with the dog then, didn't I, all around Springfield, got back about ten o'clock and I was in bed at about half past.

[My wife] in 1978 had a hysterectomy and she had to have a cyst removed, which was apparently, well they didn't actually weigh it, some of them they do, it was eight and a half inches long by six and a half inches. I heard about someone having one about twenty pounds, a cyst. But from then onwards, I was told that the prognosis was cancerous. And then she died in 1984 [. . .] Forty-one years

5.1 Campbell Park in Central Milton Keynes. The formal park near the city centre, much frequented by George Rowe and other urban residents (by courtesy of the Commission for the New Towns)

married. We celebrated our diamond wedding down there, forty years, the year before.

(*Did she like Milton Keynes?*) Loved it. [Fishermead] hadn't deteriorated up to her death, sort of thing, it has deteriorated in the last ten years. This was the house we moved into, there was very few families around, my next door neighbour, Mr Ozo, an Indian couple, they are still there, but they moved in a month after we came, and he arrived to view the house on the same day as we come down, and we met him there [. . .] They have had two sons, and been here for years, and both have done exceptionally well, been to university and got their degrees [. . .]

I have had people say 'Oh you live in Milton Keynes', and I say 'Well I love it.' There is so much going on, if you want it, doesn't mean that I need it or want it, but there is for those who want it, that is the way that I look at it, and there is going to be more and more in the future, quite frankly you know. [The theatre] got shoved back for some time, but I think it is more on the cards again now [. . .] I have been down [to Campbell Park], I used to walk down to Willen [Lake] with the dog and so forth, very nice around there, amazing that I have always found someone to walk with. Not many men want to walk really, but ladies will walk with you [. . .] They are more conversationalists, ladies [. . .]

(*So life in Milton Keynes has been fairly good to you?*) I think more so since I retired I suppose, because I am out and about so much [. . . I walk with the dog] down to the canal and have a walk round, and in fact he jumped in the canal only recently, it's filthy that is. He is eleven on the 23rd, a week. We lost the other one with leukaemia, seven years old. He [this dog] has had arthritis, according to the veterinary hospital at Cambridge, since he was a puppy, so he has done very, very well, and he has a tail that won't stop wagging, I have heard people say 'Come on wag-a-tail.' He has made my life here, quite frankly, for the last few years, he really has.

Time and event in the personal stories

The personal narratives are cast within a temporal framework – that key feature of 'story' – evident in both the past tenses and the specific time ordering of the tales. This comes out clearly in George Rowe's tale, as in Brenda Dawson's (quoted earlier). The progression may not be presented in a simple linear sequence. But *some* temporal staging always seems to be one dimension of the narrative, and particular ways of ordering this accepted as the 'natural' way to experience life's events and – in a sense the same thing – to narrate its tale.

The most prominent temporal frame is that set by the teller's *personal or family life cycle*, again evident in the two tales already quoted. Stories move through recognised stages: the teller's birth; childhood; schooling; leaving the parental home and/or first job; marriage/partnership, sometimes followed by separation/divorce and further partnerships; birth and rearing of children; then, for many older people, grandchildren, death of spouse and old age. Not all stages appear in each narrative nor are they always recounted chronologically, but they occur frequently enough to indicate a framework taken as natural and transparent. It is a common convention of our culture for individuals to classify and experience their lives in relation to the recognised life stages. The rites of passage that demarcate them, as Metcalfe and Bern point out, are not so much a 'natural process' as a 'narrative device' (1994 p. 665), well presented in the temporal orders of the narratives here.

The first move out of the parental home is often a turning point in the story's progression, a step towards the anticipated and fought-for stage of greater personal independence. Brenda Dawson presents her early life as a struggle to free herself from her mother's control. She joins the WRAC – to her mother's dismay:

Yes, oh dear, dear. But having said that, it was an acceptable way of leaving home. I had run out of things like looking for a bed-sit in London, that was frowned on, or sharing a flat with a friend, no, that was out. And sort of joining the WRAC, although she didn't really want me to, at least it was a way she felt I could leave home but still have that safety.

Further complexity is added through the turn-round from one family framework (the original natal one) to another (initiated by the teller's marriage and/or children). Through the teller's experience the tale unites two time-frames, two family time cycles.

This temporal staging is taken for granted in the personal narratives. A *family*-based orientation to time runs through most of these narratives, sometimes extended further – as will emerge later – into the longer timescale of the continuities between successive generations. What might in other types of tales be presented in 'objective' chronological terms is here narrated within the phases of family and individual life cycle. Dates are thus as often fixed by referring to marriage anniversaries or children's ages as by a named year. As Ricoeur would put it, these stories are ordered by 'human' rather than 'clock' time (1984).

Movements between different localities provide another form of temporal sequencing, and narrators sometimes relate the sequence of their lives – and stories – to where they were living at the time. The familiar travel tale is one accepted framework (De Certeau 1984 chapter 9, Robertson *et al.* 1994). But the narratives here are more often told in the context of housing and of the associated personal relationships than of place in a physical sense. Some narrators recount a particular move as a pivotal point in their story, above all if this meant their 'first house'. But though this theme is significant in many stories, further elaborated in chapter 6, the idea of 'place' seldom plays the structuring role that it does in some other tales discussed in the comparative literature (such as Bruner 1987). Family and personal stages, themselves often related to housing, take priority.

A third form for temporal ordering is through the speaker singling out particular *events* within the story's unfolding over time. Though from an outsider's viewpoint perhaps seeming of only minor interest, the narrators may present certain episodes as the highlights, more crystallised (and perhaps more frequently recounted) than other parts, symbolising some key aspect of the teller's life or view of themselves. Such events provide temporal reference points in the story. A son's motor cycle accident does this in one story – 'the worst thing that has ever ever happened' – as does the fateful moment (recounted on p. 105) when the young Peter Sutton makes his decision to leave the factory to search out his life's mission. A single episode may crucially progress the action, as when Shirley Lambert's life changes and she rejoins her family after she happens to meet her two small sisters outside a Bletchley s hop (p. 109).

Some narrations construct a sequence that seems driven by outside events – and unpredictable ones at that – rather than by the will of the teller. One speaker tells of moving to Milton Keynes because of her father's breakdown and not her own choice, and several recount the unexpected blow of a spouse's death or illness – 'when he got ill it seemed so unfair'. Time 'goes on' inexorably and in the story things 'happen' to narrators rather than are initiated by them.

Some events are described as 'coincidences', at times suggesting a mysterious or fateful import beyond the common run of ordinary life: 'odd', 'strange', 'funny'. The 20-year-old Janet Eaton's story recounts the 'weird' way a clairvoyant's words led her into a hairdressing course, while Frank Dyer's narrative emphasised how it was forty years 'exact' from his wife's death that he met the 'young lady' he fell in love with in his seventies. Judy Candy's is one of two stories to give vivid accounts of aid from near-supernatural sources. She is narrating her early days in a shared-ownership house in Milton Keynes:

Then accidently I fell pregnant with my third, which really freaked us out, we were dreadfully skint, and the place was very small, it was a case of 'Well we are going to have to move because we haven't got enough room.' The weird thing about that was we talked about getting extensions, and him travelling for a while, and letting the house out, and I was on my way up the stairs for a wee, and with nothing else on my mind at all and I heard this voice and it went 'Unlock capital!' and I went 'Ooh!' on the stairs, it was like someone had spoken to me. And I sat on the bog and I was thinking 'I wonder, I wonder', and then I joked about selling the house, and then we decided to sell the house, and it was a big decision, like having the experience on the stairs made me trust a bit more the powers that be, or whatever . . . it was a good little voice it was.

Timothy Hopkins' story related a much earlier experience, when his ship was torpedoed in the first world war and went down in twenty minutes:

Well I stood on the deck, although I couldn't swim much, even though I lived at the seaside town. And I thought 'What shall I do?', you know, and all the others was jumping over the side, and the boats were being lowered down, you know, what they keep on the sides of the boats. And do you know I stood there, and it may seem strange to you, but when I was born and I was going to die and my mother had sent for the minister to baptise me in my living room which he did, and she said 'We haven't got a godfather, vicar' and he said 'That's all right, I'll be godfather and look after him all his life.' That's the point I'm getting at, I stood on this deck, not knowing, alone, a voice suddenly said to me 'Jump.' And I turned around and there was nobody around, and it said 'Jump.' And I ran to the side and I jumped over and down. The boat was going down the side and I jumped into this boat full of men and that saved my life, because we were only about twenty yards away from the boat, rowing, when the boat went down. Now that's strange, but that is actually what happened.

Temporal framing by 'happenings', fate or coincidence, recalls the theory that a view of life as determined by outside constraints or by 'fate' is commoner among working-class narrators, while middle-class speakers stress 'agency' and 'self' (Linde 1993 pp. 128–9). But it is not easy to detect a common pattern. As is evident from their tales, many Fishermead narrators did indeed suffer harsh constraints on their choices in terms of family break-ups, financial hardship, violence, homelessness, loss. Several stories present sequential rows and confrontations which help to order the plot. But narratives recounting such 'happenings' *also* often present their heroes' positive ways of dealing with them. Paradoxically, it is sometimes the stories that highlight the narrator's energy and enterprise that are fullest of 'events'. The Ulsterman Jim Moore, for example, humorously tells of 'what you would call a misspent life, because I always did the wrong thing!'. But his story also shows him taking advantage of the sudden turns and unforeseen events which changed the direction of his life. Timothy Hopkins may have brought in a supernatural dimension to recount one striking episode, but elsewhere in his story he depicts his own self-motivation and pride. Indeed, as will emerge later in this chapter an equally if not more prominent theme, co-existing with the sequence of 'events', is of the structuring influence of character and of actions initiated by the teller.

It would be misleading to pick exclusively on one device as *the* key to the temporal structuring in any given story. Most performances intertwine several themes rather than present one systematic structure, and the presentation is complicated by back- and forward-flashes, and moments for present or future reflections. As with the elderly women narrators studied by Bennett (1986), the stories' presentation may be circular and circumlocutory, nor do the tales always have clear openings, middles or endings. Nevertheless the personal/family life cycle, movements between places and the effect of special events do emerge as common frameworks for conveying stories' temporal qualities. The first in particular, but also to some extent the others, is taken for granted as an intelligible narrative format to formulate salient features of individual lives. The story's time-ordering is less a measure of 'objective time' than a symbolically acceptable form through which people experience and convey personal continuity in a temporal framework.

This time ordering is moved on through the various dramatis personae of the stories, the next topic we must examine. The heroic 'I' may take the leading role but also interacts with other expected protagonists, depicted mainly through accepted family relationships, both dead and living, but also as friends or partners. These key protagonists will already be evident in the stories quoted so far, but another tale, that of Bessie Wyatt, can provide further illustration to lead into the discussion.

Bessie Wyatt's tale

In her late seventies in 1994, Bessie Wyatt had spent most of her life in or near Manchester. Her Scottish father died when she was a baby, and her mother brought her and her two sisters up 'on the parish' – an experience which perhaps had something to do with her expressed philosophy 'If you want something you've got to work for it.' She recounts her early studies and her jobs, joining the pay corps in the war and later supervising a typing pool where she 'loved every minute of it'. Her first and second husbands feature in her tale, the mother who supported her through her divorce, her son and daughter-in-law, sisters, grandchildren and the long-time friend whom she helped. She had moved from Manchester about ten years before to her present sheltered flat in Fishermead, near her son.

* * *

I was born in Sankey, Warrington, and there was my mother and obviously my father. I had two sisters. Anne was my eldest sister, and Mary the middle sister and I was the youngest. Now, my father he died, I was only ten weeks old when my father died. My middle sister she was two years when my father died and my eldest sister was ten, so my mother brought the three of us up. Well, she was more like a pal really to us, she was very good. You see, I didn't miss anything because I had never known a father, and Mary my middle sister she would only be two, so she really wouldn't miss him, but my eldest sister came off the worse there, and she had to sort of help with us. She got the rough end of the stick.

We were what you called in those days 'the parish' and you had to go once a week, mother had to go to get her money to keep us, and we lived in a room in a house. Just one room, and we shared a bedroom. In those days if you were on the parish they could come into your home any time and if you had cakes or biscuits on the table, that was a luxury. So you wouldn't get your money the next week, only rent, because you had bought luxuries. But we adapted to it. I don't ever remember being short of anything, though. I mean we have talked about it, and I have said to Mary 'Do you think we were short of anything?' and she said she couldn't think that we were. So, I suppose really we were all right. There was what you called 'the White Heather Club' and I suppose it was a sort of charity, and every Christmas we would get a pair of clogs off them. They were comfortable. Oh yes, clogs, and we would go to a little party they used to invite us all to a party and we used to get an apple and an orange and I don't know whether it was a threepenny bit or something, that was for Christmas, so you know, and then gradually things started to get better.

[My mother] was born in Philadelphia. And she came over to Scotland, the family came over to Scotland, the aunt came over and they lived in Scotland. And that is how she came over here then. And then what happened? Oh well of course we all went to school and I always knew – when Anne was old enough to work she wanted to be a waitress, that was the eldest sister, so she was quite happy and she worked in a shop in Manchester called 'Athwick & Browns', that is no longer there now and she got to be head waitress there and she loved it. And Mary wanted to work in a cake shop, that was my middle sister. And I was determined that I didn't want to work in a shop, because I just wasn't cut out for that sort of thing. So I made up my mind I wanted to go into an office, of course in those days education was a bit tough. It was good, you got the 'three Rs' but it was tough.

So, I went and started at night school and then I got a job as a post girl in an office, so that was the first step on the ladder. And kept going to night school and then I learnt shorthand and typing and got my certificates for that, and I thought well I am going upwards now. I got quite a decent job and then the war came along and so I joined up in the pay corps because I thought that was the nearest thing to what I wanted to do when the war was over. So I wasn't particularly clever with figures but by the time I had finished in the pay corps so that helped, you see it was all advancement. If you want something you've got to work for it.

And I came out of the ATS and I was married in 1945 and I had my son, Geoffrey, in 1946, and my husband was in the army. He was a regular but anyway he was playing about and so I thought well I am not going to put up with a life like this, so I divorced.

It was dreadful in those days. My mother stood by me, and my sister stood by me, because I had done nothing wrong. So mother looked after Geoffrey, and we stayed at mother's, because my husband never wanted a home [. . .] So then I got a job with ICI and I really worked at that and I loved every minute of it and eventually became supervisor of the typing pool, and I had forty girls under me, and I really, really loved that. All in Manchester [. . .]

I worked at ICI for many many years and I loved it, and then I met a gentleman whilst I was working at ICI, he was a sales representative, for British Insulated Cables, a very big firm, and he was area manager, and we met and we used to go out for a meal occasionally and things grew. He was a widower and things sort of grew and he was fond of Geoffrey and mother liked him, the family liked him, so eventually we got married. And then in the end he was taken so ill with Alzheimer's disease. It is a very insidious illness really, you don't really know it is happening to the person. It is dreadful, dreadful. I mean one day they are so nice and then the next day they are like a child, it is a very pitiful thing, they are like a child, and then another day they get in real tempers and gradually things go worse and then he became incontinent and then he couldn't feed or dress or wash, it was very very sad to see him because oh he was so nice, he was brilliant. But there that's the way of life isn't it, you can't help it.

So then when dad died, Geoffrey and Shirley, that is my son and daughter-in-law, they have two daughters Michaela and Elizabeth, and I lived in sheltered accommodation in Manchester. And then when dad died, they wanted me to come over here and live with them, and I said no, your ways, well we get along so well, but their ways aren't my ways, and I want to be independent and I always think what you can't see doesn't hurt you. I expect that sounds strange, but . . . So I said no to Geoffrey, I wasn't going to do anything quickly, I have got to have my space to unwind because it has been a dreadful time. Anyway I used to come over here just for a couple of weeks to Geoffrey and Shirley, just for a break, and really loved it. So I said to Geoffrey I would like to come and live here but what would be the position housing-wise, I don't want to live completely on my own, you know, and I like to feel that there is somebody around me. So I think I put my name down, or Geoffrey put my name down, for a council flat, and so we filled in the form and said I wished to move to Milton Keynes to be near to my family although I didn't want to live with them.

So one day my telephone went and this voice came on, and she said 'Mrs Wyatt, you don't know me but I know your son and we have a flat for you if you would like it at [this] sheltered accommodation', she said, 'It is Royal British Legion.' Well I know it sounds silly but you know I just burst into tears and I couldn't answer her and she said 'Shall I ring you back, you sound awfully upset?' I said I was all right I just hadn't expected it.

I was so lucky, and she said if I could 'Get in touch with your son and arrange for him to bring you over.' This was on the Monday; she said 'Come over and see the flat either Friday or Saturday of this week and let us know if you want to accept it.' So I phoned Geoffrey up and said 'I will be over.' [. . .] As soon as I walked in I said 'Yes I'll have it.' She said, 'Mrs Wyatt you've not even looked at it.' I said 'Yes I have', I knew straight away that I wanted to be here [. . .] And I moved the following Friday here, and I slept here on the Saturday. And I have never ever regretted it. I have never looked back.

And then my eldest granddaughter Michaela she got married and she went to live in Wales, and she had first of all, Emma Louise, so that was my first great granddaughter, and then six weeks ago she had Sophie, my second, and then Elizabeth, my youngest grand-daughter, she is nineteen now, she is not courting or anything. She is quite happy, you know. And when I say I don't see Geoffrey and Shirley a lot, I don't mean it like that, I never intrude on them, I feel I know they are there on the end of the phone if I want them [. . .] I just don't believe in living in their pockets. We have had our lives and we have had good lives and you shouldn't try and take off anybody else.

I had a friend in Manchester. Well we were in the ATS together, we trained at Lancaster Castle, Ella, and we did all our training at

Lancaster before we went in the ATS. And when I left Manchester she was terribly lonely because she had been brought up in an orphanage. I mean I had been lucky we had had a mother, and she had loved us dearly; but she had nobody, and she had lived in an orphanage and it was dreadful for her. So of course she came to sheltered accommodation in Manchester where I was, we had sort of followed each other and she was a lovely dear person, really, and very independent. And so when I left and came here after my husband died she was absolutely lost and she used to phone up and be in tears, and I would say 'Oh Ella you can't go on like this you will be so ill.' So I rang up the British Legion and I asked if it would be in order for Ella to come and stay with me, she already had her name down for a British Legion flat, and could she stay with me until a flat became available. They gave me consent, because they are for two people, so she stayed with me, and eventually a flat became empty here and she moved into the flat next door, here.

And you know you have your life mapped out for you, dear, it really is. Now she developed cancer and she got to the stage where she just couldn't do anything for herself. But she was only next door and so in the end she came in to me because I used to cook for her and I got an awful lot of help from the district nurse, oh they are wonderful people and Dr C—, well he is a dream. If he told me to cut my arm off, I would cut it off, he is a dream, and the Macmillan nurses I couldn't begin to tell you. So I got an awful lot of backup because I couldn't have let her go in a home after all that, she had had enough of homes. So I kept her here, and the warden, she used to come in regularly and she was so kind, and she used to say 'Now Bessie you pull that cord if you want me.' And I got so much backup here it was unbelievable, and Ella, at least she was happy for that time. So that was Ella.

Twelve months ago Ella died. But I must say that the kindness, backup, I can't see why people grumble. The only thing is there is no sea, no sea. I love the [city] centre. You see it suits me because I can't walk very far, so I get a taxi to the city centre and it is only two pounds, so if I go once a week it doesn't matter and I know I can sit down wherever I want, whenever I want. And that is why I like it and there is plenty of air. I wouldn't want to go back to Manchester to live, I go and visit my sister, but my sister comes over here to visit me more, she loves it [. . .]

> I really don't waste much time thinking about things that should be, because you can't really do very much about them really. We came up in the hard times so this is a doddle to us [. . .]

The dramatis personae

The narrations present a series of expected protagonists. These are named and unique individuals, with the drama enacted in personal not abstract terms – a contrast, therefore, to the general stories about Milton Keynes and, even more, to the academic tales of the city. But at the same time these individuals enter the stage as familiar figures.

The most common protagonists with which narrators people their stories relate to the teller's family relationships. Mother, father, grandparent, child – these are figures which carry familiar (if multi-faceted) connotations for both speaker and listeners. The story depicts the teller interacting with these figures, sometimes as identified with them.

The narrator's *parents* are prominent actors, portrayed not just as significant figures in a narrator's childhood but as shaping the teller's later pathways. Listeners readily recognise both the admirable and idealised parent, and the over-dominant figure from whom the child must escape. Agnes Farley and Brenda Dawson free themselves from their mothers, while Alison Stanley tells of taking different ideals from those of her domineering and affectionless mother. Other tales recount the deep influence of a parent's – particularly a mother's – inspiration and help both in earlier years and later. Separately or together, parents are presented as the inculcators of ideals setting the teller on track for life. In Peter Sutton's tale, 'My folks brought me up . . . never to have prejudices against another person, which I have been eternally grateful for', and Frank Dyer's describes his father as 'still alive and guiding me . . . I still love him very much and thank him for all the things he did that has made me the person that I am today.'

As in many cultures, *grandparents* are presented in a particularly warm light. They do not come into all stories, perhaps because they really were unknown to the teller or because only those episodes that fit with the expected image are remembered and recounted. Where they appear, the grandparent (usually grandmother) carries wisdom and understanding from the past, a symbol of continuity, 'like living history' (Brenda Dawson).

Similar images recur when narrators come to present their own identity as merging with one or other of these recurrent figures at particular phases of their lives. Less is now made of independence-seeking child versus constricting parent, but parents and grandparents still play a role in the continuities and ethics of the child's and future adult's life. Sometimes this is presented as cyclical. Patricia Ejikame moved out of the parental home but portrays her later regret that her mother lived so far away, because she wanted her own daughter 'to get on with my mum the same as I have'. Other narrators depict themselves taking over the role once held by their parents for handing on traditions. Children and grandchildren are not just named individuals, it seems, but representatives of the continuity and standards of families and their successive generations.

Narratives often dwell on parents' responsibilities and problems in transmitting right ideas to their children. Some depict the central actors passing their own standards to their children, whether in resisting illegal practices or, as one tale recounts, following their mother's habit of hitting back when attacked. Stories set up a comparison between children of the present and those of the teller's own up-bringing, praising the standards of their own children (unlike their neighbours'!) or recounting their efforts to train the following generation into right behaviour.

'Successive generations' start to emerge as if themselves actors in the drama. Narrators elaborating on their phase as parents stress this particularly, but others too look to the 'next generation coming up' and its importance for the future. 'The next generation after me, right, has got it made', says Shirley Lambert, 'because they have got the facilities as long as the parents drum it into them, give them the support they need, make sure they are not joyriding and all that.' The generations, past and present, lie behind the narratives, shadowy but deeply symbolic figures setting personal activities in the wider cycle of time.

Family members and generations are the most prominent, but other stock characters also appear. The *spouse* is a recurrent figure whether as husband/wife or partner. This is presented with familiar overtones: sometimes images of love, concern or loss, but often too of discomfort, competition and antagonism. The younger and middle-aged speakers, of both sexes, tell stories of violence, rejection, or struggle over life decisions, resources and children. Some depict the interplay of a series of partners and ex-partners, and of a range of step-children, complex relations with emergent rather than already-established conventions for narrating. 'The father/mother of my child(ren)' or 'my ex' are among the emerging terms, often imbued with connotations of both cooperation and hostility.

Another recognised character is *the friend*. Often this is in the plural, as narrators depict the wrench of leaving friends when moving to or from Milton Keynes, and the problems or successes of making new ones. 'I have some lovely friends here, friends like that I could really call family', says the divorced Jill Blackwell, while another young mother recounts 'the support network that Fishermead can provide for me, I have a lot of friends here'. Friends are presented as potentially like family in their support but with the different flavour of being freely chosen . Jenny Linn-Cole, now well settled in Fishermead, concludes that: 'Friends nearer to where I live are more import- ant than family, and this idealistic idea of the extended family has a bit of falsity and one can choose one's friends. With family, one's lumbered with, and why should we call upon people we may not actually like but obliged to deal with as they are family?' Sometimes it is one particular friend, perhaps a betrayer but more often loyal. Bessie Wyatt's story of caring for her long-time friend in old age is one example, while Lesley Lambert tells of a special friend sharing her experiences: 'there is so many good memories in that house, even now me and my friend, Paula, we talk about it and laugh, the things we did'.

Other protagonists that we might have expected are not evident. While there are passing references to other people at work, the 'colleague' is less prominent than 'the friend', whether because of the particular story-tellers here (many not currently in full-time jobs), the date, the circumstances of the telling, or simply because of accepted conventions for spoken life stories. Similarly, though people of course buy things and there are many references to shops, the figure of 'the consumer' – that central focus of many current academic tales – features little if at all among these personal stories' dramatis personae. There are surprisingly few, if any, 'ogre' figures. The collective category of 'teenagers' carries something of that feel in a few narrations. There are also a few vague references to 'misfits' and 'problem families' spoiling the local area, and, occasionally, to 'the planners' ('pecu- liar – not of this world . . .!'), the faceless 'them' who planned Milton Keynes or 'the council' who control housing. But there is no consistent 'them', whether government officials, traders or co-residents of Milton Keynes, even in stories by narrators whose experiences might well have led them to invoke such figures.

The protagonists discussed here perhaps seem too obvious to be worth noting – just the 'normal' way we describe our relationships when asked about our lives. But that is the point. These *are* the standard, yet emotive, figures through which tellers expect to present their narratives and marshal their experiences, knowing the understandings their listeners are likely to attach to family members, to succeeding generations or (the figure to be elaborated shortly) to the hero figure of the unique, individual, continuing 'I'. They are not 'objective' or neutral figures, but ones which convey colour and value for both teller and listener. The stories are founded, without doubt, in the personal experience and observation of their tellers. But at the same time both their narration and their reception are ordered through expected story conventions which in turn evoke shared and culturally specific symbols and evaluations.

It remains however to introduce one essential figure. In the tales we come back again and yet again to the leading protagonist: the *'I', the individual actor*. This is the central and motivating actor that both heads the dramatis personae and gives the story coherence. The final section of this chapter will be devoted to the treatment and significance of this central protagonist, preceded by some account of some other ways in which stories are structured within intelligible plots to set the role of this hero-teller in context.

Explanatory frames: continuity, avocation and the individual 'I'

The temporal sequencing within the stories, described earlier, itself gives some explanatory coherence to the narratives. It offers a satisfying and in a way predictable plot for its listeners, in keeping with their expectations about life cycle, movements and impact of 'happenings' within an individual's life. But tellers also use additional devices to give their stories coherence, a moral ordering, as it were, which distinguishes them from mere chronicles of unrelated events.

The idea of *continuity from the past* is one recurrent rationale for the plot. Narrators recount their lifelong interests as linked to one or other of their parents, or dwell on their 'roots', 'family tradition' or transition between succeeding generations. Stories commonly open with the teller's family origins, locality and inheritance from the past. George Rowe talks of his parents, and Brenda Dawson's story starts with her 'firmly working-class roots', lingering on her family's earlier background and her grandmother's tales – 'wonderful, like living history'. Values attributed to earlier family and local upbringing are invoked in several tales: Timothy Hopkins' recurrent references to his 'Dorset pride' (see pp. 91–2 and 104), another's identity as 'a Londoner', or a narrator's picture of himself as 'proud to be a Somerset man'. In 72-year-old Frank Dyer's narrative one uniting thread is the figure of his father who 'for me is still alive and guiding me'.

Continuities from the past are sometimes presented as a kind of cyclical progression, casting their shadow on the present or the future. One narrator hints at a re-enactment of the past from her 'family background, now I suppose with my mother being married to an alcoholic was pretty much terrible for us as kids, so I have come face-to-face with a lot of that stuff here'. Others speak with optimism about the future, depicting traits from the past and present recreated in the coming generations. Dennis Travers has lost the custody of his children, but still sees his son inheriting his interest in art 'from me', while another teller tells how 'We are a family of readers . . . All of us, my grandchildren are the same, and my children are the same, every house you go into in my family there are books.' As her tale continues, her daughters inherit their intelligence and sense of humour from her first husband – 'his daughters both take from him, and they have the best of him'. On a lighter note, 'We are all little and round!': a narrator justifies her bulk by recounting it in the perspective of her family inheritance.

This structuring by the past is mostly presented as direct and benign. But some stories depict the hero's struggle *not* to perpetuate some parental trait – another widespread story about inter-generational transmission (Bertaux and Thompson 1993). Agnes Farley's tale vividly narrates the turning point of winning independence as a young woman, the opportunity to 'stretch her wings' – at the same time portraying this early experience as shaping her 'rebel' personality:

I was born in Devon in 1917 and I lived on a farm until I was twenty-three, and I had two brothers, one was five years older than myself and one was ten years. And although I lived in an idyllic spot and really I didn't have anything to complain about, but on reflection I think I had a very lonely childhood because my brothers being that much older, and there were not a lot of children around, but also a very strong class distinction in that part of the world, and my mother was very aware of this and she insisted that I played only with the right children and this made life very difficult . . . The prospects were in those days that one would live at home until one married, and most of my friends did just that. I suppose it has [changed], but in the rural areas that was definitely the pattern, maybe if one was in the town at that time then one would have had more chance. I think I was a bit cheesed in my teens and always wishing I was somewhere else, very much so. I was restricted, and I became so deceitful. I think if you live that existence you either become like a dummy or a rebel and I became a rebel.

Some stories turn on that other variant on the same theme, a lament for the *loss* of continuity from earlier generations. As one young mother's tale tells it: 'The respect has gone from everything now, I mean we were brought up to respect elders, to respect property, and you were just brought up properly and it is not being kept up any more.'

Whether positive or negative, the stories are being framed in the perspective of successive generations, imaging their narrators' lives within a longer cycle of family continuity or discontinuity. Even where this is not an explicit theme, some flavour of this perspective commonly comes through: an acceptable frame, it seems, for ordering narrated experience. The precise content of this sense of continuity is unique to the individual, markedly different for each teller. But the underlying story being told is not that of a meaningless isolated individual from nowhere, but of a hero with a just base for their own identity and their place in history.

A second recurrent storyline portrays a specific *preoccupation or principle personal to the teller*. A consuming interest like music, sport or religious adherence may function as the continuing thread in a life story – effective integrating themes in that, however personal to the individual, these are recognised value-laden pathways in our culture. Such an interest, presented more as a kind of moral focus than as a mere hobby, is played as a familiar signature tune in some tales, with a meaning over and above specific chronological events. Episodes around this theme somehow convey deeper import than the 'ordinary' events of life, and are recounted with greater fluency and conviction.

An involvement with music runs through several of the Fishermead tales. When he was telling his story, 72-year-old ex-Londoner Andrew Cunningham was recovering from a stroke and finding it hard to speak, so that many of his sentences were finished off by his wife: even more of a dialogue therefore than in other stories. But once he started talking about music his narration became fluent. He told of his childhood passion to learn drumming:

I couldn't afford it, a pound an hour for lessons. Well, my dad said 'Well there you are, I can't pay for it, it's too much money.' I thought 'Well blow it, I'll find my own way' . . . [I taught myself] by sound, and a record player, you used to put the HMV records on it. Seventy-eights . . . The thing I have never learned to do properly is a roll . . . Yeh, I couldn't do it now, 'cos of the hands you see, but I could do it slowly with a good drum kit . . . Course I had a drum kit and a great big bass drum like you see in the Salvation Army up there . . . And when the war came and I went to Wales and that was when I got in the band with the *Hotshots* . . . it was good it was.

As his story tells it, his musical experience gets him into his wartime band and he continues his musical interests throughout his life.

The widower Jonathan Tyler also uses his interest in music as a central theme in his story. It depicts his pride in his long-gathered collection of 600 tapes and in his ability to identify each from just a few bars. He sets his avocation in a longer scheme of family continuity:

My love of music, well my mother used to play the piano very well, she was a good amateur pianist, and difficult things mostly Beethoven, and Schumann, and that is probably what ignited it, and that probably put it in my brother's mind, because he played jazz all his life. Off the record he listened in his leisure time to classical music, but he said jazz is for playing, but the classics are for listening to, and I agreed with him.

Music is an evocative metaphor for his experience of the city: 'I do like Milton Keynes now and I appreciate it, but it took time, it's like learning a new composer.'

Though not particularly prominent in the Fishermead narrations, adherence to a particular religion and its philosophy is another familiar framework for personal experience. It does appear up to a point. Andrea Tan tells of being led from Hong Kong to live in Fishermead by 'God's hand', while Brenda Dawson and Joy Osborne take religion as one element in their stories without expanding on it. Timothy Hopkins' tale, however, is imbued with it. His 100-year-old life story starts with his church upbringing and his long membership of his Dorset church choir. 'I almost lived in the church, I loved it.' As a young man he refused to play for his firm's football team out of loyalty to his own church team even though the result, as he recounts it, was the loss of his job. The same theme appears in the episode (pp. 91–2 above) about his godfather saving him from death and, more directly, about convalescing in Cairo during the first world war:

I said, 'Oh sister is there a church here?' She said, 'Oh yes, there is a large marquee church. Why, do you want to go?' I said, 'Well yes, the church has been my life, I would love to.' So she said 'Very well, go next Sunday.' So I went to church on the Sunday morning and the minister spoke to me when the service was over, like they do at the door. He said 'Have you always attended church?', and I said 'Yes I almost lived in the church.' He said, 'Well I wonder if you would help me with communion next Sunday, as my server?', I said, 'Yes of course, I would love to, sir.' . . . And I did that and I wasn't very old and it was a great thing to me to serve communion in a marquee church.

Religious terminology continues throughout his story, and he finally reflects 'People say oh you are fond of flowers, and I say I am, I love flowers, to me they are one of God's gifts, from tiny little seeds you get wonderful flowers like that.'

Music and religion are effective frameworks for a story. The teller does not have to work at making these commitments plausible since audiences are ready to accept their meaning to the narrator whether or not they share them themselves. Other preoccupations are less widely recognised and need more elaboration to convey their centrality for the teller. One example is Peter Sutton's tale, integrated by the lifelong passion for film he depicts throughout his life story. Now in his forties, he links this to his family roots:

My mother was a great film fan, we never had a television until I was thirteen, she adored the cinema, and in London it was a – what is the word I am looking for? – a paradise. Filmgoers' delight. There were cinemas everywhere, so consequently I spent a lot of time going to the theatres, she loved live shows as well, my father was just not interested at all. That was where I started to get a great interest before I was even eight or nine, I was totally in love with the movies . . . And when I saw the 'Wizard of the Oz', I thought 'I am in love, well this is it, I have got to do these things called movies.'

His plans to go to arts college were disrupted by his father's death. But his narration goes on to recount how he managed to carry on his love affair with film:

I stopped one afternoon [at the factory where he had had to take a job], it was the Friday I handed in my notice, I watched a chap of sixty-four, sixty-five coming up, he was planing a piece of wood, a carpenter, and doing it at a fairly slow pace, and going backwards and forwards, and I was holding the broom, and I looked at him and I said to myself 'That man has been doing that for forty years. I am not going to do that for forty years', and I went into the office to Mr Mander and I said I am so sorry but I don't think this is for me . . .

I was suddenly unemployed, which was the only time up until being made redundant, nearly three years ago now. I was out of work. I went to the Youth Unemployment and they said they wouldn't give me any money. I wasn't asking for money, I was asking how do I get into the movie business, because that is what I wanted to do in the first place, and they said we don't know, the only way to do it is you will have to knock on a few doors, and go up to that place called Wardour Street, Soho, very nasty . . . And that is just what I did, got an underground train, a bus, underground train, down to Wardour Street, started at the bottom and ended up at the top at Oxford Circus, and half way down someone said they wanted a teaboy, a rewind boy, rewinding the films, and I said, 'Great, terrific', £3 17s 6d in those days, and I had a job. And that is how I started as a teenager.

The story continues on how he 'went on from there', his professional pride in his film editing and the successful programmes he worked on; the unremitting pressures of his job were 'beautiful, phenomenal'. Sad as he was over many disappointments, his dedication to film integrates and justifies his narrated life.

The most prominent explanatory theme of all, however, centres on the idea of the *individual actor* in the story – the actor who is also the narrator. In one sense this is merely stating the obvious. Speakers were invited to recount their personal experiences in a situation of one-to-one recording, and if only for grammatical reasons many sentences naturally start with 'I'. But there is more to it than this. It is striking how forcibly the concept of the individual comes through as a key structuring theme in these Fishermead stories.

This 'I' is the continuing hero in all the tales, the unique acting and experiencing individual. It is not an individual that comes from nowhere nor one destined to maintain an isolated existence. For just as the roots and continuities of the hero's life are narrated, so too are the storied figures with which he or she interacts. The hero's actions are carried out in a world peopled by figures with familiar meanings for both teller and hearer.

But if the hero figure is not an isolated asocial individual, yet neither is it presented as primarily a member of some general category. The hero may indeed share characteristics and experiences with others, and some secondary characters may be projected in more generalised roles. But the central figure *is* that of a unique individual. Academic stories of 'identity' often define people by their membership of a particular category – by ethnic group, for example, colour, class, gender or religion. Little if anything of such identifications appears in the stories, at least for the central narrator-actor. Even the familiar roles with which the hero may successively be aligned come only into certain phases of the adventure rather than comprise the whole story. Some stories present a stronger sense of the controlling 'self' than others, and within single stories it emerges more in certain episodes than in others. But the prime integrating force which brings each story together and makes it intelligible is that of the prime actor's continuity and, in a sense, control and identity.

This is a point of some significance. Given the social constraints we all labour under, not least these narrators, the stories might equally well have emphasised the leading protagonist(s) as victim, or the determining force of external events. Something of this comes through in some narrations. But overall there is surprisingly little. The convention for telling personal narratives that both tellers and listeners seem to take for granted is that the individual teller – as the hero – is the essential reality of the story, the active pivot of its plot.

Before proceeding to a more detailed examination of the complex devices tellers use to convey this in the stories, let us take Shirley Lambert's eventful and reflective narrative as a further example.

Shirley Lambert's tale

Unlike some other narrators, Shirley Lambert reached Milton Keynes as a child. She tells how she left home in her early teens due to family violence, then supported herself by various jobs and got a

*council flat on Fishermead when she was eighteen. She later re-
sumes responsibility for her family, helping her younger sisters and
her mentally ill mother. She recounts her problems with a violent
partner and how she managed to oust him. In 1994 she was thirty-
two, living in a house on Fishermead with her ten-year-old son
Reggie. She sums up her life: 'Everybody is allowed a chance, and I
didn't have the chance and I gave myself the chance though and I
think if I can do it anybody can.'*

* * *

I came to Milton Keynes when I was roughly about ten or eleven, I
am not quite sure. We lived in Greenleys which was one of the new
estates – well, considered one of the new estates, as in Milton
Keynes. We still had the old estates like Wolverton and Bradwell,
and that is all we knew because there was no city centre, there was
no Fishermead where I live now, or anything like that.

Coming up earlier on in my life from then we didn't really know
much about anybody else, we didn't have a lot of contact because
my parents were quite strict. And being a black person you can
imagine, you know, it was like a family union, and that was all they
were interested in, and there was no outside people.

Greenleys was all right, but obviously the resources in Greenleys
was quite limited. Your city centre used to be Bletchley, like you
would have to come all the way from Greenleys to Bletchley to do
your shopping, so it was like a day trip, you know, a day trip for the
kids, and if you were bad you won't go, you know. And there was
like your corner shop, and your little community centre, but as for
pubs and clubs and things like that there was none, in the seventies,
obviously, there was none at all.

Gradually, and quite quickly, estates kept on popping up, and
there was more people and more interest in people moving in, and
you seemed to get people from London, Birmingham, all the big
cities, you would get people, and it was quite interesting the way
different people lived.

Our family personally, we had a lot of trouble with our family
because we had a violent father, we had a violent father and my
mother was actually mentally ill, she had a breakdown. We didn't
realise she had a breakdown, and because we were so close-knit we
didn't have the sense to tell anybody, we just thought well she has

gone funny, you know, and he wouldn't allow anybody to come in and help us, you know. We were very poor, and that is quite amazing looking back on, because for something like five or six years we all used to sleep on the frontroom floor, no beds or things like that, and thinking of that in the past era, and the new city, nobody realised what was going on, you know.

The older ones, like me and my sister and my brother who is younger than me, we didn't do well at school at all because we had so much trouble. Yes, we didn't do very well at school, because we had so much trouble with the family, it was more had we survived the day, you know, than actual getting down to it. My father would wake us up at three o'clock in the morning because there was dust on the stairs, so we would all have to sweep the whole house, you know what I mean, and so you didn't get a lot of sleep and then by the time you got to school you felt too tired and things like this and we didn't learn a lot. My sister has done quite good because she had a good teacher, but my teacher just thought I was disruptive and I ended up going into a children's home. About thirteen by that time.

I had actually left home by the time I went in the children's home. Because it was a residential place in Aylesbury, what we did was 'come home for the weekends'. But I had actually been kicked out of home, so they didn't realise that I wasn't going home. So what we would do like, was, we would go to the children's home during the week, come home and just walk the streets for the whole weekend, you know. There was a lot to walk, and because there were like fields and things like that you could hide in Milton Keynes then quite easily. And then when my assessment was over – we actually went to college and everything – they decided that yes, you can now go back to your family. But what they didn't know was I couldn't go back to the family, because everything was like through the courts, and as soon as I walked in the door all the abuse would start up again, the fighting. So coming up to fourteen I left home, and I actually lived with a lady who I looked after her children, and that was the only home life I knew.

Jobwise it was very difficult because I was so young I couldn't get a job in Milton Keynes. I couldn't claim, because I didn't have the sense to claim, you know, for help. I knew I was far too young, so I didn't even go and check out, or try and bang on anybody's door to beg for it, you know. So you just made do, you know.

When I was about fifteen I got a small job in a little clothes store. But I got in awful trouble there because it is like all that glitters is gold to me, and because I had worked there for a pittance and couldn't have the things that were in the store I decided to help myself! And that was that. And I remember that was my first ever job and looking back now I think to myself if only I had the sense to not see everything as glittering and you can just do that, it would have been quite good, it would have been a good memory but it is a bad memory for me to know that I had messed it up quite horribly, you know.

After that, coming up sixteen round here was quite fun. I worked for McDonald's in the city centre, and the city centre had opened then, you know, and sixteen/seventeen I worked for McDonald's until I was about nineteen, but it was great I was earning money, them days you could get a flat if you were earning money. I got a little flat and everything. And I was on like sky-high, this is brilliant you know my life is coming together and I used to earn money and that, yes, I stayed with a couple and rented a room first of all. And then the council gave me, when I was eighteen, seventeen or eighteen, a flat on Fishermead. It was just above the dentist on the corner and I moved into the flat and thought this was all great, you can buy a pair of shoes every two months, this is brilliant [. . .]

That went very well. By this time I had lost contact with my family because I couldn't go back to the house. And with all the turmoil it was easier not going back, because then I would have to think about the family and try and get my life together, and I couldn't manage the two. So up till I was about eighteen, I didn't have much contact since I left with the family, and then I went back. No, I actually went to Bletchley one day and saw my little sisters outside a shop. And they were terrified of me, and I couldn't get why they were terrified of me. And I thought 'Oh talk to me', and they said 'We are not allowed to talk to you, and you have got to go', because their father was in the shop, and I said 'This is ridiculous you know', I thought 'What is happening?' And so it was apparently he had left my mother, and taken all the kids and furniture and left her in the house with nothing, you know. So we didn't have much furniture to start off with, but he took things like the cooker, so what is she heating on, you know, took the fridge and everything, and in the conversation they kind of told me she was ill.

So me, worry, worry, worry, backed up courage and a couple of friends and we went down there, and she actually had turned mad, and she was like living off cat food and things like that, you know. In big Milton Keynes, *nobody* realised, *no* neighbours realised, how awful it was. And actually I had to commit her at eighteen to the mental hospital. And she has never forgiven me for that you know, although she has come out and is slightly better, she always every day she gives it to me, to make sure I remember that I put her in a mental home. And that is a lot of pressure, because although logically oh no I didn't I was trying to do good for you, emotionally I still think to myself, well maybe I've made it worse, why couldn't I have had the mother I had always wanted, you know, you see on 'Dynasty' [popular television soap opera] you know, why, why?

By this time, the girls had been taken off the father, and put into care. But they were so backward, I mean they didn't know basic skills like wash and scrub your teeth, they didn't know all that, and that grieved me for about a year you know, I had to get somewhere where I could get them all back. I mean I had been into care by this time, and I had come out smelling of roses, considering what a lot of kids go through. By this time I had given up on the stealing because it just wasn't paying [*laughter*], the crime was not paying at all, and I had given up on that because I had analysed the situation, when I didn't have money I stole, when I had money I forgot to steal. So when I got this job at McDonald's I actually forgot to steal, and I had the money to buy things, so that was great, and the longer you leave stealing the harder it is to go back to it. I thought it was quite important, especially in Milton Keynes, watching all the kids grow up to kind of drum it into them, it really does not pay, it is all right for today when you have taken a hundred pounds, tomorrow you could get caught, and it will put you back another year, it takes years off your life, and while everything is happening the bills they are rolling out here, and you are stuck in one place, and then when you come out it is even harder for you.

I took on a couple of children, well they weren't children, while I was in the flat. There was a young black guy and because there wasn't much black people it was so hard for him to understand the world as it was, so he used to come up to the flat and he used to eat and he was company and actually social services let me foster him although he was sixteen. And that was quite fun and I became like his big sister, he used to sleep on the settee, it was only a one-bedroomed place, you know. He was getting himself together and he found himself a little job. And it made me feel proud that I could do something for somebody else what I couldn't do for my own family.

By the time I was nineteen I met a guy and decided yes this must be it, love and everything. And it turned out he was terribly terribly violent, physiologically he mashed me up, but in between that I was still trying to deal with my mother, and deal with the rest of the family and keep on contacting them to find out what is going on, are you lot all right. And they had been mentally abused so badly that they couldn't talk, they couldn't tell me deep down inside, you know, it was like 'Do you want a biscuit?', 'Yes', 'Don't you want a biscuit?', 'No', they couldn't make up their mind what they wanted, it was what you wanted. And I could see them doing it and it would upset me, because it was like 'You tell me what you want, whatever you tell us to have', you know, and this was quite sad. They had spent time in a children's home and done really well, academically they all got 'A' levels, I'm the only idiot, I'm the only one who ain't got nothing you know. Picked up from nought, I mean none of them could read at seven, they didn't know how to spell their names, and they picked up by the time they had got to the proper age, primary school, they all picked up very well, and I was happy with that. It let me off the hook a bit to know that they were all doing well, and I didn't have to worry too much.

My mother now was gracefully getting worse. Still in hospital at that time, but we decided to take her out, because what was happening the drugs were making her drowsy, it wasn't helping her, it was stabilising her, but it wasn't helping her, and we had her there, and she was shuffling, and her hands were shaking, and all that. And I couldn't bear it any longer, so we got her taken out and she went back to the house, and what we will try and do everybody pop round and that, and when the girls, because they didn't really know my mother as a normal person, they couldn't visit her any more it upset them too much.

So it was all down to me again, by this time I was in a lot of trouble with the boyfriend. I couldn't get out of the relationship. I can understand women who get beaten up and every woman I hear get beaten up I want to go round their house and talk to them, you can get out right, but you need every support, when people say 'Why don't you leave?' that is the hardest thing to do, is to leave.

My problem was that it was my flat, my furniture, my money, where am I leaving to? Do you know what I mean? I just couldn't get this guy out, in the end thankfully for me, right, he was a criminal and it was like any day now he will get sentenced, and it was my saving grace. And he was that violent, I took out an injunction but I couldn't serve it while he was here, he would have burned me alive in the flat, he was that bad you know. So he actually got a year, he had to do a year for burglary, I served the injunction on him while he was in there. While he was in there I found out I was pregnant, just before he went in, and I thought 'Oh man, he will murder me', but I had always wanted a baby, because I always think that is unconditional love and I had never had. So, I thought to myself, 'OK, it is here now, get on with it and your life', you know. And by the time he came out, the baby was born and he wanted to come back, but once I had got him out he just wasn't coming back. He would have to burn me down, he was not coming back you know.

I had Reggie when I was twenty-two, yes, and I had a lodger. No, tell a lie, I moved into this present home a month before the baby was born, and a friend of my boyfriend's, a white guy, had nowhere to go so I said 'Well there are three rooms here, give me a bit of rent to help me out with bills and so on', you know. We got on famously and he done a lot for me and the baby, he really did, you know. He was always there, and he bought the suite for me, I couldn't afford things like that you know. Because he was working, he helped me buy my washing machine, helped me put carpet on the floor, and I will always be eternally grateful to him, because he always said as a mate he couldn't stop my old man from beating me up, he didn't have the guts, because he was that violent, and he was trying to make up for it, because he had gone, you know, and so that was fine.

Fishermead was quite funny because there were only like a few houses left there, it was like the posh area, and I felt like me – 'Dynasty', you know, 'Dynasty' roots you know, I thought to myself I lived in a posh area. I tried to make the most of it, you know, make sure that outside your house is swept dry, even if you haven't got a carpet inside, because it was a nice area and everything. It really was important you know. And gradually I met a few people on Fishermead, and you know you become friends. But it is very awkward to become friends in Milton Keynes, or have friends in Milton Keynes, because everybody comes from such different circumstances. And what it seems like is a lot of people who have had up-and-down lives, come to Milton Keynes, so everybody has got a problem, and it is very difficult to become close because nobody trusts anybody, very, very difficult. I try my best, to help out people you know where I could. But what I found was that people would take liberties, and it has made me very very cynical, I am not so free to give my help, unless I see somebody really in need of it. If people don't help themselves in Milton Keynes, they will go under.

There are so much facilities here right, to go up, if people use them, but I think that the majority of people just aren't educated to use them. Say oh like, 'I can't be bothered.' And all they know is like London, like every Saturday night you can go to a party or whatever. They can't get that Milton Keynes is a fresh start. I would never move from Milton Keynes if I could help it. I would leave the country, but never leave Milton Keynes, because as far as I am concerned it is so suitable for the children. The next generation after me, right, has got it made, because they have got the facilities as long as the parents drum it into them, give them the support they need, make sure they are not joyriding [in stolen cars] and all that, I just can't believe all this joyriding, what's the parents doing?

The majority of women round here say 'Oh I am bored in the daytime'. They irritate me, I don't have time to get bored, because there is so much that women can do now. [. . .] But they have got into so much of a rut that they can't be bothered, and the young girls around here it grieves me to see them all getting pregnant.

I had a young girl here yesterday, she used to live next door to me two years ago, and she visited me, and she is pregnant by another guy and she is with this other guy and I think it is so sad, and she is seventeen, and I tried to drum it into her. I mean she was nearly in tears, I said it is going to be hard, you will always have me here, but don't you ever think it is going to be easy, it is going to be hard, don't be telling me you are going to have two after this, three and four, learn by this mistake, everybody is allowed that one mistake. But I found the kids around here are too free, they have too much freedom and too much time to do nothing.

But up to this present day, I am doing all right, do you know that, I am floating above the norm and I want everybody to float above the norm especially if they have had a hard time. And all these rich kids who come from the privileged family and everything I haven't got time for them, and you talk to them and all they are interested in is like the drugs, I am not interested in them sort of children. All children need help, but I can't help people like that because I have got too much grievances inside of me, thinking you have had it and you have abused it. I am not interested in all the children round here, right, who haven't got it, but they have got so much like you said, talent, they have got so much of their selves to use to get them up. They just don't realise it, and I want to bring it out of them. Everybody is allowed a chance, and I didn't have the chance and I gave myself the chance though and I think if I can do it anybody can.

I mean like I said, ending the story, I went all to the ripe age of fourteen like and I couldn't even spell my own name, and I had to learn, and now like I'm the most magazine queen now, it is like I am always reading, and anybody can do it. I might not be a professional, I can't do a degree, my concentration span right doesn't, you know, I can't sit still that long, I couldn't do something like that. But then you can always do something else, I can be special somewhere else, and that is basically my life.

The creative actor and author

Shirley Lambert's tale illustrates the figure of the self-conscious narrator with particular clarity. But the leading actor-narrator plays a prominent role in all the tales, an accepted feature, it seems, of the way such stories are expected to be presented. Bruner suggests that agency is a prominent feature in autobiographical tales (Bruner 1994 p. 48). It is interesting to explore how this comes out in the Milton Keynes tales and how tellers convey this within their narrations.

One device is for the tale to centre on the narrator-hero's *character*. As Linde points out (1993), this is one accepted mode for structuring a life story. In the stories here it is often related to the complementary theme of the teller's family background and/or avocation, but also presented as a trait developed independently and individually. Sally Vincent's personal story is notable for its confrontations, as she sticks up vociferously for her rights against neighbours, partners, relations, officials. She punctuates it regularly by explanatory asides: 'I am not a very patient person', 'I have never had patience, I ain't got none', 'You couldn't change me, not after all this time.' Similar, if less confrontational, is Brenda Dawson's picture of herself as 'never very good at sort of lying quietly down like a doormat'. Though she stresses the frustrations of an army wife, her story is partly structured round how she did indeed 'complain about things' and finally, by *not* being a 'doormat', won through to an identity that she had 'lost': it was 'getting things sort of back for me – a life which wasn't just totally involved with children and looking after husband . . . It has been worthwhile.'

In some stories the individual teller's *positive action and enterprise* are depicted as the central feature. In Shirley Lambert's tale she shows herself creating her own life amidst her problems and managing step by step to 'back up courage', help others and control events. Her initial foray into fostering 'made me feel proud that I could do something for somebody else what I couldn't do for my own family', and as the story unfolds, her actions gradually enable her to help her mother and sisters, and have the confidence to advise others about the courage needed when 'it's hard'. She wants to 'be my own boss, right, and try and earn money and help everybody around me, right'.

Rachel Jacobs tells another story of individual determination and persistence (printed on pp. 138–47). Her story recounts some dire experiences. But it also notably depicts her enterprise in dealing with them, leading to the relatively happy ending as she meets her successive problems by founding her own firm, working as a cabbie, relinquishing her job to uphold a moral principle for herself and her children to observe, and finally finding a group of congenial friends.

Even where individual determination is not a major structuring device, it often enters into specific episodes. Peter Sutton's teenage persistence in finding a job in the 'movies' is one example. So too is Lucy Dale's story (pp. 124–31) of her work with the pre-school playgroup in the early days of Fishermead, followed by going back to school as an adult (no easy undertaking) and her years away from the family studying for her degree. The narrations regularly depict active decisions and follow-through, from one narrator's courage in leaving home for Milton Keynes at the age of sixteen or another's in coping alone at fourteen, to insisting on respect from others (like the bakery owner who prided herself on forbidding swearing in her shop), supporting one's own children against other people's, or sticking up for a principle whatever the consequences.

Stories involve other people and, particularly at certain life stages, the subject can be 'we'. Nevertheless the active mover is regularly 'I'. Stories recount how this active 'I' detaches itself to gain personal independence or achieve a particular aim. As mentioned earlier, extricating oneself from the parental home is one familiar turning point. Leila Birch's tale deploys the same theme to recount both the problems and her eventual satisfaction in moving out from the informal foster home she had found for herself when she was sixteen:

I got a place in North 9th Street [in Central Milton Keynes], it took me three months for me to actually tell Anne that I had got this flat, and I was going there every day and pottering about and doing bits and pieces but I found it really difficult to tell her because she had been so good to me, and I felt like I was letting her down by leaving in a way . . . In the end I told her and she was over the moon for me and she came over and saw it and so I moved in. But although I moved in, I spent most of the time out sleeping at other people's houses because Christ, I was frightened really. Eventually I remember being round a friend's house and I said 'I think I'll go home tonight, I am not going to stay, I'm going to go home', and that was the beginning of me getting into the homely type thing, and wanting to decorate and getting me stuff together. I was eighteen then, I got it just after I was eighteen, and I really enjoyed it, it was like, you know, 'This is my own pad.'

It is not always told through dramatic episodes. But the idea of keeping a sphere for the prime actor's own personality – whatever the other involvements – is an accepted theme. The stories portray people looking out for their own interests even in affectionate relationships, let alone contentious ones. Sarah Henderson, moving to Ireland with a new partner, insists 'I don't think I will give this house up, because with four kids, if there is a broken relationship . . . I need security for myself', while a single parent comments 'Whatever happens I've done my college and I can use it again.'

Individual action and control are expressed even in tales telling of constraints and disappointments, things 'happening' rather than planned. Dennis Travers' story tells of the death of his wife, leaving the army with no recognised qualifications, the removal of his adored children, the breakdown of relationships and his periods of unemployment – but still makes a funny episode of his earlier experiences and tells a tale of pride in his accomplishments as a drum major and later as a mechanic:

I keep myself to myself, and I have got all my things what I do, like my bike, and that keeps me busy. I have got to respray it, and I have got to buy some bits for it, get the exhaust modified, get cracking. I have got a few friends round here, some of them at work know where I live, because they only want me for one thing, so I can do work on their cars! . . . I really want to do a mechanical course on motor cycles, they are more interesting, they are more precision machinery than a car, anybody can work on a car, but not many people can work on a bike. There is a great difference, because they are down to the finest millimetre.

Similarly Bessie Wyatt's tale of her various 'dreadful' experiences and Brenda Dawson's of no choice over her housing also recount how they dealt with these. In similar vein Jenny Linn-Cole immediately amplifies her 'not so much a decision as something that happened' by adding 'and making the most of what happened'. And Shirley Lambert's story ends strikingly with her summing up of her scarcely easy life, 'Everybody is allowed a chance, and I didn't have the chance and I gave myself the chance though and I think if I can do it anybody can.'

The story told by Lesley Lambert (Shirley's younger sister) is one of the few that explicitly treat the narrator's *lack* of power: 'I feel like I should try and do something [for Milton Keynes]. But what can you do? When you have an idea and you go somewhere with it, they beat you down, because they are like oh you are just small fry, once you try you just get kicked down, and you can't win, unless you have got money.' But even that story unfolds into a detailed account of her effectiveness in another context, one of the liveliest episodes in her narration. It evokes resonances of the familiar themes of home and personal control.

A friend of mine that I worked with told me that there was a house going [in Netherfield] and so we moved in, it was a really big house, three bedrooms and it was a three-storey house, the wallpaper was dire and it was really really bad, it was half pink and half blue, and I used to think who in their right mind would paint their wallpaper half pink and half blue, it was like a nightmare, and so we got to painting it straight away, and there is so many good memories in that house, even now me and my friend, Paula, we talk about it and laugh, the things we did . . . Paula and I had this brainwave that we were going to decorate the little toilet, and we wanted to do something really different and Paula is really arty and I said 'Why don't we print handprints going up the wall, we can have a little border and then they could go up the wall', and she said 'That's a good idea, we could do it in the middle of the wall and go up', and then she said 'No, I think we should paint our hand and stick handprints on the wall.' So we got this paint and painted our hands and stuck our hands up the wall, and we got our friend's little brother and we painted his feet and stuck his footprints up the wall, and we signed it and it was really like, we were proud of our toilet. And everybody that came round, we would say 'Come and see our toilet', and they used to think we were crazy, and we had a house-warming party, loads of people came, we were really shocked at the amount that came, and we said 'You must come and see our toilet' and they said 'Wow!'. We were really proud of that toilet . . . The things we used to do, the memories are really good in that house, excellent.

That story ends with the narrator's confident plans for the future: 'it has all worked out really well'.

Struggles or problems – 'trouble' as Bruner terms it (1987) – are common narrative themes. But in these personal narratives they are also used to convey a sharp sense of individual control. Andrew Cunningham's story, quoted earlier, elaborates how at eleven years old he couldn't afford drumming lessons so worked at teaching himself – no light task. The divorced

Alice Phillips similarly tells of the painful conflicts with her ex-husband over her children, but also how she tries to cope: 'I don't think about it, that is the only way I can deal with it . . . There are lots of little doors in there, which get locked, and they don't get opened again, not for any reason, that is the only way I can deal with it. I mean the first few months was hell.' Many stories emphasise 'struggle', 'hard work', or 'hard times'. Individual determination is brought out through episodes about confrontations. There are vivid accounts of divisive quarrels with partners, with 'I said'/'(s)he said' interchanges, or of parents sticking up for their own children against others: they 'may not be angels', but 'I am a mum and will protect them to the end.' Jill Blackwell's tale recounts problems in the Fishermead area, but at the same time the contribution that she makes there: 'I feel, well, I haven't just come here and lived here and not put anything into the community, because I have, and that is good.' Then, asked whether 'It has made a difference to your life, being in Milton Keynes?', she responds, in words that reflect the theme running through many stories, 'Yeh it has made a difference, well, *I* have made the difference, I have gone out and made the difference.'

This theme is partly conveyed through how the story is *told*, the personal motivations and interventions recounted, the personal interpretations put onto the events. An accepted convention in presenting these tales is for the individual actor, the narrator, to be depicted not only as in the thick of the action but also as standing back, engaging in his or her own concurrent interpretations and feelings. The portrayal of the key protagonist's inner ideas and emotions is thus an expected part of the story. Partly too there is the control that, as suggested in other narrative research, lies in the personally activated processes of memory and narration, themselves playing a creative part in shaping the world. It is the self-reflective way stories are presented as much as the episodes themselves that conveys this personal determination and energy. 'It's a tough world' comments one narrator, while Shirley Lambert reflects that 'If people don't help themselves in Milton Keynes, they will go under', and Bessie Wyatt's story of getting her foot on the ladder, progressing upwards, loving her work and divorcing her husband in difficult circumstances is summed up with 'If you want something you've got to work for it.'

This individual action and control is not just part of the action, but also to an extent the guiding principle which gives the tale both coherence and its participation in somehow universal qualities. This partly consists in its formulation through familiar, acceptable plots: the transition from misfortune to success, the pioneer tale, adventure story, travel tale or the personal journey. 'Victim' tales seem less prominent in these – as in many – personal narratives. There are traces in some tales or episodes, like Dennis Travers' tale of lost children and failed relationships, or the earlier stages of Brenda Dawson's trail round after her husband, but there seems a reluctance to take this as the overt structuring device of the story as a whole. More frequent are narratives of the hero's progress upwards. Though the 'final' ending is yet to be revealed, the successes of the present represent a kind of climax to the tale. Agnes Farley is portrayed in her successful struggle for her independence, Lucy Dale for her educational qualifications, Brenda Dawson for her identity. Several narrators relate a story of beginning from almost nothing in material, educational or personal terms and gradually winning through. Elsie Simmons' story for example is of how it 'took me years to get where I am' and recalls her first move into her present house: 'There was a cardboard box. I'll never forget it. All my dishes in a cardboard box! We set the telly on it. We had the cheek to go and buy a tablecloth to sit on top of it. Oh God. Oh, I used to be really embarrassed to open the door to somebody and say "Oh, come in".'

The hero's move through life is sometimes an adventure tale. Narratives describe pioneering days in the early development of Milton Keynes, coping with mud, lack of shops and hospital, and making new friends. Others relate storied memories of childhood pleasures, the 'enjoyment' and challenge of parenthood, a job or a particular house or area. 'I have enjoyed myself in Milton Keynes', says Dennis Travers, while George Rowe's delivery takes on a special tone of excitement when he reaches the parachute-dropping episode (pp. 84–5), and Frank Dyer's tale recounts driving a tank as 'What a thrill, it was wonderful.' Accounts of excitement and enjoyment mark out particular stages of life – and thus of the plot – and again foreground the concept of the self-conscious individual, the accepted site for emotional experience as well as reflective thought.

Life imaged as a voyage of self-discovery comes in several stories. There are the episodes of making mistakes and learning from them, of gathering strength – 'becoming stronger and more resolved than carrying on the wishy washy existence I was beforehand' – or of changing views at different stages: 'What was so important isn't quite so important when you get older and you have different values actually' (Agnes Farley). Lesley Lambert's narrative is shot through with 'learning about myself as a person'. It concludes with an episode about her recent visit to America and how it 'really helped me to grow as a person . . . almost like this little flickering light and you have just come brighter'. Rachel Jacobs reflects on her own story, one with many trials: 'So it's now really that I feel good about Milton Keynes, now it's my home. A lot of it has actually been a personal journey . . . And I suspect that in five years' time I will see where I am now as yet just another stage along the way.'

Unlike many written or fictional stories, personal stories are not closed. The end of the journey has yet to come and the living teller continues. Many tales just stop with a comma, as it were, or with a recent episode that might well be less prominent in future tellings. But some tellers introduce explicit closing comments or conclusion-like reflections, whether earlier or later in the narrative. Emma Hardy sums up from the perspective of her eighties: 'it's not a very exciting life, but when we look back on it we have such great memories, it's so lovely . . . It wasn't a wasted life'; while in Frank Dyer's story: 'I have lived through a period of life with many changes. I think I have lived through sixty years of the greatest advancement in all respects, and I treasure it.' Some narratives convey a quiet ending as the narrators picture themselves as content with their present state ('I'm very satisfied with my lot'), others round things off by looking to the future. It has been observed that there is a greater sense of the 'completed' story in older people's narratives than in those of young and middle-aged narrators (Abrahams in Myerhoff 1980 p. 31). This also applies to the Milton Keynes narratives. Older narrators reflect back articulately on their lives, most explicitly in 100–year-old Timothy Hopkins' narration: 'Well that's my story . . . and as I say I went through life, and that is exactly my life story.' But younger people's stories too sometimes convey the same quality, a verbalised reflectiveness about the significance of their individual lives. Shirley Lambert concludes in her early thirties:

I mean like I said, ending the story, I went all to the ripe age of fourteen like and I couldn't even spell my own name, and I had to learn, and now like I'm the most magazine queen now, it is like I am always reading, and anybody can do it. I might not be a professional, I can't do a degree, my concentration span right doesn't, you know, I can't sit still that long, I couldn't do something like that. But then you can always do something else, I can be special somewhere else, and that is basically my life.

These story-telling conventions at the same time imply some measure of generalisation, a distancing from the contingent events reported in the tales. The personal stories are of course notably less abstract than the academic tales. They pose neither as generalised theoretical accounts nor as directed to those interested in such accounts, so are clearly near one extreme of the general/particular narrative spectrum, telling of unique individuals and their experiences. But yet there *is* also an element of the universal in these particulars.

This is partly a matter of shared understanding about the conventions that make the tales intelligible for both tellers and their audiences. The recognised images, plots and figures communicate precisely because they go beyond just single individuals. And yet, at the same time, they are effective precisely *because* they present the accepted general theme of individuals' deeds and experiences, an assertion, as it were, of their reality and significance.

It is also how the stories are told. Here we return to the dual role of the teller as both narrator and actor – the distancing eye as well as the protagonist whose past actions are reported within the narration.[1] The manner of telling conveys to the hearer that the tale is neither just a chronicle of neutral events nor an unmediated set of purely individual memories: it is a complex creation into which both narrator and actor join. The 'I as narrator' comments on the narrated tale, reminding the hearer that this is indeed a constructed narrative not a mechanical reflection of past events. The pronoun 'you' occurs as a kind of distancing and universalising device – 'you' almost in the generalising sense of 'humanity' – through such comments, inserted into the action, as 'you can imagine', 'you know', 'you can picture it'. It is not easy to assess how far such interpolations should be regarded as a personal stylistic habit, a hesitation marker or a true distancing device – or, perhaps equally likely, all three. Shirley Lambert's narration, for example, is peppered with 'you know's – in one way just a personal trick of speech and opportunity to collect her thoughts, but also in some sense and in some situations a way of adding a wider perspective to the narration. A similar point could be made about 'well', 'yeh', 'yes', 'right', 'like', 'sort of thing', even perhaps 'er': easy to dismiss (and remove) as hesitation phenomena, but also, more, or less, providing a standing-back pause in the hurry of the narrated action. There are also comments on the action like 'actually', 'really', 'Oh dear, dear!' – taking the perspective of the outside reflective commentator as it were – or rhetorical questions like 'you know what I mean?', 'isn't it?', 'wouldn't you?' which not only join the other participant(s) into the interactive process of telling but also draw in an outsider's eye on the tale. The teller also sometimes highlights the element of reflection on the events in the narrative by the present tense. Phrases like 'I suppose', 'I guess', 'I think' mark the distinction between the speaker as protagonist within the tale and as narrator outside it.

Looking through the quotations and longer texts in chapters 4–6 will show many such examples. It is of course partly a matter of degree and narrators' use of such devices varies. It is also through implication or juxtaposition – effective in oral utterance – as much as in explicit verbal formulation. The inclusion of reported speech (or thought) is an example where the actual enactment in performance can give a distancing element, moving between direct and indirect speech/thought. These distancing and universalising dimensions in the narrative are hard to pin down in the original delivery or – even more so – to convey in written transcript . Indeed many are precisely the kind of verbal and para-verbal expressions that understandably get omitted in transcription as carrying little if any cognitive meaning or as 'interrupting' the flow for the reader's eye, one reason why the artistic shaping and reflective distancing in personal tales is often under-estimated.

Narrators also use explicit reflection to impart a standing-aside quality to the telling. The comment may be quite direct, expressed in the present tense and with a proverb-like feel to the phrasing: 'It's a tough world', 'The respect has gone from everything now', 'I am a mum and will protect them to the end . . .', 'It never happens, does it? [of keeping in touch with friends]', or 'Everybody is allowed a chance.' The generalising 'you' appears again: 'If you want something you've got to work for it', 'What was so important isn't quite so important when you get older', 'You don't know what's in store for you, do you?', 'That's the way of life, isn't it, you can't help it.' Such reflections by the teller-*qua*-narrator add a Greek-chorus-like commentary on the development of the plot or on episodes in which he or she is depicted *qua* actor in the drama. The tale may centre on the idiosyncratic activities of a single individual, but – so the telling conveys – it is also more than that: a tale with wider significance. Some narratives have more of this quality than others. But all have something of it, driving a wedge between actor and narrator, and lending an unexpectedly universalising quality to the por-trayed drama.

All these devices make their own contribution to the generalising element in the stories. Most prominent of all, however, is the emphasis on individual motivation, experience and reflection. This is the basic philosophy underly-ing most of these tales – their general theory as it were. It is worth emphasis-ing this. After all, it might have been otherwise, and does not necessarily take this form in the stories of some other cultures. It may not seem so unexpected, given that so many theoretical stories stress the 'individualism' of western culture. But this portrayal of the individual's active role as the motivating, enterprising and reflecting figure in personal narratives could not just be assumed in advance, the more so since the individual is so much less prominent in the academic tales of the city. So it is indeed worthy of remark that the conventions that both frame and are formulated in these personal stories so clearly convey a theory about the significance of the individual as both actor and narrator, of the conscious, experiencing, creative self.

The cultural conventions through which these stories are fashioned thus call on the teller to foreground the individual actor-cum-narrator as the central figure. This central 'I' is complex for there is always some distancing of the narrator's role from the actor's experiences, some reflective artistry in formulating the memories, balanced differently as this is in the differing artistries of narrators' individual tales. But whatever the final balance, at the heart of the story as told remains the figure of the continuing self-aware 'I', the unique narrating and narrated teller and actor.

This chapter has covered much ground and quoted many examples. Its key points however are simple. The telling of personal stories and the lives thus marshalled through them are far from arbitrary or artless. They are formulated through a series of cultural conventions of form, structure, coverage, stock figures and (explained in chapter 4) modes of telling – conventions not necessarily consciously exercised by their tellers, but nevertheless both moulding and moulded by their tellers' experiences, their self-understanding and their performances. Far from being limited to the unique persons or events portrayed in a narration, the stories carry wider symbolic value for both teller and hearer at the same time as they constitute a resource through which individual tellers creatively formulate and experience their lives.

6   Personal narratives and urban images

The personal story-telling analysed in the last chapter was not carried out in a vacuum, nor were the stories staged in some Olympian realm without reference to particular times and places. The city of Milton Keynes provides the setting for the storied adventures or at least for their concluding episodes, and many events and reflections are related to the specificities of Milton Keynes and of Fishermead. That too is the familiar context in which they are told, a familiarity shared with their local listeners. This chapter starts from this more specific setting to turn a somewhat different spotlight on the personal stories from that of the previous discussion. Eventually it will return us to some similar themes.

The personal tales may seem at first to have little relevance for the more general stories of city life. But they do both provide a further forum in which the city is experienced, and touch on points which take them beyond individual experiences and unique settings, carrying implications about the urban images held by their narrators and relating these personal stories to other tales of the city.

This chapter is illustrated by two further stories, recounting arrivals in the city of Milton Keynes, first impressions, evaluation of urban features, views of 'community' and of belonging, and the individual ways their tellers are depicted as shaping their lives within the city. We start with a tale that introduces the specific locality of Fishermead, the Milton Keynes housing estate where the stories were recorded, told from the viewpoint of an early incomer.

Lucy Dale's tale

Lucy Dale tells how she arrived in the new estate of Fishermead in 1974, then at an early stage of its development, and of her life before and after. She and her husband had come to Milton Keynes from Kent, to get a job and a house – the same rented house in Fishermead where they were still living with their two children. Through a series of somewhat circuitous flashbacks her story depicts her work with the local playgroup in Fishermead, studying as a mature student in a local school, then a university degree. Now in her early forties, she is a qualified teacher, though so far has only held temporary teaching jobs. She recounts her abiding love of Milton Keynes but also the deterioration of Fishermead since the early pioneering days.

* * *

Well, we lived in Petts Wood, we were in a flat over the delicatessen. Petts Wood is Kent, on the borders of Chislehurst and London [. . .] We had just been married, Alec and I, he had lost his job and he had got a job on the milk round, that didn't last very long unfortunately he lost that as well. And then he managed to get a job in his trade up here from Kent, so he went for the interview and got the job. And so we moved up here and we got a house with it and we were thrilled [. . .]

Yes, [to] this house and it was brand new at the time. It [Fishermead] only went to the block at the end there and all the rest was fields [. . .] There were all fields at the bottom of the road, and at the bottom of the road it was barricaded off because you couldn't go any further than that and so it was quite safe for the kids to play outside. The boulevard was there but that was it really. Even the other side of the boulevard wasn't built although that came later.

It was wonderful when we first moved in, it was like a long holiday. We got on well with our neighbours, everybody was new in the block and everybody was young with children, and we formed quite a close-knit group and we used to go out and about, and we formed the Sports & Social Club and we had a good social life. It was there when we moved in, a lot simpler than it is now. I am not really a pub person, but we used to go out with the crowd, pubs weren't built then, it wasn't there, 'The Cricketers' wasn't there, none of the pubs were there. And the city centre wasn't open, that wasn't properly built, you used to have to go to Bletchley for our shopping [. . .]

And 'Dial-a-bus' was around then. It was brilliant. You just walked to the top of the road, and by the flats there at the top of the road, you just used to phone up and say 'I am here at the end of Penryn Road' and then a few minutes later the bus would come along and pick you up on its way through. And I used to love it and I used to go out of Fishermead – I mean you still do get the view, but there is a lot more been built – but if you turned out of Fishermead

6.1 Terraced houses and street in the Fishermead housing estate, Milton Keynes. The type of housing and setting in Fishermead to which Lucy Dale and many of the other narrators moved (photograph of terraced houses by Mike Levers, Open University; photograph of street used by courtesy of the Commission for the New Towns)

you could see across the countryside and of course that time of the year all the rape fields would be in bloom. And for me coming from – well it was a suburb, but it was very built up, we would go into the countryside at the weekends if we had a car, but I mean I didn't live surrounded by fields – and it was just wonderful like living in the countryside. It's still one of the things I like about it. Campbell Fields, Campbell Park is just up here.

(*You only had the one child then?*) Only Guy, Guy was seven when I had Laura, I had Laura in Aylesbury [about 20 miles away], because the hospital wasn't built [. . .] We accepted it because like we had moved into a new city, and there was nothing here anyway, it was just that they left it a little bit late putting a hospital here [. . .] I think they got their timing a bit stuck, because the hospital should have gone up quite quickly, let's face it [. . .] I had problems having Guy, so they decided to shoot me off to Aylesbury and it was a pain visiting for Alec and that sort of thing, you know: 'Oh God it's hospital visit!' And there I was, you know, like eight months pregnant with a stomach out here, and this bus would trundle along around the villages and I would be bumped around and I would think 'I'm going to have this baby on the way to Aylesbury' – and it was just, like, a check-up.

And so the reason we actually moved to Milton Keynes was for Alec to get a job here – and we were more than happy to move. I wasn't particularly happy at Petts Wood, I wasn't really an outgoing person. I have gained a lot more confidence since then. I made one or two friends, but basically it was quite lonely with Alec out at work and I stayed at home quite a lot with Guy [in Petts Wood], I believed that you should stay at home in those first years, although there was a spell when I went out to work, but I wasn't happy leaving him, but that was because I had to because we had big financial problems in those days.

Well I was born in Hammersmith, I was brought up mainly in south-east London, you know. I had been in other areas, as my mum and dad moved round quite a lot. My dad was a butcher and was gradually building his way up and he was quite ambitious. It wasn't easy for them either, and they went from flat to flat, and then house to house, and then moved into, just off the Ley High Road at Lewisham, and that is where we settled for quite a few years. Good memories of round there. We did all the moving around up until I was about five, and then I started at Emmersdale

School [. . .] I have got two brothers, I had a brother at the time, I grew up with a brother, but there was another brother, my youngest brother was born when I was twelve, they are both in America, today [. . .]

I loved him [my dad], but he was – well, marriage problems. He and my mum were divorced and there was – marriage problems. I didn't see him that often because he remarried again. It was quite a long hard bitter divorce, you know. In the twenties, let me see, they were separated for my wedding, just before my twentieth birthday, and they started a divorce about a year later, so I was in the twenties. It [hurt] me in the sense of a child, like the marriage was never, well like I say it had its happy times, but it was a very bitter long divorce and it did affect me a great deal, yes, and the marriage itself, growing up in the marriage itself, do you know what I mean? I am not saying that I wasn't happy, I mean my parents were good parents, my dad was selfish but on the whole he was good, he did care for us and I did love him, my dad, and that was it. I am very very close to my mum but I don't see her as often as I would like, although she was up this weekend. She has remarried now, and lives on the borders of Cambridge, she has got a thatched cottage out that way, and it is lovely and I go out there [. . .]

I did manage to work for one term last year and I managed to get a little work and we did manage a holiday as a family last year, and it is the first holiday we had since Laura was born. I did manage to get a bit of supply teaching at summer but only because the school fought for me, and they said it is ridiculous, she knows the children, she knows the school and you know she would be better than another teacher coming in, stranger coming in. So they gave me a little bit of supply teaching over the summer, but the supply people said all right but she can only do it at that school. I had to make a break from that school, you see, they kept me on for a while and kept me going, and I didn't get a job for the September, and I am still struggling to get a job for this September, now [. . .]

After doing playgroup, I developed the playgroup at Fishermead over a few years with lots of other people, but I sort of took it over and then watched its development right the way through, and I did a lot of community work in those years, and I also trained a lot through the Pre-school Playgroup Association. And I decided that when I went back to education I wanted to get something out of it for myself. So instead of doing the Bachelor of Education which is basically child development, I wanted to do something that I could develop on my own. So I went and did English literature and drama and what I did was BA with qualified teacher status, and I did the course which was at my level, which was a bit more, like a degree with a post-graduate [teaching certificate] thrown in and put together. It was very good on both angles really, and I enjoyed the course.

It took me two years to get A levels [pre-university qualification], which I did at Stantonbury [school]. I did that in the sixth form and had a wonderful time, absolutely brilliant time I had at Stantonbury. And then I did this [university] course and I had to live away from home [. . .] I stayed in the hall for the first year and then I found lodgings in the second year and stayed there for the rest of the three years. My landlady was a character, just down the road from the university, and I was happier with her, because she was nearer my age, and I got on really well with younger people, she was a one-parent family with a little boy, and he – I just liked the home atmosphere with a child and everything

I found it quite lonely first of all. Oh it was terrible. After the first year I nearly, well after the first term . . . Very very hard that first year, packing up my gear and going up there, and then I got used to it and then I started to enjoy it and have my own space and my own room, and I got used to it, and you just acclimatise. Well, I used to come home on a Wednesday night to do Guides, I have always done Guides and drop everything else and all the committees and playgroups and everything else but I did keep my Guides going right the way through because I felt I needed it. Something away from studying and everything. I do a Guide company and I take them away and camping and everything [. . .]

I love Milton Keynes, I love living here. I think it is a shame, I think this particular estate has deteriorated, it seems to be getting noisier and more trouble, and it doesn't seem to be as peaceful as it used to be, and when you cruise through this estate, my son and I because he is unemployed, we are both unemployed, we will often go bird watching a lot, and we go to different woodlands. But at the same time we are interested and when a new estate goes up we will cruise the estate and look at the houses, and other respects too, just to look at the houses, look at the gardens, look at how they are developing. And this estate just does not seem to be as peaceful as other estates.

Just over the last five years, about five years, it has gradually started, maybe a wee bit longer than that, it started, and there seems to be a lot of – em . . ., I don't think it is as bad as its reputation is. It seems to have a reputation and people talk about it, and they say 'Oh it has a terrible reputation and I wouldn't live on there', but certainly if you are living on here the rubbish and the state of the streets and the rubbish . . . And you know it isn't all the families, it is just the odd few, and I wish they would do something about that. I don't like to victimise people or anything but I think something could be done.

I've been a bit out of it in all fairness. I mean at one time, at one time when I did the playgroup I couldn't walk down the road without someone saying hello to me and I knew all the young mums on here and I had good connections with all the schools, and was very much in the community. But since doing my course, I haven't been, and I have lost contact, and have come across the occasional person I knew, but basically I have lost contact, and it is quite nice because there always seemed to me when I worked at the playgroup the people that were supportive of the playgroup were the same people, and it is the same with Guides. It is always the same people, and there seems to be quite a lethargy amongst some people, but it is quite nice to feel that there is a community spirit.

I did hear through the grapevine that [the playgroup] did have problems at one time. But I was talking to a young mum the other day and she was talking and we had a really long chat, and she was saying that it has changed now and saying that people at the playgroup were taking up PPA [Pre-school Playgroups Association] courses again, and you know it's developing, but then that is what playgroups are about, they have their ups and downs and it is the people that take over it, you know. Well they develop with the parents that are running it, you know, they certainly had problems when I first started. Well, when you think how difficult it is to get those kinds of projects going . . . Well, like I said, there used to be Youth Club round at the Trinity Centre, and I know there has been like a judo class and dance classes but you have to have money to send your kids there, I mean it might not be over expensive but you still have to have money.

It's lovely to be able to walk up the road. I mean we have got the car now, [but] I remember being pregnant with Laura and having to walk right over to the other side to Waitrose [supermarket], and it used to be on the other side to the city centre, and carry my bags back at like seven months pregnant. And I used to have about six or seven carrier bags to cart back, and I used to think 'What the flaming hell am I doing this for!' But now it is much easier [. . .]

I love Milton Keynes, I love the area, and I love the fact that you can be in the countryside within five minutes' walk. Ideally, if I could get a job I would like to buy a house, and ideally I would like to lift this one and plonk it on another estate. That's what I would like to do. I love this house because of the windows and the light, we are all fresh air fanatics, the worst, and I love the fact that I can lay in bed at night and watch the stars with the windows open [. . .] And I love sitting in this room with the windows open. First thing in the morning, it is lovely, the sun comes in, I love the house, and it's out the back in the afternoon and evenings, it is very good. I would like to pick it up and ideally take it to the country really, if ever I had the chance to buy, that is the environment, I would like to overlook fields and things like that, because we are such nature fans [. . .]

Tales of Fishermead and the place of 'place'

The housing estate within Milton Keynes to which Lucy Dale so enthusiastically moved and where other narrators eventually found acceptable homes was that of Fishermead. There too was where the narrators were living at the time their tales were recorded. Even if they had moved to that particular estate only recently, their stories to some extent refer to it and to their lives there. The narrations present both personal experience and more widespread images of locality and community.

Fishermead was one of the earliest 'new city' estates or 'grid squares', started in 1974 with further building in the 1980s. Its name comes from an old field name in the locality, and, as in many Milton Keynes estates, the street names have a common theme: this time Cornish fishing connections. Like other new city estates, it was planned both to communicate with others and to have its own local facilities, but was to be distinctive in being close to the city centre and more dense and 'urban' in its buildings and spacing. The housing is largely grouped round squares and along the central boulevard. Much of the earlier housing was built in three-storey blocks with wide windows, carports and, initially, flat roofs (which later had to be replaced); this was complemented by the later more varied designs which included two-storeyed and bungalow housing for sale. Public open space is prominent, with tree-planted landscaping and Kernow Crescent curving around a local park (Fig. 6.3 on p. 153).

As an estate, Fishermead has attracted varying opinions, from enthusiasm in the early days to more derogatory opinions recently. The terraced houses round the public squares were a conscious attempt by the planners 'to create

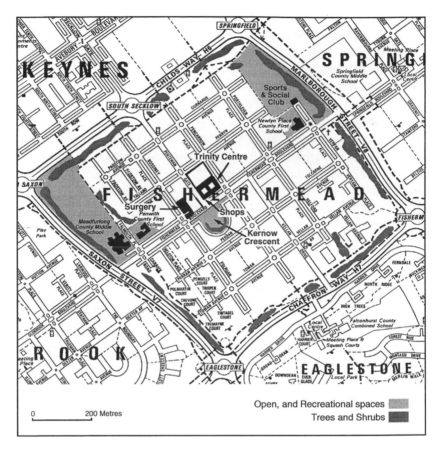

6.2 Map of Fishermead: the setting for the personal stories. This shows places
mentioned in the tales such as the local centre (site of the Co-op and other shops,
and of the doctor's surgery), the Trinity Centre (incorporating the church), sports
and social club, schools, public squares, recreational spaces and planted areas (by
courtesy of the Commission for the New Towns, revised by John Hunt)

street orientated low rise urban housing with direct access for the car and
the pedestrian' ('Housing 1 and 2 . . .' 1977 p. 880). Kernow Crescent at the
heart of the estate lies on the central boulevard, described by one enthusiast
as 'a fine crescent of rental houses and flats in the eighteenth century style of
Bath or Cheltenham' (*A Brief Guide* . . . 1987 p. 6). Many non-dwellers in
Fishermead dislike its terraced housing and what is now seen as repetitive
regularity, but it has had admirers too. Eugene Fisk sums up his 'personal
view':

There is a continental feel to [Fishermead], flat-fronted yet with balconies but with no front gardens. So the dwellings are immediately adjacent to the streets which are wide, in fact 'boulevards', alive with shrubs and trees. There is a hint of the Georgian about the continuous levels and the regular patterns of windows. The inclusion of a crescent of terraced houses in this style further states the Georgian motif [while] Mullion Place suggests the quiet seclusion of a London square. (Fisk 1981)

In 1994, when these personal narratives were recorded, Fishermead contained about 4,000 people in just under 1,500 households; the figures from the previous census (1991) are summarised below. Despite Fishermead's external reputation as a run-down and poor-class area, the population came from varied backgrounds and was in some respects fairly typical of that in Milton Keynes more generally. However, in common with other estates near the city centre, there were fewer older people and more small households, among them many single-person households and lone parents. There was also a higher proportion of terraced housing, flats/bed-sits and rented housing. This was the setting for the narrators recorded here, most of whom lived in the terraced areas round the centre of the estate.

Population and households in Fishermead, 1991

POPULATION	**3,930**
Male	1, 912
Female	2,018
Pre-school age (0–4 years)	10.7%
School age (5–15 years)	22.7%
Over retirement age	6%
Born outside the UK (the majority coming from the New Commonwealth)	9.6%
Economically active	71%
Moved in previous 12 months	13%
HOUSEHOLDS	**1,418**
Average household size	2.77
'Lone parent'	11%
Containing pensioner(s) only	10%
Owner- occupiers	41.3%
Car-owners	66%
With central heating	100%

(Based on the 1991 census returns as summarised in Milton Keynes Borough Council 1993 pp. 97–100 and Buckinghamshire County Council 1993 pp. 171, 286)

The personal narratives sometimes represent Fishermead as a locality about which it is possible to generalise. People live 'on Fishermead', and 'you either love it or hate it' (Richard Walker). The stories refer to the type of housing or to landmarks like the local shops (especially the Co-op), the doctor's surgery, chemist, baker's, 'Trinity Centre', schools, the pub or the social club. Such features, it seems, are assumed as part of the stock setting for the stories' local action, in a parallel way to the church and bridge at the heart of what Frake terms the 'cultural construction' of the English country-side (1996). Kernow Crescent is mentioned too, sometimes depicted as at the heart of Fishermead, as well as Fishermead Boulevard, the wide street running through the estate, which in the spring, as one story has it, 'is just two rows of daffodil and tulip all the way up'.

The distinctively *local* nature of Fishermead is emphasised in some tales. A mother portrays Fishermead as 'very much like a self-contained environment, in some ways you get stuck in the confines of it, because of the transport when you have kids it is so difficult to travel on the buses . . . That is one thing about Fishermead that being so self-contained the kids they are very territorial with their attitudes' (Sarah Henderson). It is also contrasted with other Milton Keynes estates. 'I have been here a year' comments Sally Vincent after moving from Conniburrow, 'I am getting to like it.' Another narrator ponders the conflicts between estates:

I mean we have wars as it is between Conniburrow and here, and here and Bletchley, and it is all gang warfare. The boys hate each other. I mean S – 's boy he was up here for a year and he couldn't stand it, he had to go back and live with his nan in Bletchley because they wouldn't accept him, because he came from Bletch-ley . . . every time he stepped outside the door there was trouble.

There are also negative generalisations about Fishermead. The layout and the over-spreading bushes on roundabouts are criticised, as are the potential dangers to pedestrians, and the architecture.

Then take the houses, flat roofs, costs a fortune to put bitumen on afterwards. Why did they have flat roofs, oh they wanted it to match the city centre, that sort of thing. I mean the houses, apart from flat roofs, they have done a wonderful job enclosing a large house into a small exterior, but, look at the driveways they are inches, you can't put a mini on them. So what happens, everybody parks in the street. (Ernest Brown)

Whether critical or complimentary, such accounts picture Fishermead as a physical location – a *place* – with its own characteristics.

It is also sometimes presented as a 'community', not so much a physical place as a focus for social interaction and support. Judy Candy had finally managed after many troubles (p. 150 below) to get her house on Fishermead and her tale continues:

I got involved, and I do find on Fishermead, I mean my own personal view of Fishermead is that it is like a big village, it is an estate but it is like a village, but the other estates that I have lived on there hasn't been such a community spirit, even though I mean it is a bit of a dive and a lot of criminal activities . . . I do like Fishermead actually, there is a lot going on, a lot of energy and a lot of noise, which is a bit much sometimes . . . I love it, I love to walk down the street on a sunny day and hear reggae coming from one place, and rock 'n' roll from another place up the street and somebody else playing a bit of rave or something. And you know, I think this place is happening, that it is not too stuffy even though there is a negative side to that, the criminal stuff . . . I think I would like to move eventually, but right now I need the support network that Fishermead can provide for me, I have a lot of friends here.

Similarly Lucy Dale recounts being 'very much in the community' in her early days, and others describe activities centring on the playgroup or on support from their friends. Twenty-year-old Janet Eaton glories in the street life:

I do like it down here, it is a really friendly street, loads happening, if you look out your bedroom window every night you will see something happen . . . I suppose I am just a nosy neighbour, but there are arguments down the street, and the police down here, you know, and I open my window up and hang out and everyone is hanging around. And you don't have to have your music on because you can hear it anyway and you are sitting out there in the summer and someone says well come over . . . I just sit out there on the brick wall and that and everybody sits out there, crowds of you sitting outside your house.

Fishermead's poor external reputation also gives it a kind of identity. This is the background to Judy Candy's 'I do like Fishermead actually' or Lucy Dale's 'I don't think it is as bad as its reputation is', as narrators express their positive counters to the image. Others too insist that Fishermead is 'not as bad as people make it out to be' or 'I ain't had no trouble since I've been here, so that has been lucky, but I like it.' Richard Walker tackles it explicitly:

Status wise, I suppose if I was very much a snob I wouldn't live here, it is very low-key, I suppose is the word, in terms of places to live. If you speak to what I term as a 'Milton Keyney', you know been here over five years, if you say you live on Fishermead, it is not quite seen, you know – well it is one better than living on Netherfield or The Lakes [estate in Bletchley].
    Personally I don't see the stigma, having lived here for two and a half years. I

think people here are very different, their values seem to be a lot lower, they don't have this sort of 'being like the Joneses' attitude that I have experienced in the rest of Milton Keynes. I think, to use the wrong term maybe, they are working class and they tend to have the man go out, man and woman now, and go out and earn their money and come back and enjoy – and that is life and they don't seem to feel there is a stigma. If you speak to anybody on Fishermead they don't think there is a stigma. I only see the stigma because I have lived in Bletchley, west Bletchley, for most of the time I have been up here, and see the stigma because people would say 'Oh I wouldn't live on Fishermead.'

The younger Patricia Ejikame's story tells how she relishes Fishermead life and rejects others' accounts:

You hear so many stories about – oh, you know, it is this and it is that. But I like it personally, because ever since I have moved up from London I have always lived on Fishermead and couldn't imagine living anywhere else. There is a few bad things going on and that, but me personally I like it, and I couldn't imagine living anywhere else.

Fishermead's 'deterioration' is a common motif. Lucy Dale's story recounts her glowing memories of earlier community, then the later falling away: 'I think it is a shame, I think this particular estate has deteriorated, it seems to be getting noisier and more trouble, and it doesn't seem to be as peaceful as it used to be.' Other tales speak regretfully of the Youth Club, now closed down, the community newspaper or the festival: 'as Fishermead has gone on they have lost it' (Joy Osborne). There are constant references to increasing 'noise', burglaries, drugs, unreliable youngsters or anti-social incomers.

We have been on Fishermead, I think about fifteen years. Fishermead in those days, to be honest about it, was a nicer place than it is now. The people were nicer. Quite a few of the inhabitants I regret to say are rapidly deteriorating . . . I mean it was a lovely turning at one time, it really was. There is a family moved in, I won't tell you exactly where, but they moved in, their house had burnt down, they used to live on the Lakes Estate, they had rehoused them here, and now all you get is swearing and everything . . . it has brought the place down tremendously, and there are a lot of people unfortunately moving into Fishermead like that. They built this estate with the idea of it being one of their plum estates. (Ernest Brown)

These accounts too give Fishermead a kind of identity through their appeal to potentially shared memories of a common past or a call to unity against changes and newcomers. The details vary. One narrator states as self-evident that 'it has deteriorated in the last ten years', others speak of 'five years'. But in general terms the 'deterioration of Fishermead' has emerged as an accepted myth among the longer-established residents, invoking among other things the conventional nostalgia characteristic of so many representations of 'community'. Barbara Johnstone's analysis of American Midwest stories suggests that people are 'at home in a place when the place evokes stories and, conversely, stories can serve to create places' and pictures a community of speakers as those 'who share previous stories, or conventions for making stories, and who jointly tell new stories' (1990 p. 5). On the same lines, the widely (though not universally) accepted story of Fishermead's deterioration to an extent shapes it as an identifiable and shared locale for its narrators.

Fishermead is not self-contained and themes of local identity are balanced by outward-looking links. Most stories depict their protagonists as going outside Fishermead for their shopping, for work, leisure activities, friends, external support, church events or visiting relatives. Rachel Jacobs calls on the external 'Letnet' scheme to help her cope with poverty (below, p. 145), while Joy Osborne recounts her non-Fishermead church affiliation: 'I have got my own sort of people and we work as a team together you see . . . There is a church on Fishermead, but . . . I like a lively church. The one I go to is more a spiritual church.' Incomers from London tell of keeping up their London links for a time, and even when acclimatised to the new city do not set their stories solely within Fishermead. Those moving in from other parts of Milton Keynes – over half of the narrators – regularly portray retaining previous connections like doctor, club membership or friends elsewhere in the city. As elsewhere in Milton Keynes – and in keeping with the planners' view of the estates as *not* self-contained units – people go outside for many of their activities.

Despite these indications of a 'community of interests' rather than of 'contiguity' (as Ward has it, 1993) Fishermead is the stage for many of the stories' events. There is little indication in the tales that 'global' links or the new 'information nexus' suggested by analysts like Meyrowitz (1985) have replaced people's local foundations. The label of 'no sense of place' could not really be applied to the Fishermead dwellers' narratives, although the broadness or narrowness of the local focus in the stories does vary with the teller. Tales of young mothers often focus more on the locality, tales of those with full-time work less so; those of older people revolve more round memories of earlier community activity. In all however, the Milton Keynes narrators do not use the concept of 'place' for the structuring role found in some life narratives elsewhere (Bruner 1987 p. 26), nor do they give it the prominence we might have expected from those academic tales that emphasise the local as counterpoint to 'global'. Despite the interest in personal and family *housing*, an overt preoccupation with 'place' or with 'the local' as such does not strongly mould the Fishermead personal stories.

The perspective is an ambiguous one however. For there is also some moral implication in the stories that 'place' and 'neighbourhood' somehow *ought* to be important. Narrators depicting extra-Fishermead links recount their lack of local involvement with regret, even guilt, or wish there were more 'community' activities. The tales imply an ideal – an unachieved ideal – of community identity and cooperation if not in the estate as a whole then at least in some local neighbourhood. The implication is that, whatever the present practice, people's roots and activities essentially do, or ideally should, somehow pertain to a *place*. Whether critical, commendatory or idiosyncratic, the stories often step uneasily around the familiar themes of a tension between local and extra-local interests, in a tone of discomfort about their protagonists' lack of greater local involvement.

The tellers' personal relation to their locality and its relevance or otherwise to their personal journey also comes out in other aspects of the stories. Particularly illuminating are the adventures they have to narrate about their moves and settling, their assessment of 'belonging' or of 'home', and their views of Milton Keynes as a town. The final story to be printed at length, that of Rachel Jacobs, illustrates how some of these issues – among many other of the themes discussed so far – can be treated in narrative form.

Rachel Jacobs' tale

About forty in 1994, Rachel Jacobs recounts her 1984 move to Bletchley (the long-established town incorporated within the 'new city' boundaries), accompanying her then partner, the father of her three children. Her dramatic narrative portrays the disasters connected with her separation from her partner, and how, having been left destitute, she became a taxi-driver. She managed to buy a house on Fishermead, was for some time on income support, but is now gradually recovering and back in regular work. As she tells her 'personal journey', she has at last found a group of congenial friends and 'so it's now really that I feel good about Milton Keynes, now it's my home'.

* * *

My earliest memories weren't here, because I didn't grow up here, I was born in Ilford in Essex, and I stayed in Ilford until I was coming up to thirty. It is ten years ago, ten years this summer, I moved here.

I moved here because my children's father's company moved head office up here and they wanted to establish a head office full of young and hopefully settled couples [. . .] They asked him if we would move up here.

And I didn't want to. I came here a couple of weekends because we were house hunting. And I hated it, I hated it, it was awful. Because when you drive along the H and V roads [the main grid roads], as a stranger, you don't see anything other than road. There is nothing, is there, I mean there is nothing. Trees and bushes, but nothing, no cats and dogs, no cyclists, and couldn't help but feel it was a ghost town.

I felt very uncomfortable with the whole thing, and apart from that I was a lousy map reader, and if you can't read maps you can't survive in Milton Keynes. It took me three months to work out that the V in the V roads meant vertical and the H in the H roads meant horizontal. I couldn't get from Bletchley to the city centre without a map, and even then I used to get lost.

(*It was different from where you lived before?*) Yeh I mean Ilford was a British town, with an established community. I felt like I belonged there, all my roots were there, every time I walked past a shop, or a street, or into a turning, it had a memory of some sort for me.

Milton Keynes had nothing for me. And I didn't like it at all. It wasn't helped by the fact that for the first year that we lived here I was still going to college, in London, so I spent a working day down there, come back here evenings and weekends, so I never really got to know anybody. I used to arrange to meet friends socially down in London, and then come home to sleep in Milton Keynes, and I still didn't like it, to be honest with you. The only people I knew were the people who'd moved with us from London with John's company – and I didn't really like any of them either! They were all computer buffs and they were definitely not my scene, and there were just no soul mates for me amongst them. And I felt very alone actually.

We moved into Bletchley, west Bletchley, so quite an established part of Bletchley, and I never saw the neighbour, I felt completely estranged, I didn't feel like I fitted in, I didn't like it, I felt . . . Oh, I can actually remember I had been living in Milton Keynes for eighteen months and was decorating the front room and there was a knock at the door and it was the postman, with a parcel too big to go through the letterbox, and he not only handed me the parcel through the front-room window, but he spoke to me. And when he had gone I cried because he was the first person in Milton Keynes who had spoken to me voluntarily, which I know sounds daft, but I guess it was just a sign of how isolated I felt.

The whole layout of Milton Keynes was different, the infrastructure is different, a lot of what is in Milton Keynes today was not there then, I didn't know where to go to meet people that I would want to be friends with, so it was very difficult. I tried standing outside the school gate, along with all the other mothers, to wait for my kids. But that wasn't my cup of tea anyway, and I still didn't hit it off because I wasn't really that interested in how so-and-so did in her ballet lessons or where little Johnny came in his maths exam.

So I was very, very isolated. And that actually went on for quite a while, I never really felt like I knew Milton Keynes. And then for various personal reasons to do with my friendship with John, I became a cab driver. There is nothing like being a cab driver for getting to know Milton Keynes. I suddenly felt like I knew the place. There's something to do with knowing actually where things are in a place, that make you feel like you belong. It's not a real feeling, it is actually quite a superficial feeling, because it doesn't have a lot to do with people. So that was when I started to feel that I belonged here, that was when on my occasional trips back down to London I didn't think 'Oh aren't I pleased to be back.' I used to start going back down to London and thinking 'I don't want to be here, this is not for me.'

I have to say, that whilst for me on a personal level it hadn't worked up to then, for the children it had, because for very young children there is a huge range of activities that are absolutely free and carefully organised and planned and brilliant. There is nothing better, really. I mean walk outside your front door for a hundred yards wherever you go in Milton Keynes and you are in a green bit and the kids loved it, that was marvellous. In the summer we would go and pick up John from work with a picnic and we'd open the map of Milton Keynes and just point to a green bit and say 'Well, we will go and see what is there.' And we used to go off and explore with the children, the green bits. So the children had actually settled, very quickly, and I appreciated what it had for children [. . .]

Yeh, so being a cabbie helped me, suddenly I got to know where things were, and I didn't need my map any more. I used to walk down the high street in Bletchley sometimes and people would stop me and say 'Hi, how are you?', and I wouldn't have the faintest idea of who they were, and yes it makes you feel you belong [. . .]

Three years. It was very hard work, it becomes almost an addiction. You feel like you have a lot of freedom when you do a job like that, you choose whether you go out to work, you choose when you stop, that can get addictive, and you start to think well I could never work for a proper company because I would have to do what I am told and work within certain limitations. No, you kid yourself really, but to be honest the money is not good on an hourly rate it is actually appalling, it is only if you work twelve or fifteen hours a day that it becomes worthwhile. It is one of these things that look good on paper but when you add all the bits and pieces and put them together it is no longer a good deal, is it? So one day I woke up to this fact, and I stopped basically.

It was an interesting experience. One of the reasons I gave up is because for all sorts of reasons, the vast majority of cab drivers are at best amoral and have one foot perched very perilously either side of the fence [. . .] Even though I didn't break the law, I actually realised that I had been very accepting of what was going on, and I knew that I had reached a fairly dangerous point for me when my car reached an age when it couldn't be re-plated [licensed] by the council. Because you are only allowed to use cars as taxis up to an age, and I didn't have the where with all for a new one. And the thought went through my head, 'Oh, I know what I will do, I will go to so and so, because he will be able to get me a nicked car.' And the moment I thought that thought, I thought 'Hang on, what are you saying?' And that is actually when I made the decision to leave. Because even though I didn't do the things that they did, by association I felt uncomfortable with it. And while purely as individuals many of these people were charming, they would come into my home, they would be talking, and my children would be here absorbing thoughts, it is hard to say. I mean kids aren't stupid, kids know what is going on, and I thought 'No, how can I on the one hand say to my children "It is wrong to steal, it is wrong to take drugs, it is wrong to threaten someone with a shot gun just because they haven't paid you your fare", and then say but it is OK for these people to come into my home and talk about it' – because it isn't really OK is it? I had got into it slowly, you don't realise because it is so pervasive [. . .]

You feel a real pratt you know, you stand up and you say to someone 'No this is wrong.' [. . .] They used to think I was crazy. I used to get some real abuse. And the things they all used to get up to, you don't even know [. . .] So you are in a very difficult position. So I decided for all sorts of reasons, that being one of them, I got out. And the moment I did it, it was like you had shed a weight from your shoulders, because it just wasn't the right environment – it wasn't emotionally healthy, that was the problem. I stopped cabbying three years ago.

When I moved here [1984] I was at college. I stayed in college for a year in London [. . .] and then at the end of my first year here I was offered a full-time job in London, which I took because it was a wonderfully prestigious job, and it flattered my ego no end. But the problem was, that it was one of these jobs where you can't leave the office until about 7.30–8 p.m. and then back to Milton Keynes and it is time to crawl into bed and get up the next day for work. So I lasted at that for about eighteen months.

The kids' dad was brilliant basically. During the week he basically looked after the kids, he worked locally, and had time for them. We had a nanny, and if he hadn't been prepared to look after them I couldn't have done it.

But the job, well it was one of these, a self-defacing job really, it was full of ego and prestige and a flash job title and all that. And it sounded so damn swank, it doesn't mean a damn thing. I found it flattering, but in the end that is all it is, it's a fancy job title and OK perhaps it is a fairly fancy salary, but in fairness by the time you have taken off the cost of your daily train fare and the cost of a full-time nanny you are actually no better off than if you had worked in Milton Keynes in a slightly less prestigious position. It suited me at the time I suppose. But it didn't suit me for much longer than about eighteen months and then I had to make some decisions because I knew I couldn't go on that way, it wasn't right.

And what I decided to do was to start up my business from home, still with John, still living in Bletchley. And I started up a word-processing secretarial service. And I managed to start that just at the right time [. . .] and I managed to build that up quite nicely. And it was good because I was working and dealing with the kids and still earning a decent whack, so that was fine.

Through all of this to be fair, John and I hadn't really been getting on too well. It was all a bit dodgy I suppose, but it came to a head when I'd been having my own business for about eighteen months – I'm sorry about dates here, but they just blur after a while don't they – and I really got it to a stage where it was self-perpetuating. I had enough business coming in and I was pretty much always doing something, and that was really nice.

And his company asked us if we would go and live in Brussels on a two-year contract, and he came home and told me about it. And I said 'Well we will think about it', and he said 'You've got until tomorrow morning.' He said 'Well it has come up at short notice and they have to know by tomorrow morning.' And I said 'What do you mean you've got till tomorrow morning!' And if we say yes, then it is six weeks to the day until we leave, which is no time to pack up your house and find somewhere else to live, get schooling for the children! Oh it was a nightmare.

So I mulled it over and being the adventurous sort, I said 'Yes.' John my ex, at the time, being the conservative sort, didn't get it in writing from his company. So basically they told him to pack up and me to pack up but they said that because they themselves didn't have a contract with NATO at that moment in time, that we shouldn't do anything irrevocable, which was a bit of a difficult thing to say. So we waited until a week before we were due to fly out, we couldn't wait any longer and I sold my business, and we got people in to rent where we were living in Bletchley and all the rest of it. And that was when the phone rang, and it was John's company saying 'It's off.' Well, my words aren't actually repeatable here. They're particularly not repeatable because when we said 'What about the money for me?' – because I'd actually had to give John all the money from my business so he could pay for air tickets and all sorts – they said 'Tough.' Basically 'Tough', that's what they said.

I was really angry with John because he wouldn't fight for me, he wouldn't stand up for me, and I felt that they had really done the dirty. You cannot say to someone 'You're flying out here's your plane ticket', but on the other hand say 'Don't do anything irrevocable', you can't. There comes a point where you have to make a decision, you have to say 'OK we are renting out our house.' And I feel I was stitched up. I feel John should have fought for me. But he took it.

And ultimately what I felt was well it is OK for him. He has his 30,000 grand a year job, hasn't he, but I had nothing, I had sold to someone else. I couldn't say 'Please can I have it back, but I haven't

got the money to give you because I've given that to my other half.'
And then again I couldn't open up in direct competition because
that wouldn't have been right either. And the pits was when a
couple of weeks later John came back and said 'And by the way I
think you should go and get yourself a job.' He wasn't very tactful.
That was really the straw that broke the camel's back between John
and I. I mean there had been a lot wrong between us, and both of us
had contributed to that. And maybe both of us contributed to this
whole sort of Brussels deal going down. But we played a game
together knowing that it was going to come crashing, maybe, I don't
know. And I left three months later.

That was a really difficult time for me. We had been living
together for a long time, but we weren't married you see, and he
wanted our separation to be done properly, legally, and I said 'OK'.
And we went to our respective solicitors and were told that because
we'd not been married, and because even though I had always been
working and paying bills – I tended to pay the bills like the food bill,
or the kids' shoes, or stuff like that, and he tended to pay the gas,
mortgage, the electric and stuff like that – and while it worked out
about quits, in the end, he had receipts and I didn't and I was
entitled to nothing, nothing, nothing. The other damning thing for
me was that because he had been really upset one night, he'd come
home and said 'I can't stand living in the same house as you and I
know you want to leave', and to save him his dignity I had left. I
shouldn't have left the family home, should I, silly move to have
made.

Well, four years ago found me with not a penny because I had just
lost all the money to the business, and nothing, absolutely nothing,
absolutely destitute. The only things I was allowed to have was the
things that I could show reasonably that I had owned before I had
known him, so it was all [. . .]

But somehow that was four years ago, and it was then that I
found this house, and I found that very difficult as well, and basically I had to buy it with a mortgage. I bought it on the basis that I
was working as a taxi-driver. And I had all these wonderful
schemes for renting out a room, free of charge in return for like
baby-sitting, and it never worked, so I could never put in the hours
to pay the mortgage. And of course ever since then I have been here
with debts, you can imagine, but it's getting better now, it's getting
better now.

But it is only in the past year that I've really felt that I really do belong here in Milton Keynes, that I've met a group of people that I really like. I've found a number of places to go where the sort of people that I'm likely to like will go. So it's now really that I feel good about Milton Keynes, now it's my home.

A lot of it has actually been a personal journey, not just a financial one. A lot of it has been to do with me, trying to find a way of existing that I feel comfortable about. Judging by a lot of the people I know, it seems to be a journey that is . . . I think that most of the difficulties I've had, looking back, in one way or another have been self-inflicted, not consciously necessarily, but they have all been self-inflicted. And it's been about me trying to find – I don't know what the words are – a sort of whole-life existence, rather than packaging off my life and saying these hours of my day are work and these hours of my day are children, and these hours of the day are me, whatever – trying to find a way of existing that almost merges them all, something that feels comfortable. And it has been difficult.

And I suspect that in five years' time I will see where I am now as yet just another stage along the way.

(*Do you think you will still be here in five years' time?*) If I am in England I think so, yes, yes, I do, actually, I am not sure why. I think Milton Keynes has now become mixed up in my head with other feelings of well-being, which aren't necessarily inherent in Milton Keynes itself, although some of the things I've found here, and where I have found them, I mean I am not sure what exists, elsewhere, but my children have found a lovely place called 'Inter-Action' [Centre for Community Arts], do you know it? at Peartree Bridge. They go there in their holidays, and it has to be one of the loveliest places to go, and it's a nice healthy sort of place that you would want your kids to go to and that's just down the road.

And I have joined something called Letnet here, as well. How do you explain it, it's a scheme where you buy or sell, you buy other people's time, skills, whatever, with your own time, yes. I know it does exist in various other places in England. Right now it exists here in Milton Keynes, and by its very nature a certain person will join it. And so again it is a way of meeting and that feels really nice as well. It's a way of people helping themselves and each other and incidentally sticking two fingers up at the government, if you like, because you can completely bypass that system, and it's very empowering. And that's how I got the kitchen built. Come back and see it when it is clean and tidy, but basically that is how I got it done. It was something that I needed to have done, my other kitchen was a more traditional one, and it gradually fell apart and I found it really embarrassing but I couldn't do anything about it, because you have to have money. And then I found out about this scheme here and now I can do something about it, and for as long as that scheme lasts and for as long as I'm in a position and can't just snap my fingers and pay for things, that's going to be very important to me, and we've met people through the scheme, that are really good people to know.

So yeh, I feel very comfortable here. But – when I think of myself living in Milton Keynes I think of myself living in this house and I see it as shut off and closed off from the rest of Fishermead. I mean I don't know many people in Fishermead at all, and those I have met I actually don't get on very well with, it is awful, isn't it. So I suppose I just keep myself to myself in that sense, because if in my heart of hearts I don't like someone I'm just not friends with them, I'm not nasty but I just avoid them. For a while when I was living here I was stuck on income support, and that's got to be one of the most depressing things. You have all the time in the world and not a penny to do anything, and that I found very very isolating.

(*What about the facilities on Fishermead?*) What facilities, on Fishermead!? Ultimately it's the pub! Well, there is the local Sports & Social Club, a place where you can get really drunk. That sounds really awful but I can't stand it. You go there to get really legless so it appears, yes, and I've never been. And you have a Co-op [small local supermarket], a very limited and very expensive one, and the Post Office is fine, and a doctor's surgery which I don't use actually. The thing is that I have a doctor on Netherfield, who I like, and I'm loath to leave him and discover I don't like the new place [. . .]

What other facilities are there? Lots of lovely bits of green covered in dogs' poop. People simply think it's really OK here to take your dog for a walk and watch it poop where they know all these kids are going to be in a few hours' time. I don't understand their mentality, I really don't. A lot of theft and burglary, I mean I've been burgled about six times in the past two years. As far as I know everyone in this bit of cul-de-sac has been done at least once in the past year [. . .] A few weeks ago they came in through the front door, that is why I have got a board there, you know, I mean the question I have to ask myself is, is it worth replacing? They just kick the door in. To be honest with you the general feeling that I have is that they are determined, and also that they are kids [. . .]

And again this is going to sound really awful, and I know it can't be true, it can only be my perceptions of things, but the people that I've met on Fishermead seem to think that it is OK to bring up your kids to do this kind of thing. This is one of the reasons I don't particularly mix with them very much [. . .] I actually used to be friends with a woman, until I discovered that her son used to fence all the stuff that got nicked, and when I challenged her on it, she said 'But it's OK because he doesn't nick it', and I said 'Yes but he arranges for it to be nicked', and she said 'Yes.' I said 'Can't you see that that is just as wrong?', and she said 'No'. So I am not friends with her any more. It seems it's very pervasive [. . .]

I think I probably would stay [in Fishermead]. But if I had the money what I'd do would be to find a way of making the house secure, which you could do, with enough money you can make it secure. So yeh I probably would, mainly because I think that money spent purely on bricks and mortar nowadays isn't necessarily valued, and there are other things that I would do with my money, rather than spend it on bricks and mortar [. . .]

Adventures of moving, housing and home

The intertwined themes of people and of place come into the personal stories in several contexts. Episodes about moving to a new dwelling, of struggling for a place to live or of establishing a home feature commonly in the narrations by the Fishermead dwellers within Milton Keynes. The experiences portrayed are personal ones, enacted in a wide variety of circumstances and personalities. But far from being purely idiosyncratic, their narrative formulations represent accepted themes for story-telling, ordered in creative but familiar ways by their individual tellers.

As in Lucy Dale's and Rachel Jacobs' tales, the move to Milton Keynes figures in many of the narrations. This was a subject on which the tellers readily expressed themselves, with familiar themes to draw on. Their adventures often turn on the importance of house or job, and the relation between house moves and the heroes' developing personal and family life cycle. The stories tell, variously, of the pulls of existing links in the area, of 'accident' or of a leap into the unknown.

Several stories portray their heroes as pioneers, moving into Milton Keynes when the city or the estate was still at an early stage of its creation.

This is especially to the fore in accounts picturing the move as a new start, so that the narrator's tale and that of the city unfold together. As Lucy Dale tells it:

We moved up here and we got a house with it and we were thrilled . . . It only went to the block at the end there and all the rest was fields . . . It was wonderful when we first moved in, it was like a long holiday. We got on well with our neighbours, everybody was new in the block and everybody was young with children.

George Rowe comes at a later stage in life but still conveys the drama of coming to a newly developing town soon after its 'birth':

All of a sudden my wife's sister said to her about they were going to go to Hackney Town Hall and saw about Milton Keynes being born, because that was what it was called, 'being born' . . . There wasn't much around at that particular time, in 1976 . . . Near the roundabout just down the bottom here, there wasn't anything beyond there at all, they used to walk down to the railway lines with all the overhead electricity pylons down there as well, and it was all fields all the way down.

Not all narrators recount these episodes as happy, especially those like Brenda Dawson or Rachel Jacobs who came at the behest of others. But a sense of adventure is still a frequent theme. Jenny Linn-Cole's tale is of coming from south-west London in 1982 to get cheap housing:

So we moved into this new house in sort of a lot of mud, a quagmire, the road was continually covered in this mud. I gave a name for it, 'sloo' I called it, which was a combination of glue and slurry I suppose. A machine used to come down to clear it away but it actually mixed it up into this sort of 'sloo', and we were running motor bikes at the time and we sort of didn't have mud flaps on the back and we would go up the road on these things, not the end, and we would have this line of mud going up sort of whipped up by the wheel and actually come up on to the back of our jackets and so it looked as though we had done something really nasty, accident wise and had problems with our bowels or something, you know. It was an interesting time, it was sort of like living in frontier country.

In some tales moving to Milton Keynes is the turning point, particularly if it results in the first 'proper house'. In others it is merely one of several urban moves, with nothing exceptional about its being to Milton Keynes. Some narrators move into estates that are already well developed – by then with little feel of a 'frontier' – or come first to the older settlements of Bletchley or Stony Stratford, only later moving into Fishermead. Jill Blackwell's story shows her escaping from her ex-husband: 'I knew that if I was around my brothers my life would be easier, and I did move into Milton Keynes . . . [but] it is not like a new thing to come here, because I have always moved.' Another narrator wants to leave London for both business and personal reasons and considers Milton Keynes since some of his friends had moved there, ending up by taking a house in west Bletchley and a shop in Stony Stratford – long-established towns in their own right. Andrew Cunningham comes later in life, to the sheltered flats in Fishermead. After several years' wait the final decision is rapid: 'We said yes, we liked this one, and we would have it, and she said "Sign here", and "there are your keys", and that was that!' Such episodes are not depicted as revolutionary moves to 'a new city' or new life, merely as connected to the familiar migrant themes of the unfolding family cycle, friends or relatives in the locality, or relinquishing previous entanglements for a 'new start'.

The moves may be portrayed as carefully planned, expressing personal choice as well as family connection. Richard Walker's story represents an extreme case:

I knew of Milton Keynes, not colossal. It was my aunt, in fact it is my mother's brother's family who lived in Bletchley, so after getting married the thoughts were like 'Where shall we live?' . . . and we both decided to look outwards and get a map out and sort of draw little circles of where you want to go, and it kind of started at Harrow which is where most of my friends from college are, we did a circle as it were around Wembley [where they then lived], got to Harrow & Wealdstone and Watford, and I remember King's Langley coming into this as well, and then eventually because as I say I had family up here, we come up to Bletchley and then worked backwards going towards Leighton Buzzard way. And at the time my aunt was going through a stage where she wanted to move to Mitcham, London, and the plan was to buy her house . . . which ultimately didn't come through, and seeing as we had already made up our minds on Milton Keynes, we then bought our first house on . . . the Rivers Estate [Bletchley].

The first step to Milton Keynes is often the prelude to further moves *within* the city. Well over half of the Fishermead narrators had first come to some other area of Milton Keynes, and nearly half had moved two, three, four or more times since first arriving in the city – not an uncommon pattern in Milton Keynes, a 'mobile' district with a high proportion of 'within-migration' (Buckinghamshire County Council 1991 p. 4).

The intra-city moves are sometimes presented as part of an 'upward trend' as it is labelled in Richard Walker's narrative. He recounts people's attempts to move up and out from estates like Netherfield or Fishermead, then to a series of increasingly prestigious peripheral villages in the surrounding area. In some tales the heroes circle round a sequence of friends or partners. Lesley Lambert comes to the Lakes Estate in Bletchley as a child, later joins her sister Shirley in Fishermead, then goes successively to the new estates of Springfield, Netherfield, Coffee Hall and back to Fishermead. Another narrator lives on the estates of Stantonbury, Great Linford, Fishermead, Great Holm, Fullers Slade and Bradwell in the nine years since coming to Milton Keynes to join his step-mother. For such tellers coming to Milton Keynes is only one step in a tale of movements.

Others narrate lurid and intensely felt tales of eviction or homelessness before reaching their present dwelling. By 1994 Judy Candy was in a house in Fishermead with her partner and three children, but earlier episodes recount her falling out with their then landlord and becoming homeless:

It was a dreadful dreadful time actually, because Carlos [her son] had just recovered from double pneumonia, and was in hospital, it started off with bronchitis and Shanghai flu, to asthma and bronchitis and double pneumonia and he was really ill, he didn't eat anything for a week, ulcers all over his mouth, really poorly, he was only two/three. And I suppose with the stress coming out, Ivan [partner] was having asthma attacks and I was anorexic and we had a little boy baby. And oh it was completely mad. And then it was Luther [eldest son]'s first day at school and we were homeless and we had to go to this bed-and-breakfast in Luton, and I felt sick because I didn't know what to expect, . . . we thought it would be a hell-hole and that you would have to be out all day. But as it went, for bed-and-breakfast, it was a nice place, and we had a telly in there, toilet in our room and a shower and a cot for the baby and the boys were in bunk beds, and we had access to the kitchen for an hour a day, and we didn't have to go out all day. And so we put Luther in school just up the road from us for the twenty-eight days that we were there. And then we got moved to a hostel in Church Street, Wolverton and it was bloody horrible. I cried when we got there, and said 'Oh my God no', it was disgusting and filthy, and ashtrays with ash everywhere and empty pans in the sink . . . [It] was horrid, people were nicking food off each other, wee all over the toilets, just disgusting, really filthy and smelly, and everybody, well not everybody but a lot of people living off each other and the caretaker was like something out of Steptoe, and this man cleaner well he was a joke, really it was filthy . . .

And [then] we were rehoused, to this house. We had actually been living on Fishermead before and had been involved with playgroups, like working for the committee and you know, and I was quite active in the community, I suppose, and C– P– [the local Liberal Democrat councillor] really helped us, he actually visited us in Luton. And it was my birthday, as well like, a coincidence, but he came to visit us and see how we were, what we were doing, and what the state of the place was in this bed-and-breakfast. All the way from Milton Keynes, just to visit us in our bed-and-breakfast. I am sure he put some words in for us and that is how we managed to get this place and it was a godsend . . . it was heaven!

Elsie Simmons' story portrays similar trials, but starts with what appears to be a stroke of luck.

I came down [from Scotland] for a holiday to visit my big brother at Christmas and never went home because someone offered me the keys to the house. And I took them and stayed here. Then she gave the house up and that was me stuck because I gave up my house when I came down here. This was about six months later. But like she'd told me she was going to find the service man. She never, she just went down to London. She sent the Council a note saying she was giving up the tenancy.

I got evicted. I was pregnant. I was in tears not knowing what to do. I had to phone the probation officer and they told me to get a taxi to the Council offices for they're up there and the Council sent me to a b & b in Dunstable. I'd have done anything to get out. I hated it . . . I was in there for two months from September to November . . . It was horrible. I never knew anybody. I'd never been to Dunstable in my life. I was terrified.

But her tale too concludes in the happy ending of getting a home. 'And then they gave me this, and I moved in here. I remember when I first moved in. There was a cardboard box. I'll never forget it. All my dishes in a cardboard box . . . My first home in Fishermead, my first home of my own. This is my first real house in Milton Keynes.'

Other episodes use images that are by now part of the developing mythology of Milton Keynes and its growth. There is the 'mud' of the early building work, getting lost, the roads that go nowhere, or the long trail to the shops before the shopping centre was built. Transport is another recurrent theme. The early 'Dial-a-bus' scheme evokes rosy memories but more recent bus episodes are expected to be horror tales.

There was one particular time I came over from Fishermead to Heelands with my bag, I had the buggy, couldn't take the plastic stuff, didn't have enough room, and two little toddlers and on the way back I had been given a few bags of clothing and I was well laden and one of the children went to sleep on the bus, it was raining and I had to get off the bus with the buggy, Ellie, and the other two kids, one of them asleep, and nobody helped me and I put my back out. Because I couldn't manage the plastic, the baby in the buggy was getting wet, and I put my back out getting off the bus. And I thought never ever again am I going to get on a bus with the kids. (Judy Candy)

Other adventures centre on hospitals and medical treatment – a common narrative topic in our culture, again sometimes told as horror tales. The Milton Keynes general hospital was completed well after the peopling of the first estates, and several narrations depict the travails of hard journeys to Aylesbury, Northampton and other hospitals outside the city.

Settling into a new place provides another acceptable focus for vividly told episodes and reflections. Some tales portray this as a delightful period in their narrators' lives, cooperating with friends and neighbours on new estates, as in Lucy Dale's story. Joy Osborne's story presents similar themes:

I had been married about three years, and we were living in London in two rooms. And there was mould up the walls, and there was mice, and they used to eat all the food. And my husband went to a Job Centre . . . and they said, well if you get a job in Milton Keynes they will give you a house, with a garden. So that weekend we came up to Milton Keynes and he had about five interviews and he got a few of the jobs and started a week afterwards. And within a week we were housed in Milton Keynes, in Netherfield.

Well to us Netherfield was wonderful then, I mean I know people knock it now, and I think that is sad because in those days it was lovely. Yeh there was a community spirit and there was a neighbourhood house, which I think was a good thing. Then it was everybody from a new community moving in to Netherfield . . .

When we moved up I thought it was absolutely wonderful, we moved up with a cot and a freezer, because it was a furnished room. One cot and a freezer. And we started from that and we bought a bed for two pounds, and it was only a couple of years I got rid of that, a secondhand bed. And we started from there and built up our home around it.

Others recount unhappy experiences. Rachel Jacobs' pain of isolation is epitomised in the episode of bursting into tears when someone actually spoke to her. Loneliness – a familiar motif – is pictured sometimes as the result of moving from elsewhere, but also in the context of personal situations and stages of the domestic life cycle. Both are evident in 24-year-old Patricia Ejikame's story. She had moved with her parents in her teens and was now in Fishermead, tied by her 15-month-old daughter but still talking of London: 'I have got all my real friends and family down there, but I do feel because I have got nobody up here I do feel alone, I haven't got anybody to talk to, you know.'

The adventures of moving and settling – getting the necessary 'bricks and mortar', settling down into a local area – are told partly in terms of a place. Even more strongly, however, they dwell on the narrator's relations to other people in or beyond the immediate locality. This interweaving of themes about locality on the one hand and relationships with people of like mind on the other is a recurrent pattern, relevant both for images of the local estate and for 'community'.

The stories' celebration of both the exploits and the troubles of their hero-tellers is the more effective because they are narrated within familiar frameworks. They touch on the emotive themes of moving into or within a city, of loneliness and of companionship, of finding a home, and of struggling towards some measure of success or of repose in face of difficulties, with housing and residential moves accepted by both tellers and listeners as

6.3 Kernow Crescent and park in the centre of Fishermead (by courtesy of the Commission for the New Towns)

resonant contexts for the stories' episodes. These are familiar spheres in which people's plans, struggles and successes can be acceptably portrayed. Such episodes often conclude with the provisional 'happy ending' of in some sense finding and building a home, some kind of settled resting place. In these contexts too, the stories are shot through with the ambivalent and two-sided theme of involvements with both place and people.

Intimations of community

Ambivalent themes about 'community' are thus woven through the personal tales. This 'community' is portrayed as ideally resting in local cooperation and joint interaction with neighbours in a specific locality. But the stories actually portray few concrete illustrations of community as neighbourly action. Rather, their narrators refer uncomfortably to *not* interacting regularly with their neighbours in the locality.

Thus Joy Osborne's tale insists that 'it is a good thing working for your own area' but continues 'as I work as well, I can really say that I know the neighbours just to chat but I don't actually really know them really well, because I am working', while in Rachel Jacobs' tale, 'I don't know many people in Fishermead at all, and those I have met I actually don't get on very well with, it is awful.' Other narratives present their heroes as 'being out of it' due to commitments outside the area, as no longer being 'in the community' or not interacting with other people locally. Though the tellers portray contributions to projects and groups elsewhere, many also imply uneasily that this does not extend enough to local neighbourliness. The model of 'community' as ideally based on the *local* area is combined with a picture of its infrequent actualisation in specific events.

The notion of 'community' thus comes into many narratives as something unfulfilled, as lost or as existing only in the past . The 'traditional' ways of community life – now gone – are looked back to as part of the narrator's early life when children were brought up 'better than now' or 'happiness oozed the whole time'. Stories highlight the 'traditional' ways of doing things, with rural associations especially to the fore: woods, gardens, farms, cows, blackberries and the villages of the past. A similar nostalgia appears in accounts of the more recent past too. Joy Osborne's 'Netherfield was wonderful then' is a prelude to an account of how this 'community spirit' disappeared: 'You lose that newness and the thing that you had, and the people start to move out, and the people that you have known all the time are gradually disappearing, and new people come in.' Her story continues by depicting her sorrow for the lack of community spirit in Fishermead. Both Lucy Dale's narration regretting changes in Fishermead and the recurrent 'deterioration of Fishermead' myth harp on the same theme. The essence of 'community' is projected as lying in its existence in the past and loss in the present.

Ambiguous reactions to the pictured opposition between the harmonious traditional 'community' and externally induced heterogeneity sometimes play below the surface. In one way the stories presuppose Milton Keynes' dependence on incomers with differing backgrounds, even the attractions of urban heterogeneity. But differing backgrounds are also portrayed as spelling lack of harmony, evoking narrative motifs of loneliness and alienation. The true (but lost) community ideal is, by contrast, hinted at as somehow more natural, belonging to people with shared roots. Shirley Lambert depicts the difficulty of making friends when 'everybody comes from such different circumstances', and, in another tale, 'we are such a mixture here, and that is why Milton Keynes hasn't worked'. Peter Sutton similarly portrays Milton Keynes as an artificial setting for diverse people, not conducive to true community:

You can't put all your eggs in one basket and that is what they have done. It doesn't take a psychologist to work that one out, and that is no disrespect. But, that is what they did, they welcomed all persons from different sections of community, you have got the East End . . . you have them from Wales, from Aberdeen, Scotland, Norfolk, everywhere, and they have said, 'Right, you will all live in this community, there you go, aren't you wonderful, we have provided all these nice big houses, which you all want, off you go'; and it didn't work, and it is still not working.

The evocative term 'community' gives a strong evaluative tone to any narration, linking the teller and the tale to widely shared stories and meanings. The *ideal* vision comes through prominently, resting on a wishful identification of community and place that chimes with a deeply entrenched English mythology. There is also the counter-pull, the other side of that same myth. For community is equally figured as something too often now vanished – belonging to the once-natural world of a teller's younger days or of harmonious past times now lost.

Urban mythology, new city and the creativity of narrative

The personal narrations also convey images of Milton Keynes as a whole. These bring us back not only to themes from previous chapters but also to the other stories of urban life.

As always, the particular twists in the personal stories vary. Some portray Milton Keynes warmly, telling a tale of having now settled in a congenial resting place – 'we wouldn't move back if you paid me' (Ruth Curtis), 'I love Milton Keynes, I love living here' (Lucy Dale), or 'I do like Milton Keynes now and I appreciate it, but it took time, it's like learning a new composer' (Jonathan Tyler). Sometimes such accounts link the teller's personal tale to that of the planners, speaking of the 'wonderful job' made of Milton Keynes (Timothy Hopkins).

Other narrators associate parts of their stories with the pessimistic tales of Milton Keynes or recount the city's difficulties with education, transport, lack of a theatre and art gallery, or teenage indiscipline. Lesley Lambert's tale presents this as Milton Keynes' failure to live up to its plans. 'The whole idea of Milton Keynes was a great idea to start off with', she says, 'the shopping complex linked up with the rail, the station. And then what happens? It is miles away, the railway station, and I don't even want to get started on the bus service, because it is unbelievable, it is really dire.'

Other tales again emphatically reject the story of Milton Keynes as a poor place to live, or speak more moderately of both advantages and disadvantages. 'I know people knock it', says Brenda Dawson, but 'I've actually liked living in Milton Keynes.' Emma Hardy similarly concludes that 'What you don't like about Milton Keynes is really outshone by what you do like' and

Richard Walker sets it in further perspective by 'I only notice how good it is when I go to London, and you start seeing the dirt on the streets. [Visitors] always leave saying they wish they were living here. To my mind that is enough of an advert and it is the right place to be.'

What is interesting however is less whether the stories end up 'pro' or 'con' Milton Keynes than the terms in which they do so and their relation to other tales about the city. Through the personal narratives come more general images about both Milton Keynes and urban life more generally.

One of these is the view of a city or town as ideally a locale with opportunities for its people's activities both now and in the coming generations. How individual stories deal with this idea varies according to their tellers' personal situations and viewpoints. Many tales describe the huge range of activities in Milton Keynes, especially for children – 'geared really for the children' (Jim Moore). Others complain of little for young people, with the implication that in a city there really should be, or (in Richard Walker's case) of the lack of 'West Indian social events' for those in the 'thirty-plus age bracket'. Brenda Dawson's account – 'there is a lot going on' – is very different from Roger Vaughan's 'nothing on', 'nothing for the youth at all' (Lesley Lambert) or the plaint in Patricia Ejikame's tale:

When I first came to Milton Keynes [aged fifteen], to me it was like a ghost town, there was nothing going on, because I had come from London there was such a lot going on in London. It was like, it was like going into a time-warp and I used to just sit in my bedroom and play my music and the time used to waste away and I never did anything constructive until I started work ... Like I said, it wasn't until I started going to work that I started to meet people, like even now, Milton Keynes is OK I suppose, growing up, like living environment in a way it is very nice, but as for entertainment – like being my age, I'm twenty-four, and coming from London, there is nothing really going on ... I'm just utterly bored and I hate Milton Keynes, I really do. I mean there is really not anything to do, I mean you have got the parks, but you know ...

The elderly George Rowe concludes: 'There is so much going on, if you want it, doesn't mean that I need it or want it, but there is for those who want it.' Whether or not the aspirations are actually fulfilled in personal terms, the stories can draw on the familiar ideal of the city as the place of opportunity.

The related idea of Milton Keynes as a place to find freedom or a 'new start' also comes into many stories – a variation on the 'City air makes free' theme of the city as route to new opportunities and independence. There is also the idea of looking to the future and of a place where the next generation can grow up in fine conditions. Other tales applaud the idea that unlike traditional settlements Milton Keynes is a 'new' and 'modern city', 'progressive', 'up-to-date [and] fast moving' (or – if it is not – that it ought to be), or revive the organic metaphor of garden city tales by which Milton Keynes is pictured 'growing' like a natural organism: being 'born', reaching a 'baby stage', going on to old age. Such themes are expressed through personal stories rather than stated in general terms, and the vision can be frustrated as well as fulfilled. But the basic image of urban life as offering opportunities is often there, playing on similar chords to those in the planners', garden city and Utopian tales.

A few tales evoke the contrasting theme of the 'artificial' character of Milton Keynes, recalling the pessimistic tone of academic tales and of the concrete cows narrative. For local narrators it is mostly the 'new town' aspect of Milton Keynes rather than urban life generally that provides the direct focus for such evaluations. One repeated image pictures the town as 'spoiling the countryside'. It has been 'heartbreaking', says Peter Sutton, seeing the 'countryside being destroyed' and losing the old villages, 'but that is what a new city does'. There are contrasts between the 'established', 'traditional' communities elsewhere, with their 'winding roads', their roots and their memories, and the imposed newness of Milton Keynes, its anonymous roundabouts and maze of unpeopled roads.

These ideas surface most explicitly in the accounts of first impressions of Milton Keynes – a stock context for representing the city as devoid of humanity with roads leading nowhere. Rachel Jacobs' story paints it as a 'ghost town' – the same term as in Patricia Ejikame's tale – with no people, no memories, no living roots.

I came here a couple of weekends because we were house hunting. And I hated it, I hated it, it was awful. Because when you drive along the H and V roads, as a stranger, you don't see anything other than road. There is nothing, is there, I mean there is nothing. Trees and bushes, but nothing, no cats and dogs, no cyclists, and couldn't help but feel it was a ghost town . . . Yeh I mean Ilford [where she grew up] was a British town, with an established community. I felt like I belonged there, all my roots were there, every time I walked past a shop, or a street, or into a turning, it had a memory of some sort for me.

Such notions are less prominent in later episodes in the stories. As Richard Walker meditatively sums it up:

We all know that it is artificial, we all know that the city is artificial, I mean, as in, you know, Milton Keynes started from one end straight to the other, we know it is artificial I suppose, being built – but the point of the matter is that it is not artificial to those who are born here, it is home. We know it is artificial because we weren't born here, but to them it is home.

In their personal tales narrators are thus not only telling of their own experiences in their own way by formulating them through narrative conventions like those discussed earlier, they also play on images of urban life likely to be both familiar and intelligible for themselves and their listeners. They deploy resonant images of towns as places for freedom and opportunity as well as that of the profound opposition between 'artificial' town and 'natural' country. The oppositional imagery is further strengthened by the overtones of 'community' as essentially something of the lost past, resting in the burnished memories of earlier days in the country or remembered roots in established towns and families. It could not be found, it is implied, in a new, planned town, built artificially and from above. That old set of oppositions is still potent: harmonious community as against diverse association, rural life as opposed to artificial city, natural and traditional ways set against the imposition of the town.

In their marshalling of these familiar themes from our established urban mythologies the narrators are doing something other than just repeating outsiders' tales from the past. Rather they are building creatively on the set of accepted narrative resources, known to themselves and their listeners, to organise their own personal stories and (in a sense the same thing) their own unique lives within an urban context. In creating these individual tales of actors/narrators, furthermore, they are also formulating – creating – the city and its life.

The creative role of this personal story-telling comes through even more strongly in two further dimensions. For the two most prominent recurrent themes of all in these tales adopt a very different storyline from that told through the dichotomies of the classic urban tales.

The first of these brings us back to the creative agents portrayed and expressed in these stories. The narrative conventions discussed earlier are directly relevant for the picture of individuals and their lives within the setting of urban Milton Keynes. The heroes are depicted as winning through in their adventure tales of settling and moving within the city, above all as narrators recount and reflect on how these heroes start to identify with Milton Keynes and shape their experience of it as 'home'. Sarah Henderson, coming to Milton Keynes aged eleven, now 'always think[s] I've lived in Milton Keynes, but I never did if you know what I mean, because I moved out for two years . . . but I came back and had the children and stayed here, you know'. Other tales narrate how from first feeling that their roots were elsewhere their teller-heroes have gradually come to think of Milton Keynes as home. After Brenda Dawson's horrendous first impressions, she then 'got into the sort of swing of being here'.

Amidst the ambiguous tensions between place and people discussed earlier, the idea of the personal wins out when the stories treat of settling down and thinking of Milton Keynes as 'home'. The narratives rank 'place' as secondary to personal relationships, shared interests or a subjective sense of 'belonging'. Janet Eaton recounts her distress after leaving Milton Keynes: she 'really really hated it because I missed everybody here and my mum and my dad'; while Leila Birch's story is not about moving to a place but about being accepted by a substitute mother and sister: 'I felt I belonged somewhere.' Similarly the importance of the personal dimension is expressed neatly by Frank Dyer who came to Milton Keynes because his son was there, but then fell in love:

From the first four years of being up here, I didn't feel much of Milton Keynes, and I had come up, I thought, for a new future, but alas it didn't happen. I was on my own, and I had no one. And then this young lady came along, and you have already heard the start of it, my life has changed, and Milton Keynes is a wonderful place, and it has given me someone to care about and love.

In its low-key way Dennis Travers' narrative verbalises the common theme: 'I have enjoyed myself in Milton Keynes, I have met a lot of people who have taken an interest in the things I do.'

Richard Walker's story is a particularly explicit representation of the idea of home as subjective experience created through individuals' actions, transcending locality while recognising it:

My upbringing was that of a West Indian through and through, but when I reached six my parents packed up and went back to the West Indies and off I went, and so I am one of these unusual children who was born here, started schooling here at an early age and then switched to the West Indies and then came back at eleven and then finished here and then went to the States for a couple of years, and then came back here.

His story portrays Milton Keynes as 'home' but continues with his decision to keep on his mother's London flat, 'so my base is very much Milton Keynes ... [but], I suppose, in staying in London, I am part-time, a cross between the two'. He then speaks of Jamaica:

I love my home country, as it were, purely and simply because (a) my mum is out there and I love it anyway, and (b) it is what I consider as my base, home, you know if I am really looking at home, where you go back to your roots and such, that is my roots ... Jamaica is what I identify with like, so you will understand, and London is where I was born, and I was born in Whittington Hospital in Hornsey and so every time I pass there I give it a salute to say this is where I was born, you know.

Rachel Jacobs' reflective narrative similarly weaves together the intertwined themes of people and place. After the earlier episodes of isolation and bewilderment, when 'Milton Keynes had nothing for me', taxi-driving gives a new view:

There is nothing like being a cab driver for getting to know Milton Keynes. I suddenly felt like I knew the place. There's something to do with knowing actually where things are in a place, that makes you feel like you belong. It's not a real feeling, it is actually quite a superficial feeling, because it doesn't have a lot to do with people. So that was when I started to feel that I belonged here . . . But it is only in the past year that I've really felt that I really do belong here in Milton Keynes, that I've met a group of people that I really like. I've found a number of places to go where the sort of people that I'm likely to like will go. So it's now really that I feel good about Milton Keynes, now it's my home.

The interaction with congenial companions ultimately wins out.

This focus on creative individuals runs counter to the images of urban alienation or standardisation portrayed in most academic urban tales. It emerges in familiar and recognisable form in the personal stories, linked to the creative role of their hero – the 'I' discussed in the last chapter – and the narrative conventions through which individuals acceptably shape their storied experiences. It plays too on that other prominent cultural theme, downplayed in classic urban theories but elsewhere another significant myth of our culture retold in parts of the planners' and garden city tales: of the active role of the conscious individual.

The second major theme in the personal tales is a striking one, for it emphatically delineates the 'country' characteristics of Milton Keynes and, ultimately, of urban living more generally. Given the deep-seated myth of the classic oppositions between 'town' and 'country' this is somewhat unexpected. Nevertheless it comes through as one of the most prominent themes of all in the personal narratives.

This comes out in story after story. 'Trees, shrubbery, flowers . . . three million trees' are the essential 'thing that [makes] Milton Keynes different to anywhere else' (Frank Dyer). The millions of trees are a particular focus in the narratives.

I think Milton Keynes is absolutely marvellous and we were very fortunate because we knew the forester who planted all the trees and everything and he said it won't look anything for several years but eventually we will say it is wonderful. And only about a fortnight ago I was standing out and looking at the different bits of foliage and planting and I said well – he's dead now – 'You did it and you said you had and there it is and it is beautiful.' (Emma Hardy)

Or again:

I think we need all the trees we can get, quite honestly, it is one thing I like about Milton Keynes, is its trees and parks policy. I went to Little Linford Wood on Sunday for their open day and they were talking about how, well I overheard this, that MK is built in a park as opposed to the other way round, which I thought was an interesting notion. (Jenny Linn-Cole)

Similar images appear strongly in practically all the narratives. Speaker after speaker refers to the parks, the green and the trees: the 'peaceful, clean air, green, lots of trees' (Andrea Tan); 'it always seems that at the back of the house is either a field or a park' (Sally Vincent); 'fresh air and space' (Brenda Dawson); 'all the flowers and the trees and all that . . . clean' (Joy Osborne); 'walk outside your front door for a hundred yards . . . and you are in a green bit' (Rachel Jacobs); 'they have made a wonderful job of [Milton Keynes], it's lovely, I think, the flowers and the trees and the coloured flowering trees' (Timothy Hopkins). Andrew and Irene Cunningham describe their move to Milton Keynes as 'like moving to the country . . . clean air, no smoke fumes', and Lucy Dale, though she would ideally like to take her house into the 'country' in the middle of fields, still portrays the 'countryside' element as the central attraction of Milton Keynes: 'It was just wonderful like living in the countryside. It's still one of the things I like about it . . . I love Milton Keynes, I love the area, and I love the fact that you can be in the countryside within five minutes' walk.'

There are still a few evocations of the classic story that what are thought of as 'rural' characteristics are incongruous in an urban environment, and that 'country' and 'town' lives are somehow essentially opposed. One 72-year-old narrator reflects on his early Somerset upbringing, then his recent years in Milton Keynes: 'So I have the best of two things. I know the country life – "A Somerset Man I be"! Funny isn't it? I now live in Milton Keynes, you wouldn't think I was the same person would you?' Another tale portrays Milton Keynes as unparalleled and surprising:

Wonderful . . . trees, shrubbery, flowers . . . three million trees . . . it is this thing that makes Milton Keynes different to anywhere else. Greenery, greenery, we are in a city, and yet five minutes up the road we are in the centre getting a loaf of bread from Sainsbury's, or a packet of rolls from Waitrose . . . it is wonderful when you come to think of it.

Even those relishing the 'country' qualities of Milton Keynes view *further* building as encroachment. 'I hate to see fields disappearing under bricks and

6.4 The 'city in a park'. Lodge Lake in the Loughton Brook Valley, about twenty minutes' walk from the city centre: one of the many 'linear parks' throughout Milton Keynes (by courtesy of the Commission for the New Towns)

mortar', and 'Milton Keynes is big enough now, and they should stop now and leave all this lovely countryside.' The wheel has come full circle for it is developments threatening the now-established order against which the old images are once again invoked.

The overwhelming image in the narratives, however, is one that overlies and challenges that other binary myth. It is a story depicting *co*-existence, in theory and in practice, of both 'green' *and* 'urban' characteristics, of old *and* new. Brenda Dawson emphasises the open spaces and fresh air within Milton Keynes and the way it has developed as a new kind of city: 'I quite like the original idea of Milton Keynes, was that you didn't sort of have your inner city areas . . . The city centre is light and airy, and the shops, and it is not this horrible dark place, crammed full of industry and stuff like that.' Andrew Cunningham's tale presents urban Milton Keynes as 'marvellous. New town, no chimneys, . . . daffodils', and Ernest Brown sums it up as 'Such a wonderful mixture of old and new . . . you have got the olde-worlde in Stony Stratford and things like that and the beautiful little villages, and of course you have got the ultra-modern in between.'

In one sense perhaps the most interesting thing about the view of the city in the personal narratives is that in one way there is not a view. By that I mean that mostly it is taken for granted that an urban environment, far from being a new artificial constraint on their lives, is merely the natural background for human stories rather than – as in the academic or the 'concrete cows' narratives – a problem needing special explanation. In this sense the city is a natural human setting, not something with a new and external 'impact'. In another way, however, dwellers in Milton Keynes frequently come up against external images of the city and are used to articulating their own views. It is remarkable how clearly and regularly they recount a positive story that unites together the features of 'green-ness' and 'urban-ness' as a fit and actualised setting for human life. As in the stories of history and humanity considered in chapter 3, the city does not after all contradict nature but is merely another context in which to experience it.

Though not from the Fishermead personal narratives, Anita Packwood's 'In the Sinking Sunlight' is worth quoting for the way this local poet formulates a vision that also emerges in the personal tales. Her version is expressed in poetic and romantic language about a 'fairy tale land', but essentially revolves round the same theme. She tells how the spring, flowers, trees, lights, 'Point' (the prominent multi-screen cinema and night club), housing estates and sky combine in the evening light of Milton Keynes:

> Softness settles over Milton Keynes
> Everywhere gentle spring softness
> Like a fairy tale land
> Everything sparkling
> Serene, silent, beautiful
> Myriads of golden daffodils
> Dancing slightly in the evening breeze
> The new 'point' distinct, dominant
> Dazzling, gleaming in the glow
> Of sinking sunlight
> Streetlights already on
> Sprinkling light over small estates
> So picturesque and new
> Small young trees swaying
> Wearing their new summer styles
> Majestic multitudes, green
> Sky pure powder blue
> With pale pink ribbons
> Soon to be serenaded by starlight.   (Packwood 1986 p. 31)

Here, as in so many of the personal narratives, the tale brings together, rather than opposes, the natural, planted and built features of the city.

To conclude, each personal narrative is unique. These are accounts created by individual narrators, rooted in their own unique life stories. But their authors also creatively recompose on widely recognised themes. Even the most personal of the episodes has overtones of generality and explanation: the familiar struggles and travels of the individual hero-teller, the pioneer's adventures, the fitting conclusion of coming to a home, the leaning towards personal relationships as much as or more than place. We also encounter the stories' recurrent images of community and of urban life. Differ among themselves as they most certainly do, the tales nevertheless draw on and recreate the narrative themes of classic urban myths to formulate the personal experiences. They sing the familiar threnody for lost community. They retell too the tale of the concrete artificialness of urban life replacing the traditional ways of localised community and countryside: that well-honed mythology of incongruity between older harmonious nature and modern alienated town.

But at the same time, and strikingly laid over this, the Milton Keynes narrators are also creating a strongly emerging storyline both of a 'green' city – nature within, rather than opposed to, the town – and of urban life as the domain of creative and conscious individuals. Not everything may be perfect in cities – or in a given city – but the tellers here portray cities as an accepted arena for people to enact their struggles, joys, sorrows, triumphs, their ambiguously experienced narrations of 'community', their storied interactions with the natural world. Such themes have some presence in other tales of the city but have been little to the fore in recent academic narratives. As they deploy these images of cities within their tales, the authors are marshalling their personal and narrative resources to challenge the mythic binary oppositions and to develop instead a contrasting myth for thinking about and experiencing towns, one in which urban life is a natural setting for creative human lives, no more artificial or alien than that of the countryside.

7 Conclusion: whose stories of the city?

Our imaginary Martian anthropologist would gradually have become aware of the co-existence of a wide range of stories about the city, more than appeared at first sight. There are the abstract academic accounts; the stories of Milton Keynes itself, partly overlapping with academic stories but distinctive too; and the manifold personal narratives, formulated through narrative conventions but also unique to their tellers.

This multiplicity of stories might seem too obvious to state. We scarcely need telling that there are differing viewpoints – individual, political, moral – and arguments between them. And of course the stories in this volume are only a small selection. The personal narratives come from only thirty-five of the 4,000 individuals then (1994) in Fishermead or the 150,000 or so then living in the new city of Milton Keynes (with yet more to add since then as the population of the city and its surrounding areas rises to the 200,000 mark). And even laying aside individuals' tales, many other stories could supplement those told here. Not only are the many groupings and interests of our culture likely to have their versions (group and family narratives of the kind discussed in Rubin 1996 part IV for example) but even for the categories here there are as many stories as tellings.

So in one way it should be no surprise to find this plurality of many differing narrations of the city, apparently a significant feature of our culture. But we now rightly challenge older glib assumptions about the complex heterogeneity of the 'modern industrial west' as against the supposedly homogeneous and uncontested thought-systems of 'traditional' cultures and can no longer just take it for granted without examining the practice that our story-telling around a specific topic will indeed be multiple rather than homogeneous. So it is still worth remarking that we find this *multiplicity* of articulated and differing stories about urban life delineated in this study. Some tales are widely agreed among particular groups of people, others told in specific contexts or for individual purposes. Some recount the general characteristics of the city, others overtly tell of specific cities or of the unique individuals who people them. There are the abstract verbal accounts distilled by intellectuals; tales of planners and bureaucrats narrating their deeds amidst the specificities of particular cities; differing stories about the same city: the 'concrete cows' story recounting the tellers' revulsion for the dead hand of imposed inhuman planning contrasting with tales celebrating the continuities of history, tradition and human creativities; and the multitudinous personal tales in which individuals transmute and mould the images of their time through the narration of their own experience.

It is only too easy to screen out this variety. There is always the insider's temptation to attach greatest influence to stories in whose telling or listening we ourselves directly participate, a particular seduction for the academic story-tellers perhaps, and for those, like the planners, responsible for persuading people of the truth of their version. It has also been the tradition in much social science to consider personal narratives within a different framework from other studies, if at all. But cities are made up of individuals. And each individual has his or her own stories. These differing personal narratives are equally part of the whole, intertwining and co-existing with the other stories to formulate the images and experiences of urban life. To explore only certain types of tales or to focus primarily on putatively 'opposed' categories (those of 'actors' as against 'theorists', perhaps, or ruling-class as against proletarian stories, resistant and struggling against 'dominant' tales) is tacitly to ignore the reality of other voices and the complex plurality of the co-existent tellings.

Interacting stories

The stories' multiplicity raises the contentious issue of the relation between these narrative genres. Is it one of equality, for example, of dominance or, alternatively, too multifaceted to make such judgements at all? These questions are scarcely easy, if only because here if anywhere replies depend on where the answer is coming from. But they are at least worth raising rather than – as often – just assuming.

One position is that all stories are equally acceptable. No one story is or should be predominant, including that of the academic analyst. This view has a long history but recently has been particularly pressed by writers in the postmodernist style. Many studies of personal narratives take the similar line of explicitly rejecting a 'realist' or a correspondence view of truth (e.g. Linde 1993 pp. 14ff., Rosenwald and Ochberg 1992 pp. 2ff.). Johnstone posits that 'narrative creates truth', recalling Dineson's comment that 'truth, like time, is an idea arising from, and dependent upon, human intercourse' (Johnstone 1990 pp. 9, 126, Dineson 1961 p. 165). This general approach is often linked to relativist perspectives, whether of the moderate kind that remind us that outsiders should not rush in with uninformed and perhaps self-interested judgements, or in the sharper version by which all tales are

equally good and the analyst is merely telling another story, no more authoritative than any other. So when all voices are valid, let them all sound.

Such an approach has its appeal, albeit resting as much on moral and
philosophical underpinnings as on empirical findings. Gathering and
analysing tales about urban life (or whatever) need not entail a commitment
for or against the 'truth' of any one of them, whether in terms of the tellers'
'actual' experience or of some external reality. This approach also follows
the common methodology in social research that narratives are studied less
for their truth or falsity than as manifestations of particular cultural ways,
whether as guiding people's actions, formulated as literary texts, providing
sanctions for the current order, modes of aesthetic expression or self-
understanding, or pathways for conducting human lives. Uncovering the
multiplicity of stories or the cultural conventions of story-telling does not
depend on adjudicating their literal accurateness.

Perhaps the question of 'truth' cannot be totally left aside however. The
more sophisticated studies of personal narratives – even those going out of
their way to reject correspondence theories of truth or to stress the narrative
construction of experience – recognise that a crude equation between experience and narration is over-simple and that, while narratives may control
some aspects of the world for their tellers and listeners, they may not control
them all. As Mumby puts it, narrative may be a central notion guiding social
analysis but there is no 'simple isomorphism between narrative . . . and the
social realm' (Mumby 1993 p. 5). Similarly Rosenwald and Ochberg broadly
argue for non-realist interpretations of life stories but continue:

At its limit, however, this line of reasoning can be taken to support the notion that
social life counts for nothing outside of discourse. On this tack the improvement of
life can be accomplished if one tells a better story about it. But life is not merely
talk; inequalities of opportunity, for example, are not redressed if individuals, or
even whole classes, tell more 'agentic,' optimistic autobiographies. (1992 p. 7)

The narrators themselves would also claim their stories to be true rather
than false or fictional – an important point that it is surely patronising to
brush aside by insisting that all stories are essentially the same in this
respect. The tellers of academic stories, local tales and the self-narratives are
alike in classing them neither as imaginative literature nor as fiction but as
accounts of the world, expressed perhaps in tangential or impressionistic
form but basically as something true. Some stories, admittedly, seem more
variable or embroiderable in their tellings and less crystallised over time.
Others are more fixed and their content seemingly less liable to change. But
some kind of assumption that the stories can ultimately and in some degree

be judged by evidence and experience underlies their telling. The claim to truth is not irrelevant for the tellers and listeners themselves.

There is no simple solution to such issues, now increasingly discussed in the literature (e.g. Neisser 1994, Plummer 1995 esp. pp. 170ff.). Correspondence models have their attractions, but in thoroughgoing and exclusive form carry problems for narrative analysis (summed up in the familiar point about 'the facts' being themselves shaped and selected by the narrative in question); they also miss the important notions of the subjective coherence of stories for their tellers/listeners and of the role of story-telling in shaping experience. Coherence models are essential for a full understanding of stories and story-telling in context, but if taken to extremes would seem to deny any independent concept of falsehood or of empirical evidence, and allow no grounds for differentiating among different types or functions of story-telling. For present purposes I am continuing with a dual perspective of (1) broadly following a coherence-view of truth as an analytic perspective on the stories (combining this, as we proceed, with the concept not of propositional truth but of artistry) while also (2) refusing to abandon some sense of appealing to evidential criteria for the analyst's own conclusions and, in parallel, recognising that from the tellers' viewpoint their stories are indeed presented as corresponding to reality and in *that* sense open to judgement as to their truth or falsity.

In any case relativism needs its limits too and it is surely not sufficient just to retell the stories and leave it there. We should not be forced into an artificial choice between what is represented as old-style scientistic positivism and a nihilistic relativism. As is now increasingly recognised, there are strong arguments for maintaining the scholar's traditional responsibility to attempt a detached perspective in light of the evidence (see for example Kuper 1994, Layder 1996). This responsibility may remain near-impossible to fulfil in its completeness, but it has not been removed by our sensitivities to the subjectivities of research or the postmodernist scepticism of academic 'metanarratives' (Lyotard 1984 p. xxiv).

What other kinds of overview, then, could be given of this multiplicity, and of the relations between the various stories? A number of established perspectives are still worth considering.

One position is to regard all the stories as in practice equal – not in the sense of postmodern abstract theory but rather of an empirical statement that all stories are in fact equally relevant or effective for their particular participants. Another influential viewpoint suggests that 'power' largely shapes which versions are dominant, whether by determining the perceptions of relatively passive, deprived or powerless groups or, in more Gramscian vein, interacting with other factors to gain their acquiescence. Such analyses could point for example to the economic and political sanctions supporting the Milton Keynes planners' story, or the struggles in other stories to contest this version. Often the implication is that the 'contesting' versions are somehow truer, with the dominant stories essentially a veil for power.

Both positions have the merit of considering relationships between differing story-genres rather than treating them in isolation. It is not so easy to assess their validity in the real world of tellers and listeners. Picturing stories as equal is fine as far as it goes, but it does have a tincture of over-optimistic pluralism and of rather easy acceptance about it: is there really evidence for what is perhaps ultimately an evaluative wish rather than documented conclusion? The second position is equally open to empirical challenge. It rests on the (usually unargued) assumption that we can tell which story is truth, which smokescreen. It also downplays the narratives' heterogeneity and individuality by focusing on broadbrush contrasts between, say, the stories of 'dominant' or 'privileged' as against 'resisting' or at best 'appropriating' and 'consuming' tellers, or (in the reductive Marxist versions) on the contrasting tales of just two, putatively antagonistic, parties set within a conflictual model of society.

Seeking for *general* conclusions on these or similar lines may not be productive. If we view stories as process – tellings rather than texts – then the influence of these various tellings must be relative rather than absolute, contingent on the individuals or purposes involved and varying with the situation. The realisation of 'power' or of 'function' is surely related to people and situations rather than monolithic or permanent qualities in particular narratives. What counts is thus not some absolute sense of equality, hegemony or power, but which stories *and their tellings* are dominant or meaningful for particular participants. The answers are likely to be variegated rather than uniform.

A similar point about variety and overlap may well apply to that other established distinction: between the accounts of 'theorists' and of 'actors', or (similarly) between 'analytical' and 'folk models'. These are influential and still illuminating juxtapositions in social science and on the face of it applicable to our many stories of the city. But there are complications. Not only are there more than two parties or two sets of stories, but their participants are far from distinct from each other. Their themes and tellings overlap. Further, *all* the stories are in some sense those of actors and all convey elements of theory. In his recent collection Robin Horton concludes that theory plays a part in all the patterns of thought (African and western) that he is discussing, modifying his earlier contrast between 'theory' and 'ordinary' or 'commonsense' knowledge (1993 pp. 11–12). The same point can be made here: the tellers of and listeners to the stories are *all* in a sense both implicated in the drama they portray and involved in theorising through their narrative. What begins as a helpful distinction for some contexts, turns out unavoidably oversimplified as a summary conspectus for the overlapping multiplicity of our tales of the city and their tellers.

This is worth emphasising, for it is easy to fall into the habit of assuming this distinction and then making further assumptions about which stories come 'first' and who, in a sense, 'owns' them. Take the story of the binary opposition between town and country. This appears in many narratives in this volume, notably in the academic and the 'concrete cows' tales. We could conclude that the intellectuals' distilled versions start things off and they then filter down to other tellers. Certainly the academic stories tend to be more crystallised, and thus *look* prior in terms of textual permanency. But we should not succumb without reflection to the intellectuals' temptation of seeing academic theory as the 'real' story and less formalised accounts as merely its fragmentary reflections.

We could turn it the other way round. A possible parallel is suggested in a recent field study of the implicit economic conceptions of Colombian farmers (Gudeman and Rivera 1990) which led the ethnographers to suggest not – as some might have it – that these farmers were influenced by European economic theory but that the earlier Spanish peasant immigrants to Colombia shared certain European folk ideas about economics which were then crystallised in the theorists' writing:

To judge by the Colombian ethnography it would appear that many of those 'voices in the air' [from the academic texts of economists or political philosophers] come first from the practices and articulations of living folk and are then . . . distilled and transformed by academic economists into textual forms. (Gudeman and Rivera 1990 p. 182; cf. also Kuper 1992, 1994)

Might it be similarly plausible to see our academic urban theories as drawing on ideas expressed in more widespread story-telling?

That could be an equally valid way to approach interactions between stories, and one that is now considered with more sympathy. Given the multiplicity of the story-telling about the city reported in this volume, generalised conclusions, whether descriptive or exhortatory, are actually rather difficult to justify. And, as argued earlier, juxtaposing 'theorist' to 'folk' stories is over-simplifying a complex situation. But in so far as that juxtaposition *is* still appealing (as it will doubtless remain for some purposes), then there is nothing to say that looking at the relation the other way round is inherently less plausible than assuming that the normal process is for the intellectuals' stories to come first.

The artificiality of town as against the 'natural' ways of the country, to continue with the same example, is indeed a central theme in the academic stories. But it also comes through forcefully in the 'concrete cows' tales and (if less strongly) in other stories too. So might both the academic theories and the recently enacted narrations represent formulations of more widely held narrative themes rather than something originated 'from above' by the theorist and philosopher? This was certainly Hannerz's view when he described the parallel 'folk/city' dichotomy as the celebration of 'established wisdom' (Hannerz 1980 p. 64). Similarly themes highlighting the significance of individual agency, so prominent in the personal stories and in the humanistic–historical tales of Milton Keynes, have their paler (but perhaps re-emerging) reflection in some aspects of academic social theory. And perhaps we can ultimately relate the theoretical formulations about the fragmentation and alienation of modern urban life to that same long-sung lament for lost community expressed (among other places) in personal narratives.

The issue then becomes not so much the interaction between different genres of stories as their relation to more deeply rooted story-telling resources. The social construction of reality, to use Berger and Luckmann's fine terminology (1966), is not just a matter of how intellectuals construct it when they philosophise but also encompasses all the accepted stories and story-telling conventions of the culture.

Story-telling for the city and its tellers

There is, then, one further slant on the multiplicity of stories of the city. This involves turning our gaze away from the relations between different types of existent stories and more towards the processes by which they are constructed and told.

The tales considered here exist as performed tellings rather than as decontextualised texts with purely cognitive import; they carry overtones beyond a merely 'information' function for their narrators and listeners. This is obvious enough for live presentations. But written texts too, like the academics' stories here, have parallel performance attributes, increasingly explored in recent work on the active processes involved in reading and in writing (for example Keller-Cohen 1994, Street 1993).

Regarded as performance, story-tellings are not closed in either themes or number. In a way they vary infinitely in being differently told and heard on

different occasions and by different participants, drawing on both recognised themes and the creative wordsmithing of their narrators. Written texts
too, though more crystallised and in that sense more permanent than oral
forms, are constructed on the same principles, drawing differentially on
both traditional and innovative resources, and actively formulated and
reperformed by their audiences. They continue less as completed and closed
products than as fluid and emergent processes actualised in specific situations.

   Story-tellings are for this reason used for a whole range of purposes. Such
uses are familiar from comparative research. Story-telling can act as mythical charter, sanctioning and formulating the current order and its history (or
a particular view of it) – a relevant context for some of the stories told here.
Narrative forms give individuals pathways for existing and for experiencing
– for the 'implicit organization of experience into set, satisfying patterns' as
Hymes has it of Native American narratives (1982 p. 122). Story-tellings are
used in the claiming or maintenance of identity, for self-legitimation and the
validation of experience. They provide a way of coping with struggle, anxiety
or sorrow, if only by setting them within intelligible plots and figures, or of
removing the teller from the mundane constraints of the present. They can
both shape and contest social realities, both uphold and challenge power.
They can express the underlying preoccupations and symbolisms of both
individuals and groups. Like other speech acts their cognitive and informa-
tion-conveying elements may constitute only a small part of their functions,
especially when the narrations are presented in rites of passage and other
rituals (familiar contexts for some academic story-telling). They are used too
for creation. Cancel's comment on oral narration – 'sense-making in public
becomes world making' (1989 p. 207) – could equally be applied to the
stories here; so too could Bauman's view of narrative as 'constitutive of
social life in the act of storytelling' (1986 p. 113). Or let me extend some
earlier remarks on poetry to these stories of the city – for in the large sense of
that word they too have something of poetry:

What is involved is not the passive repetition of externally determined words –
artistic or ritual or utilitarian – but people actively moulding the world around
them: the world of symbols which, ultimately, constitutes the world we experience
and live in. It is through poetry – not exclusively, certainly, but surely pre-eminent-
ly – that people create and recreate that world. (Finnegan 1977 p. 274)

   The above merely sketches some common uses of stories (for other
discussions see e.g. Finnegan 1992 esp. pp. 125ff., Plummer 1995). It is
worth remembering this potential multiplicity of role, the basis for my

scepticism about *generalised* conclusions about the relations between
stories. Certainly we can surmise that some types of stories are used
more typically for some purposes than others: academic story-telling for
crystallising abstract communications and for demarcating an elite through
esoteric language; personal tales for formulating and validating experience
or to satisfy an inquirer. But if stories are realised in their tellings, their roles
must depend on the participants in that enactment (listeners/readers as well
as tellers) and on *how* the tales are told and heard. Some tellers are more
powerful than others in particular situations or for particular people, or
deploy their skills and formulate their ideas more effectively, or draw larger
audiences. Because there are multifarious individuals and multifarious
tellings so too are there multiple uses, both foreseen and unforeseen.

So it is not just story texts that need exploring but also how stories are
created and understood. Returning to this issue draws us back to the varying
story conventions analysed in earlier chapters, those narrative resources
which listeners recognise and which tellers recreate and deploy in their
tellings. To review these briefly, let us return to the varying patterns through
which people can narrate the stories of the city – the story features discussed
in earlier chapters.

The conventions for temporal ordering both overlap and differ between
the various story-telling genres through which people tell of the city. Academic narratives often tell of large-scale historical sequences, especially
those revolving round the grand stages to do with industrialisation. The
Milton Keynes planners' tale has a more limited and explicit timescale,
mostly opening in 1967 and concluding in the 1990s, though with glances
back or onwards in the more elaborate tellings. In the garden city stories we
encounter relative rather than absolute time, that of the growth and matur-
ing of cities. The concrete cows tale often coincides with the planners'
timescale, sometimes also evoking the wider timeframes of the classic urban
theories, while the more humanistic celebratory story calls on a narrative
running through many centuries as the backdrop for more recent developments. The personal stories are not without some reference to broader
timescales and vary according to personal experience and teller, but the
ordering is often of turning-points within a single life or in what Hareven
calls 'family time' (1977), where cycles of family and personal life rather
than numerical dates provide the framework.

The contrasts are striking. But whatever their other focus, the stories and
their tellers regularly build in *some* temporal frame through which the
action must eventually move. Several also contain a look to the future,
whether cyclical or linear, depicted either as part of the tale or – as in the

Utopian visions of urban life – as a foreshadowed sequel to it. Underlying the stories is the idea of an intelligible sequence of episodes over time, of locating the present within a wider ordering, and of a concern for the processes of continuity whether in urban, personal or family terms.

Conventions about how the genres are actually told form another differentiating feature, one which accomplished story-tellers must learn. Their expected tellers differ. So too do the media considered appropriate for their delivery. Academic stories are mostly confined to word-based communications in print, supplemented by occasional live performance rituals. Others draw on a wider range of media, among them illustrations, photographs, auditory forms, video, broadcast and personal interaction. Their expected audiences and settings differ too: academic peers and students for the academic narrators; the hoped-for sponsors, government agencies and potential or actual residents for the planners' and to some extent garden city exponents; largely friends, relatives or visitors for the personal tellers. Once again, there are both contrasts and continuities.

There are also the ways tellers present their plots as coherent and persuasive. Within the differing genres of city tales there are differing expectations about the crucial cause likely to drive the action and render it intelligible to teller and listener, often embodied in the protagonists presented as the central or contributory movers in the plot. The academic tales introduce characters clad in abstract garb: such figures as 'industrialisation', 'modernity' and 'postmodernity', 'capitalism', 'community', 'alienation', as well as generalised beings like 'the consumer', 'the elite', 'urban man'. The movers and shakers in the planners' story are, naturally, the planners, architects and bureaucrats, sometimes interacting with the insubstantial secondary actors encountered on their way like the 'natural forces' which create cities or 'the people' – figures that move to centre stage in the partially overlapping garden city tales. Other narratives foreground the dragon of the soulless planners and, through the image of the self-contradictory concrete cows, call in shadowy abstract figures from the academics' tales, while in yet others still we see the effects of the long 'history' and 'traditions' of the area and the beneficial actions of human beings. The personal stories, finally, while containing many themes and figures, turn on the creative deeds of named individuals, acting in a series of recognised family and personal roles, above all the active reflective 'I' of the teller-hero.

The plots are distinctive and lead to differing ends. But there are significant similarities too. On the face of it their scope varies greatly: experiences of one individual in a single generation; Milton Keynes as one unique town; thousands of years of Buckinghamshire history; the founding and growth of a garden city over a limited time span; the stages of western history through recent centuries. So do their conclusions. Some tell of the success of the individual 'I' in winning through to the present after the sufferings on the way; others of the dire results for humankind of planners' heartless impositions or, alternatively, the 'natural growth' and happiness they can engender; the rich historical continuities and human creativity conveyed in the alternative tale of Milton Keynes; or, different yet again, the dreaded alien ation or fragmentation to which humans are fated in most academic stories.

What they share is the sense of moral ordering. To a greater or lesser degree, the stories all in their way carry implicit claims to speak for more than just individual tellers or unique episodes. They are parables that go beyond specifics and hint at universals about what is of value for human beings. Differ as the plots do in episodes and actors, they still partake of this same idea of good and of evil and are understood as such by their participants. They recount success, failure, trouble, destiny, loss, the Golden Age of the past or the future, and the struggle against adversity.

The recurring themes in the stories add to this impression. There is no one overarching message, for the actual narrations are heterogeneous, with overlaps and complexity rather than single grand schemes. Their relation to 'the city' varies too, some stories addressing it directly as a problem or setting it against the concept of free individuals, others, like the personal tales, mostly taking it as a given backdrop rather than an issue. Nevertheless, amidst the fluidity certain themes draw attention. While certainly not the only ones in play and emerging differently in different stories, they are seemingly of some abiding importance.

The first of these centres on *'community'*: its celebration, its existence in the past, its loss, attempts to achieve or refine it, and guilt for its apparent abandonment. Often, but not always, closely related to this are the motifs clustering round the famous *opposition between country and town*. Some tellers recount the reinforcing of this division. They depict the artificiality of the town with its 'impact' on human life and destruction of age-old rhythms of the natural rural world, and set up contrasts between nature and man-made urban life or between engineered constraints and the free traditions we have lost. Others introduce the same array of protagonists to reach differing conclusions, notably in the many Milton Keynes personal stories telling of a green city, the country within the town. Here lies a set of preoccupations about the nature of our being, seemingly at the heart of our imagery. The figures playing out the differing outcomes within the overall drama about community, city or country enact and re-enact a kind of cosmic myth of our culture.

We are also brought back to the timeframe of the stories, for another recurrent issue is that of *continuity*. Not that there is agreement among the differing stories: some academic tales for example recount the abrupt ruptures of past history, others its gradual shifts. But a preoccupation with continuity and its problems is a prominent theme. We hear of questions of family and personal roots; of traditions, lost or retained in memory; of the actor-tellers' relation to earlier and succeeding generations and the transmission between them; of historical continuities beyond the confines of the present.

The final prominent theme lies in the concept of *active experiencing individuals*, ones who can also reflect on – tell stories about – their experiences. This is most to the fore in the personal stories where, it seems, one of our accepted narrative conventions is to foreground ideas of agency (Bruner 1994). But it is not confined to them. It comes through as an understated sub-theme in stories at first sight inimical to individual creativity like the planners' tale, and frames the historical riposte to the concrete cows tale. Paradoxically, even the bleak academic tales might be said to gain their effect through playing on the unstated image of the natural and free individual, now destroyed, of the lost Golden Age.

Might this dwelling on the active reflective individual in our story-telling also be a significant preoccupation of our culture? Certainly there is a vast philosophical, literary, social and historical literature on ideas of the individual, of the continuing self and of self-awareness in western civilisation, some of it proposing contrasts with alternative ideas of the self or the person in other cultures.[1] How exactly to delineate the significance of this cluster of notions is controversial, especially since the tales here involve actor-tellers rooted in social settings rather than the atomistic single individuals of some philosophical traditions. But the world-creating qualities of the overall narrative imagery focused round the reality of individual agents/experiencers can scarcely be denied. The personal stories draw on it in full measure, a mythic theme evoking deep cultural resonances for both tellers and listeners. It is relatively absent in most current academic stories about the city. But is this perhaps equally to be interpreted as an indication that the figure of the active and reflective individual is due for a revival in the more theoretical genres? Or that its studied down-playing there is actually stating a position and a tacit invitation to further challenge in the same continuing interplay of themes?

These emotive issues of town/country oppositions (or not), of community, of continuity and of the action-cum-experience of creative individuals are not fixed and literal. Nor does each always appear with equal force in all tellings. But they are sufficiently widely shared to be evoked without explicit narration or even deliberate cognitive intent, alluded to in differing and contrasting ways in the many tellings. They appear in one form in the planners' narratives, in another in concrete cows stories, garden city tales, or the multifarious and unique personal narratives. The personal narratives lay more stress on individual agency and on challenges to the binary town/country opposition than do most academic stories – as things now stand. But the balance around these recurrent themes may well change in future tellings. The key issues provide resonant chords which can be used through the many tellings, deployed in varying guises and combinations, sometimes more deeply explored, sometimes only briefly sketched, sometimes portrayed with passion, sometimes only lightly alluded to or mischievously played with. The narrative themes draw participants beyond the present contingent tellings into more far-reaching dramas, as story-tellers of all kinds exploit these notions in their otherwise differing narratives about the nature of humanity, of society, of history.

Underlying the tellings are a series of plots well recognised by both tellers and hearers. There is the myth of the lost Golden Age; of a coming Golden Age of the future, perhaps a cyclical refinding of what was earlier lost; of an individual's adventures and at least moderate success against trials and tribulations, maybe looking forward to yet more struggles in a linear or cyclical sequel; of a great plan laid down at the start and fulfilled over time, whether 'evolution' or the Milton Keynes Master Plan; or a tale of stages in the age-old unfolding of history over the generations. Such plots appear again and again irrespective of the particular protagonists, common tales of our time. It might be going too far to see them as drawing on cosmic myths universal to all human narration. But our stories are at once unique in their tellings and evocative of deep-seated plots which strike a profoundly familiar chime to tellers and listeners alike.

Such stories do not spring up from nothing. But, equally, neither are they transmitted through a literal process of rote memory or some mechanical and unchanging social conditioning. It is more illuminating to look to people's practised and accomplished arts for enacting stories, both their telling and their hearing. Participants in any given culture or situation actualise their learned ability to create their own stories through marshalling the narrative storylines recognised by their fellow participants and deploying – more, or less – the conventional features of the differing genres. Neither the institutions of communication in our society nor individuals' grasp on experience and analysis could exist without these learned arts for narration and their creative realisation. In one way this recalls Albert Lord's famous *The Singer of Tales* (1960), which showed how epic singers composed and performed their heroic narrative songs by delving into a traditional store of formulae, themes and styles so as to construct their unique creations following the established conventions. This picture of a kind of treasure-house is one way of conveying the resources on which accomplished tellers in a society can draw. An alternative metaphor is Jerome Bruner's 'tool kit' image which can be applied not only to self-narratives (his original focus) but also to other narrative genres:

> One important way of characterizing a culture is by the narrative models it makes available for describing the course of a life. And the tool kit of any culture is replete not only with a stock of canonical life narratives (heroes, Marthas, tricksters, etc.), but with combinable formal constituents from which its members can construct their own life narratives: canonical stances and circumstances. (Bruner 1987 p. 15, also Bruner 1991)

Similarly, linguistic anthropologists and other writers on the ethnography of speaking have pointed to the ways that speakers, poets, singers and writers – indeed competent members of a culture generally – develop the capacity to recognise and manipulate appropriate genres in appropriate situations by drawing, perhaps differentially, on the recognised generic conventions (e.g. Bauman 1986, Briggs 1988, Hymes 1981, Sherzer 1990, Tedlock 1983, Yankah 1995; also Bakhtin 1986). The artistries of verbal genres and their conventions regularly prove much richer and more flexible than outsiders at first appreciate. So do the art-ful ways that people create, change and manipulate these complex resources.

And if this is true of the verbalised arts in cultures traditionally studied by anthropologists, so too does it apply to our own. Here too tellers and listeners are able to deploy the narrative resources of themes, plots, motifs and other conventions to create their stories, organising their understanding and control of the world they live in. Whether or not one accepts the view that a narrative potential is universally inbuilt into humankind or that it pervades *every* form of thought or expression – open questions both – the striking thing is our capacity not only to enact stories but to recognise the due conventions of the appropriate genres. Without being overtly instructed, as it were, people already have the creative narrative resources to tell and hear stories in recognised ways. Some generic conventions are more formally taught, true, one example being the expected patterning for academic story-telling. But, whether or not it is consciously recognised, all story-telling means to one extent or another deploying learned and sophisticated arts.

These basic processes underlie the tellings of all the story genres treated here, good reason for considering them together. Some tellings may be more crystallised, literary and abstract than others, or reach one type of audience rather than another. But all are individual *and* exploit the store of themes, plots and conventions to express and communicate their tales to their audiences, realising and moulding our cultural resources. For all that the stories draw on the great myths of our time, the way they are retold is not immutable. Each telling draws on the wealth of narrative resources to construct its individual insight, and the prominence and treatment of key issues in one narration can be re-ordered or challenged by other narrators. It is through their story-tellers' creative shaping – transmuting and selecting as they re-enact the tales – that the myths of our time are realised in their multifarious tellings.

We end, then, with a picture of our many stories of the city being created by active tellers with the capacity to draw from the continually recreated narrative resources of our culture: among them those stirring motifs of individual agency, of human action in urban settings, of community, of continuity over the generations. In this sense our processes of story-telling turn out to have parallels with those of other cultures, not least those which in the past have been regarded as 'traditional' and characterised by oral more than literate communication. We meet again that essential dynamic between individual creativity and cultural resources, between tradition and innovation. The narrators are individuals, but this is not the old 'individual versus society' metaphor. Rather story-telling represents one potent form in which individuals both create, and draw creatively on, a shared cultural potential for their own unique but communicable performances.

It would be easy and in one sense correct to be critical of these tales and their tellings. The academic stories may persuade us into seeing the world and its history in ways which in other genres would be heard as highly unconvincing: is there really such a thing, for example, as the 'modern' or the 'postmodern' city (a query pertinently raised in Scott 1995 p. 469)? Or is either the planners' upbeat tale or the pessimistic concrete cows story really matched by what goes on in Milton Keynes? And should we always accept at face value the narrated lauding of personal achievement or the heritage tales told by those celebrating the development of local histories?

Such critical reactions are justified and by now well rehearsed. But there is also the other side. It is true that the stories we tell may be used for what in a personal evaluation could be adjudged 'good' or 'bad' purposes or carry more, or less, conviction as 'true stories'. But the cultural capacity they represent – in the same way as language itself, or music – is a positive not negative aspect of our culture. Our narrative resources give us a handle to catch the world and to debate the great issues of community, of individuals with their struggles and triumphs, of our built and planted environment, and of our continuities over time. Here we have the tools to use, if we choose, to create and understand human experiences, in cities as elsewhere.

All the tales in this volume can thus be brought within the same perspective, one which turns the spotlight less on the limitations than on the benefits of our narrative resources. Our cultural riches include the potential for the crystallised and articulate tellings which make up the wealth of our academic narratives. They also offer us narrative tools for grasping 'the rich and messy domain of human interaction', as Bruner has it (1991 p. 4), and for the creative formulation by individuals and groups of tales of their lived experiences, among them the emergent tales of the city as the expression, not the antagonist, of humanity.

Narration is not the whole of life. But it is no small part of our culture that we can create storied pathways to live by through our performance conventions, themes, plots, orders, cosmic myths. In deploying these narrative arts, individuals can formulate, create and extend their own and others' condition. They can challenge the truth of their own and others' stories and use the established conventions to develop new twists to the tale. These narrative resources for creating and experiencing the city are surely in the end the stories of us all, the creative artistry and resource through which we form our lives and the world around us.

Appendix 1 Note on sources and methods

The central sources for this study were personal interviews, documentary sources on Milton Keynes, participant observation, and, for the 'academic stories' in chapter 2, theoretical writing by social scientists on urbanism and related topics. I also drew extensively on secondary sources for background and inspiration: especially work on narrative, myth and performance; folklore; oral history; urban anthropology/sociology; and social theory.

The once-conventional – and still useful – distinction between primary and secondary sources does not altogether work in this context. Official publications about Milton Keynes, theoretical sociological analyses of cities or the personal narratives are all treated as in a sense forms of story-telling, therefore all in this sense 'primary'. Some sources however are more foregrounded than others in this study, especially the personal stories.

The personal narratives

These were told by thirty-five individuals who were at the time of the recordings (1994) living in the new-city estate of Fishermead (see maps in Figs. 4.1 and 6.2). The selection and approach are explained in chapter 4, pp. 57–9, but, briefly, they were found by mainly snowball methods (with some attention to a range of ages and backgrounds) and were recorded by Delia Gray, research assistant on the project, through undirected sessions lasting about one hour each. The tapes were transcribed by Dianne Cook and the transcripts sent to their authors. I was then responsible for further visits to some of the authors and further processing of the initial transcripts to reach an acceptable text for quotation in printed form (see chapter 4, pp. 75ff.). Conventions used in the transcripts are:

Words in *italics* (within brackets)	Spoken by Delia Gray, the interviewer
Non-italicised words in square brackets	Inserted later for intelligibility or explanation
[. . .]	Words or passages omitted in the lengthy transcripts
. . .	Omissions in the short excerpts

All narrators gave explicit permission for their stories to be used and quoted in the research, but their real names are mostly not given. This common practice is helpful for preserving confidentiality, but has also sometimes been used by researchers to minimise individuality, give a perhaps spurious impression of 'objectivity', or even avoid acknowledging the authors' intellectual property. I undertook not to divulge names or addresses in any public report so, apart from the few cases where authors specifically stated that their true names were to appear, I have used pseudonyms – with some reluctance, as in other respects I would prefer these articulate personal speakers to have the credit under their own names.

Eight pilot interviews were also conducted in 1993 (in Milton Keynes but not Fishermead): not used directly in the study but providing useful supplementary background.

Other sources

Published sources giving one or another story about Milton Keynes are manifold. The main categories I drew on were official reports and publications of various kinds, especially those by the Milton Keynes Development Corporation (MKDC); national and local newspapers; posters and other visual displays; broadcasts; books about Milton Keynes by a variety of authors including local residents and specialists in such topics as planning, architecture or 'new towns'; articles in specialist journals; books etc. from the People's Press of Milton Keynes and other local publishers.

Participant observation also made some contribution. Except for three years in the 1970s I have lived in Bletchley (now part of Milton Keynes) since 1969, thus personally seeing and experiencing twenty-five years or so of the development of Milton Keynes. This was supplemented by follow-up discussion with several of the narrators represented here, and by more systematic participant observation on local music-makers in the early 1980s (see Finnegan 1989, esp. pp. 342ff.), which, though with a different focus and published esp., also provided significant background for the present study.

Finally, participant observation was an important source for the 'academic stories' considered in chapter 2, undertaken over many years of teaching, reading and interacting with colleagues and students in the social sciences. Many of these academic tales – convincing or the opposite, true or false – are stories in whose narration I too have been involved.

Appendix 2   The personal narrators

The following notes on the thirty-five narrators of the personal tales may be convenient for reference. Fuller information is in many cases given in the main text, and lengthy extracts from the transcribed tales of six of these speakers are printed in chapters 4–6. Unless otherwise indicated, names are pseudonyms, and present tenses refer to 1994 (the date of the recorded narrations). The various local estates mentioned can be located on the Milton Keynes map in Figure 4.1.

Leila Birch
Grew up in Mitcham, south London, but left own family at sixteen, on her last day at school, to join friends in Milton Keynes who became a kind of foster family. Worked in various jobs, including dentist's surgery. Lived in various locations in Milton Keynes, then came to Fishermead eight years ago where she is now living with her eight-year-old son; his father visits from time to time. Aged about thirty.

Jill Blackwell
Constantly on move as a child, around Liverpool and Lancashire. Came to Milton Keynes, where her sister and two brothers were living, largely for support against pressures from her ex-husband. Divorced with two children of eighteen and eight. Currently unemployed but doing voluntary work with teenagers. Has lived in Fishermead for six years. Late thirties.

Ernest Brown
Spent most of his life in north-west London, in business. Wanted to leave London so looked round Milton Keynes, where several of his friends had moved. Came to west Bletchley in 1977, then, after various moves of house and shop (dry-cleaning) within Milton Keynes, moved to Fishermead about fifteen years ago. Now living in own house, bought out from the corporation. Three sons nearby. Now retired, about seventy-three.

Judy Candy
Brought up in Sussex, left home at eighteen to live with partner in Twickenham. After birth of first child moved to Milton Keynes (Heelands) for shared-ownership scheme. After various intra-Milton Keynes moves and period of homelessness, rehoused four years ago in present house in Fishermead, where now lives with partner and their three sons. Loves 'community spirit of Fishermead'. Aged about twenty-eight.

Andrew Cunningham
Brought up and lived much of life in Hounslow. In army during war. Moved to Milton Keynes because unable to get council house locally (no mortgage available

as he was diabetic), also disliked changes in Hounslow. Several years after his first inquiry, finally moved to Milton Keynes with his wife about sixteen years ago, worked till retirement. Keen self-taught amateur drummer. Recovering from a stroke and finding speaking difficult, but aided by his wife Irene. Aged seventy-two.

Ruth Curtis
Born in Lake District but due to her cerebral palsy had lived in hospital or residential home for much of her life. Moved to Milton Keynes about thirteen years ago to get more independence, first to Neath Hill, then eight years ago to Fishermead where she lives independently with her husband and her many pets. Probably in thirties.

Lucy Dale
Grew up mainly in south-east London, with many moves in childhood – her father was a butcher, gradually working his way up; parents later divorced. In 1974 moved from Kent with husband, to get a job and house – straight to present rented house in Fishermead where she still lives with her husband and two children (twenty-one and fourteen). Worked with local playgroup, then took A levels as mature student in Milton Keynes and a university degree (outside Milton Keynes). Qualified teacher but by 1994 only some supply teaching, not yet a permanent job. Early forties.

Brenda Dawson
Grew up mainly in Southall with 'firmly working-class roots', left home to join WRAC. Met husband in army and moved round for many years as army wife, came to Milton Keynes (Tinkers Bridge) in 1976 when her husband left the army, for housing – 'not planned' – then to Fishermead in 1980, following her husband's job. Once her three children were at school, started work, at first unqualified then took diploma in social work, now working with disabled adults. Forty-nine years old.

Francis (Frank) Dyer
'A Somerset man and very proud of it'. Joined army in 1938 and spent ten years on various assignments round the world, which he also followed up as a civilian. A widower for forty years. Moved to his present sheltered accommodation in Fishermead five years ago – near his son – and has now fallen in love and starting a new life. Aged seventy-two.

Janet Eaton
Grew up in Brixton. Moved to Milton Keynes (New Bradwell, then Fishermead) in 1976 with her family because of her father's job (a milkman); other members of her wider family also already in or moving to Milton Keynes. Went to school in Fishermead. Moved out of family home when fifteen to live with a series of friends, then many moves in and outside Milton Keynes, now back in friend's house in Fishermead. Currently doing hairdressing course. Twenty years old.

Patricia Ejikame
Grew up in Edgware, came unwillingly to Milton Keynes with her parents when she was fifteen following her father's breakdown. Moved out to flat/bed-sit with boyfriend, but currently living with her brother in her parents' house in Fishermead as they have now moved to Richmond for her father's job. Working locally. Aged twenty-four.

Agnes Farley
Lonely childhood in Devon till twenty-three when left for job in Admiralty during war. Various moves within England following her husband's job (civil engineering), then to Bletchley for thirty-nine years. Worked in Bletchley Park once children were in their teens. Has two daughters and several grandchildren of whom she is very proud. Now in sheltered accommodation in Fishermead with her husband. Mid-seventies.

Emma Hardy
Grew up in Southwold in Suffolk, very happy memories of childhood. Brother and sister died of leukaemia (attributed to Sizewell nuclear station). Trained and worked in physiotherapy till 1971, started Red Cross team in Suffolk. Moved in 1984 from cottage on Duke of Bedford's estate to present sheltered flat in Fishermead because of her husband's heart trouble; he died recently. Two children, several grandchildren. Aged eighty-two.

Sarah Henderson
Brought up by mother in grandparents' large house in West Hampstead. Mother then married and they moved to Milton Keynes (Conniburrow) in 1977. Moved out of family home when seventeen, due to problems with stepfather. Various moves in and outside Milton Keynes, including period in homeless hostel and women's refuge, then to present house in Fishermead. Four young children. Considering moving to Ireland with present partner but intends to keep her house for security. About twenty-eight.

Timothy Hopkins
Grew up in Dorset. Various jobs in Weymouth, army telephonist in first world war, then worked in London between wars and as Post Office telephonist during and following second world war. Retired 1959. A widower since 1970, two daughters. Tells vivid tales of his adventures and his lifelong church interests. Came to Milton Keynes in 1984 to sheltered flat in Fishermead. 100 years old.

Rachel Jacobs
Lived in Ilford, Essex, till nearly thirty, moved to Bletchley in 1984 to accompany the father of her three children. First commuted to job in London, then started own firm in Bletchley, but after a series of disasters leading up to and following separation from her partner she was left destitute and became a taxi-driver for three years. Bought house on Fishermead with mortgage about 1990, for some time on income support, now back in work. About forty.

Lesley Lambert

When three years old moved to Milton Keynes with father (in RAF in Oxford); in children's home for four years, then to Lakes Estate in Bletchley and at school locally. Supported herself by part-time jobs while studying diploma in performing arts in Northampton, now in part-time drama youth work. Moved in with her elder sister Shirley (below) in Fishermead for two years when eighteen, then various moves within Milton Keynes sharing houses with friends, a year in New York (uncle in Barbadian Embassy there), now back with her sister in Fishermead. Aged twenty-four.

Shirley Lambert

Elder sister of Lesley (above). West Indian background. Left home at fourteen due to family violence, supported herself by various jobs, got council flat on Fishermead when eighteen. Resumed responsibility for her family, helped younger sisters and mother after her breakdown. Problems with a violent partner whom she was able to eject when he was sent to prison. Now lives in rented house on Fishermead with her ten-year-old son. Aged thirty-two.

Jenny Linn-Cole (own name)

Brought up in small village in Essex. Parents both teachers. Has degree as graphics artist, cartoonist, also recently qualified in homoeopathy. Moved with partner to Milton Keynes in 1982 because of cheap housing: bought house in Two Mile Ash but had to sell after four years. After various moves within Milton Keynes, and breaking with partner, now lives with six-year-old son in three-bedroomed rented house on Fishermead. Currently on benefit as single parent but aiming to set up in homoeopathy practice. Aged thirty-six.

Jim Moore

Born and brought up in Belfast where his father owned pub. Began studying medicine, but gave up; in civil service for some years, then running own business (a struggle). A widower with four children, of whom two live locally, one is in Canada. Wife died suddenly in 1986 when planning to move to flat in N. Ireland, but daughter persuaded him to come to Milton Keynes, first with her, then to Springfield, then to sheltered accommodation in Fishermead. Seventy-nine years old.

Joy Osborne

Grew up in London East End (Forest Gate). Came to Milton Keynes in 1978 with her first husband, moving to a house on Netherfield from a miserable flat in East London. Three older children by first husband, baby by second husband. Moved to Fishermead six years ago, working in local bakery. Keen member of spiritual church. Late thirties.

Alice Phillips

Brought up in Eastbourne till eight, then went with parents (ex-railway/crane driver and nurse) to farm in Wales. Secretarial training at college in Wales, then left home for Stevenage and London. After period of homelessness, got house in Fishermead about nine years ago where living with her two children by her first husband (now divorced but still taking some care of the children). Aged thirty-one.

Douglas Ramsey
Early years divided between London and Derby. Came to Milton Keynes in 1985 when sixteen to join his mother and get away from his stepmother. Resumed education in Milton Keynes but failed to complete A levels successfully after spending six months in Jamaica, his parents' birthplace. Had moved round between six or more different Milton Keynes estates. Would like to do social work training eventually. Living temporarily in hostel for unemployed in Fishermead. Aged twenty-five.

James Richards
Joined accounting firm in London in 1930 and stayed for forty-seven years; in civil defence during war. Married to much younger wife for ten years (no children), then divorced, did not remarry. Moved to bungalow in Beanhill in 1976, then in 1983 to present sheltered flat in Fishermead. Aged eighty-two.

George Rowe (own name)
Till nineteen lived in Cranfield (village near Milton Keynes) where his parents had also been born. Started work in local brickfields aged fourteen. In RAF in war, then a job in a luggage factory in London, moving up to management. While in sixth floor flat in Hackney drove up to look round Milton Keynes and decided to move. Came to present rented house in Fishermead in 1976, at same time as his wife's sister and husband moved into a house opposite. A widower since 1984, one son. Aged seventy-two.

Elsie Simmons
Grew up in Scotland, mainly in suburbs of Glasgow, with her grandparents and father (long-distance lorry driver). Came to Milton Keynes through her brothers, who lived in Bletchley. After a mix-up over a borrowed house, in bed-and-breakfast accommodation for a time; then allocated a house in Fishermead five years ago shortly after the birth of her daughter. Would not want to go back to Scotland since most of her family are now 'down here'. Late twenties/early thirties.

Alison Stanley
Brought up in Glasgow, where her father was a toolmaker with a leading Glasgow firm. Worked on switchboard in Vyella before marriage, then various small jobs. Married at twenty-one; her husband was working his way up in the Singer Company but died of cancer at forty-one. She and her two daughters worked 'as a team' while they were growing up; both daughters are now journalists: 'we are a family of readers'. Moved to Bletchley, where her sister lived, when her daughter got job on Milton Keynes paper. Since 1984 warden of sheltered flats in Fishermead. Aged sixty.

Peter Sutton

Brought up London, father (adoptive) in building business, mother with interest in films which she passed on to him. Had intended to study at Battersea Art College, but on death of father had to find work at fifteen. Managed to get into film industry where he became an editor; later in BBC television for twenty-five years and moved with them to the Open University BBC Centre in Milton Keynes. Made redundant in 1992, partly by choice. Married three times; still sees the two children from the second marriage. Depressed about his redundancy and unsettled marriage. Currently in hostel in Fishermead, but still full of enthusiasm for film. Aged forty-five.

Andrea Tan

Born and brought up in Hong Kong. Had come to Milton Keynes two months before through contact with a previous resident of Fishermead who had returned to Hong Kong for Bible study. Renting flat for six months, felt she had been led there 'by God's hand'. About thirty.

Dennis Travers

Born in Sussex. In orphanage in Woking for seven years as his father (electric plate welder with Southern Rail) died when he was a baby, then rejoined his mother in Lancing on her remarriage when he was ten. Sixteen years in army in the Persian Gulf, Cyprus and Germany as supply specialist, then joined army cadet force as instructor in 1985. His Irish wife (epileptic) died in 1989 and his three children now 'taken off me'; subsequently had other partners and children. Has lived in various locations in Milton Keynes since 1984, currently in unemployed hostel in Fishermead. Has worked with cars as semi-skilled mechanic and is hoping to gain further City and Guilds qualifications. Aged forty.

Jonathan Tyler

Partly brought up by his mother's parents in Yorkshire; later at boarding school in Bedford, then moved with his mother to south-east London. His father was a teacher in India with only brief visits to England. Married and lived in London (which he loved); bought house in south-east London then gradually moved up-market. In army during war, prisoner from 1942; from 1947 till retirement in 1977 in civil service (Customs and Excise). Widower since 1972, with two daughters. After a heart attack, wanted 'a quiet place to live' and chose Milton Keynes because younger brother lived nearby. Moved into present sheltered flat in Fishermead about 1992. Extremely knowledgeable and enthusiastic about his record collection. Aged seventy-eight.

Roger Vaughan

Moved around as a child (father a pilot), including in the area near Milton Keynes where three sisters and two brothers now live. Previously a school caretaker in Leighton Buzzard (near Milton Keynes). Now selling jewellery etc. in Milton Keynes for which he needs to live locally. Since 1993 has shared a housing association house in Fishermead with his sister. Age uncertain (thirties?).

Sally Vincent

Grew up in Lambeth and Marylebone, moved to Milton Keynes aged twelve with her mother and siblings. Stayed on when her mother returned to London. Job in local factory (where her mother had also worked) for five to six years after leaving school. Stormy relationship with violent boyfriend whom she has recently married. For a time in homeless hostel in Wolverton; now living on social security in rented housing association house in Fishermead with their four children. Aged thirty-one.

Richard Walker

Born and brought up in Wembley, also spent some childhood years with his parents in West Indies. In army (REME) between seventeen and twenty; came out to care for his mother after she had a nervous breakdown. Married girl from Wembley when twenty-four. They decided on Milton Keynes by drawing concentric circles on map, also had relatives in the area. Bought 'our first house' in Bletchley in 1983. Now divorced; the two children live in Stony Stratford, being brought up as 'black British children' with regular visits to Jamaica. Living with new girlfriend in her house in Fishermead, but also keeping up his mother's ex-flat in East London, convenient for his current university studies. Aged thirty-five.

Bessie Wyatt

Most of her life spent in or near Manchester. Her Scottish father died when she was a baby and her mother (from Philadelphia) brought her and her two sisters up 'on the parish'. Ambitious to work in an office, unlike her shop-working sisters, and studied in night school. Joined pay corps in the war, later worked as supervisor of a typing pool: 'loved every minute of it'. Divorced her army husband with her mother's support. Remarried about 1958, a widower who subsequently died of Alzheimer's disease. In sheltered accommodation in Manchester for some years, then moved to present flat in Fishermead in 1983, near her son. Late seventies.

Notes

1 Story: 'the orders by which we live our lives'

1 This volume does not try to engage with the many controversies over the detailed definition or classification of cities, towns etc., nor to chart their diversities (for such issues see Flanagan 1993, Cohen and Fukui 1993, esp. Introduction). For the purposes of this volume, the terms 'city', 'town', 'urban environment' etc. are used more or less interchangeably.

2 For example Sherzer 1990 on the forms of verbal art among the Kuna Indians of Panama, Briggs 1988 on the creativity of tradition in Mexicano verbal genres, and Tonkin's analysis (1992) of the narrations of the Jlao Kru of Liberia; also Howell 1986 on treating together all forms of discourse within a culture (the Malaysian Chewong). None exactly parallel my investigation here; they take ethnopoetic and linguistic issues further than I have been able to do here, for example, and focus less on the idea of contrasting 'stories' and of self-narratives. But all share the aspiration of bringing together differing forms of verbalised discourse within a single conspectus.

3 For references on personal narratives and life stories see chapter 4, note 1.

4 For example Clifford and Marcus 1986, Van Maanen 1988 (anthropology); Cronon 1992, Mink 1987, White 1973, 1987 (history); LaRue 1995 (law); McCloskey 1990 (economics); also examples in Hanne forthcoming.

5 Additional fields where the views/preconceptions of individuals, groups or organisations are approached as 'stories' include (among others) social and community work, policy studies, war propaganda and experiences, fashion, biblical studies, education, law, ecology, media studies. For recent overviews see Riessman 1993, Hanne forthcoming, also ongoing research in *Journal of Narrative and Life History*. For further analyses of theory as story see Plummer 1995 esp. p. 181, Riessman 1993, esp. Introduction, also the narrative account of social science methodology in Polkinghorne 1988.

6 For example Bauman 1986, 1992, Bauman and Briggs 1990, Bauman and Sherzer 1989, Finnegan 1977, 1992, Sherzer and Woodbury 1987, Urban 1991, or, in parallel if partly differing ways, Gee 1991, Gergen 1994, Smith 1981.

7 Narrative specialists will recognise the partially controversial nature of my approach, not least the inclusion of the fourth feature indicating process and performance rather than just 'text'. It is both narrower and broader than some other approaches. I assume 'story' to be one category within the broader field of 'narrative'; thus all the 'stories' here are also 'narratives' and in most, though not

190

quite all, cases I use the two terms interchangeably (occasionally distinguishing 'story' – with its plot, coherence or moral shaping – from 'chronicle'). The study focuses mainly on stories told primarily in verbal terms (though words are not the only things they consist of). It thus does not extend into the wider sense of 'narrative' adopted by Barthes (e.g. 1975 p. 37) and his many followers, which includes presentations through media such as pictures or tapestries. On the other hand I am not adopting the formalist distinction between *fabula* (story material) and *sjuzet* (plot) but using 'story' in the broad sense which includes both. I am also avoiding the sense of story which assumes that it is essentially to be equated with political praxis and the exercise or rejection of power – though a political setting and function can be features of particular narrations. I mostly side-step the contentious issues of 'truth and falsity' (though see the comments in chapter 7) and of the relative priority as between narrative and 'life' (cf. MacIntyre 1985 pp. 197ff.). For further discussion and references on the nature and study of narrative and/or story see – to foreground some recent publications – Johnstone 1990, Linde 1993, Mumby 1993, Plummer 1995, Prince 1994, Riessman 1993, Rosenwald and Ochberg 1992, Tonkin 1992; also Bakhtin 1981, Chatman 1978, Genette 1982, Langellier 1989, Mitchell 1981, Prince 1982, 1987, 1989, Samuel and Thompson 1990.

2 Abstract tales of cities: the narrative in urban theory

1 The academic urban theories are well known and easily accessible from the voluminous writings on the subject. Recent surveys, giving further references, include Dickens 1990, Fainstein and Campbell 1996, Flanagan 1993, Giddens 1989, Kemper 1991, Savage and Warde 1993, Schwab 1992. Although theoretical writing has an international rather than national scope, I have given primacy to theories typically circulating within British academic circles (American work, though in many respects overlapping with the stories presented here, tends also to include some more optimistic tales of urban life). This chapter also focuses primarily on accounts which are presented and recognised as articulated theories, mostly crystallised in the form of theoretical sociological writing, rather than on ethnographic studies (like some of those reported in Sanjek 1990 or in *Urban Life: A Journal of Ethnographic Research*) which sometimes imply a rather different set of narratives.

3 Storying a concrete city: cows, gardens and other urban tales

1 For fuller accounts of the garden city movement see Howard 1898, 1902/1946, also Hardy 1991a, 1991b, Munzer and Vogel 1974, Osborn and Whittick 1977, Ward 1993.

4 Storied lives: the tales of individual urban dwellers

1 In particular Abrahams 1985b, Bennett 1986, Bruner 1987, 1991, 1994 (among others), Bruner and Feldman 1996, Byron 1992, Johnstone 1990, Josselson and Lieblich 1993, Langness and Frank 1981, Myerhoff 1980, Personal Narratives Group 1989, Polanyi 1979, Rosenwald and Ochberg 1992, Titon 1980; also the useful overviews in Langellier 1989, Linde 1993 and Riessman 1993, the psychology collections by Neisser and Fivush 1994, Rubin 1996, the sociological/psychological analysis in Pahl 1995 and (for a more philosophical approach) MacIntyre 1985. Though the terms are often used interchangeably, 'life stories' are sometimes distinguished as taking a wider span, with 'personal narratives' focusing on selected episodes; other overlapping terms include 'self-narrative', 'first-person narrative', 'personal experience stories'. These self-narrated forms are often broadly contrasted with 'life histories' (narratives compiled by others) and frequently refer to oral rather than written narratives; however (as Stanley 1992 rightly argues) they also clearly overlap with written autobiographies.

2 My account of the recording situation is confined to sketching its main features. A detailed analysis of the situation and its dynamics would be too lengthy to include here, and perhaps not necessary for purposes of this specific analysis. For the issues involved see Briggs 1986, Mishler 1986, Yow 1994 and references there.

5 'That's my story': narrative conventions in personal tales

1 I have found Bauman 1986, Stanley 1992 and Tonkin 1992 especially helpful on this issue; see also Denzin 1989 pp. 20ff. on 'the subject in the text', Lanser 1981 on point of view, Linde 1993 pp. 120ff. on reflexivity, Prince 1982, 1987 on 'autodiegetic narrative' and the 'narrator-I'/'character-I'.

7 Conclusion: whose stories of the city?

1 Recent works relevant in this connection include Brown and Ouroussoff 1994, Carrithers *et al.* 1985, Cohen 1993, 1994, Giddens 1991, Hall 1991, Morris 1994, Ouroussoff 1993, Rorty 1987, Seidler 1994, Shotter and Gergen 1989.

References

Abrahams, Roger D. (1985a) 'A note on neck riddles in the West Indies as they comment on emergent genre theory', *Journal of American Folklore* 98 (387): 85–94

(1985b) 'Our native notions of story', *New York Folklore* 11 (1/4): 37–47

Bakhtin, M. M. (1981) *The Dialogic Imagination: Four Essays*, Eng. trans., ed. M. Holquist, Austin: University of Texas Press

(1986) *Speech Genres and Other Late Essays*, Eng. trans., ed. C. Emerson and M. Holquist, Austin: University of Texas Press

Barker, Greta (1980) *Buckinghamshire Born*, Milton Keynes: The People's Press

Barthes, Roland (1972) *Mythologies*, Eng. trans., London: Cape

(1975) 'An introduction to the structural analysis of narrative', *New Literary History* 6: 237–72

Bauman, Richard (1986) *Story, Performance, and Event: Contextual Studies of Oral Narrative*, Cambridge: Cambridge University Press

(1992) 'Performance', in Bauman, Richard (ed.) *Folklore, Cultural Performances and Popular Entertainments: a Communications-centred Handbook*, New York: Oxford University Press

Bauman, Richard and Briggs, Charles L. (1990) 'Poetics and performance as critical perspectives on language and social life', *Annual Review of Anthropology* 19: 59–88

Bauman, R. and Sherzer, J. (1989) (eds.) *Explorations in the Ethnography of Speaking* 2nd edn, London: Cambridge University Press

Bauman, Zygmunt (1987) *Legislators and Interpreters: on Modernity, Post-modernity and Intellectuals*, Cambridge: Polity

Becker, Howard (1986) *Writing for Social Scientists*, Chicago and London: University of Chicago Press

Bell, Hilary (1994) (comp.) *A Lifetime Away: Childhood Memories of Stony Stratford*, Wolverton: Living Archive Press

Bendixson, Terence and Platt, John (1992) *Milton Keynes: Image and Reality*, Cambridge: Granta Editions

Bennett, Gillian (1986) 'Narrative as expository discourse', *Journal of American Folklore* 99: 415–34

Berger, Peter and Luckmann, Thomas (1966) *The Social Construction of Reality*, London: Allen Lane

Bertaux, Daniel and Thompson, Paul (1993) (eds.) *Between Generations: Family Models, Myths and Memories*, International Yearbook of Oral History and Life Stories, Oxford: Oxford University Press

193

Billings, Bill (*c.* 1981) *Bill Billings . . . Poet 'Assassin'*, Milton Keynes: the author (no pagination)

Birch, Clive (1987) (comp.) *Around Milton Keynes in Camera*, Buckingham: Quotes Ltd

  (1992) (comp.) *Old Milton Keynes in Camera*, Buckingham: Quotes Ltd

Bird, Jon, Curtis, Barry, Putnam, Tim, Robertson, George and Tickner, Lisa (1993) (eds.) *Mapping the Futures: Local Cultures, Global Change*, London and New York: Routledge

Boje, David M. (1991) 'The storytelling organization: a study of story performance in an office-supply firm', *Administrative Science Quarterly* 36: 106–26

Bornat, Joanna (1989) 'Oral history as a social movement: reminiscence and older people', *Oral History* 17: 16–24

A Brief Guide to Places in Milton Keynes (1987), Milton Keynes: City Discovery Urban Studies

Briggs, Charles L. (1986) *Learning How to Ask: a Sociolinguistic Appraisal of the Role of the Interview in Social Science Research*, Cambridge: Cambridge University Press

  (1988) *Competence in Performance: the Creativity of Tradition in Mexicano Verbal Art*, Philadelphia: University of Pennsylvania Press

Brown, Donald E. and Ouroussoff, Alexandra (1994) 'Anthropologists, comparison, the West, and the individual', *Man* 29: 975–6

Bruner, Jerome (1986) *Actual Minds, Possible Worlds*, Cambridge Mass.: Harvard University Press

  (1987) 'Life as narrative', *Social Research* 54: 11–32

  (1990) *Acts of Meaning*, Cambridge Mass.: Harvard University Press

  (1991) 'The narrative construction of reality', *Critical Inquiry* 18: 1–21

  (1994) 'The "remembered" self', in Neisser and Fivush

Bruner, Jerome and Feldman, Carol Fleisher (1996) 'Group narratives as a cultural context of autobiography', in Rubin

Buckinghamshire County Council (1991) *The Buckinghamshire Migration Report 1991*, Aylesbury: Planning Department

  (1993) *Parishes and Towns in Buckinghamshire Part 1*, Aylesbury: Planning and Transportation Department

Burke, Kenneth (1945) *The Grammar of Motives*, New York: Prentice-Hall

Byron, Reg (1992) 'Ethnography and biography: on the understanding of culture', *Ethnos* 57 (3/4): 169–82

Cancel, Robert (1989) *Allegorical Speculation in an Oral Society: the Tabwa Narrative Tradition*, Berkeley: University of California Press

Carrithers, M., Collins, S. and Lukes, S. (1985) (eds.) *The Category of the Person: Anthropology, Philosophy, History*, Cambridge: Cambridge University Press

Castells, Manuel (1977) *The Urban Question: a Marxist Approach*, London: Edward Arnold

  (1983) *The City and the Grassroots: a Cross-cultural Theory of Urban Social*

Movements, London: Edward

(1989) *The Informational City,* Oxford: Blackwell

Chambers, Iain (1993) 'Cities without maps', in Bird *et al.*

Chatman, Seymour (1978) *Story and Discourse: Narrative Structure in Fiction and Film,* Ithaca and London: Cornell University Press

Clark, T. and Salaman, G. (1996) 'The management guru as organisational witch-doctor', *Organisation* 3 (1): 85–107

Clegg, Stewart R. (1993) 'Narrative, power, and social theory', in Mumby

Clifford, J. and Marcus, G. E. (1986) (eds.) *Writing Culture: the Poetics and Politics of Ethnography,* Berkeley: University of California Press

Cohen, Anthony P. (1993) 'The future of the self', in Cohen and Fukui

(1994) *Self Consciousness: an Alternative Anthropology of Identity,* London and New York: Routledge

Cohen, Anthony P. and Fukui, Katsuyoshi (1993) (eds.) *Humanising the City? Social Contexts of Urban Life at the Turn of the Millennium,* Edinburgh: Edinburgh University Press

Connerton, Paul (1989) *How Societies Remember,* Cambridge: Cambridge University Press

Croft, R. A. (1984) (ed.) *Victorian and Edwardian Milton Keynes: a Photographic Collection,* Luton: White Crescent for Wolverton and District Archaeological Society

Cronon, William (1992) 'A place for stories: nature, history, and narrative', *The Journal of American History* 78: 1347–76

Daily Telegraph (1992), 'Milton Keynes', 23 January

Dalby, Stewart (1990) 'Survey: Milton Keynes', *Financial Times* 18 January

(1992) 'Survey of Milton Keynes', *Financial Times* 3 April

Davis, Rib (1980) (ed.) *Write here: Poetry and Short Stories from Writers in Milton Keynes,* Milton Keynes: The People's Press

De Certeau, Michel (1984) *The Practice of Everyday Life,* Eng. trans., Berkeley: University of California Press

Denzin, Norman (1989) *Interpretive Biography,* Newbury Park: Sage

Dickens, Peter (1990) *Urban Sociology: Society, Locality and Human Nature,* New York and London: Harvester Wheatsheaf

Dineson, Isak (1961) *Seven Gothic Tales,* New York: Random House

Epston, David and White, Michael (1992) *Experience, Contradiction, Narrative and Imagination,* Adelaide: Dulwich Centre Publications

Fainstein, Susan and Campbell, Scott (1996) (eds.) *Readings in Urban Theory,* Blackwell: Oxford

Featherstone, Mike (1993) 'Global and local cultures', in Bird *et al.*

Fine, Elizabeth C. (1984) *The Folklore Text: from Performance to Print,* Bloomington: Indiana University Press

Finnegan, Ruth (1977) *Oral Poetry: its Nature, Significance and Social Context,* Cambridge: Cambridge University Press (2nd edn Indiana University Press 1992)

(1989) *The Hidden Musicians: Music-making in an English Town*, Cambridge: Cambridge University Press

(1992) *Oral Traditions and the Verbal Arts: a Guide to Research Practices*, London: Routledge

(1996) 'Personal narratives and urban theory in Milton Keynes', *Auto/Biography* 4 (2/3): 13–25

Fisk, Eugene (1981) *Milton Keynes: a Personal View*, Milton Keynes: The People's Press (no pagination)

Flanagan, William G. (1993) *Contemporary Urban Sociology*, Cambridge: Cambridge University Press

Flie, Jonathan (1994) <u>*Not*</u> *the Concrete Cows: a Kaleidoscope through the City of Milton Keynes*, Milton Keynes: Padstow Books

Foucault, Michel (1972) *The Archaeology of Knowledge*, Eng. trans., New York: Harper and Row

(1980) *Power/Knowledge: Selected Interviews and Other Writings 1972–1977*, Brighton: Harvester Press

Frake, Charles O. (1996) 'A church too far near a bridge oddly placed: the cultural construction of the Norfolk countryside', in Ellen, Roy and Fukui, Katsuyoshi (eds.) *Redefining Nature: Ecology, Culture and Domestication*, Oxford: Berg

Freedman, Jill and Combs, Gene (1996) *Narrative Therapy, the Social Construction of Preferred Realities*, New York and London: Norton

Gee, J. P. (1991) 'A linguistic approach to narrative', *Journal of Narrative and Life History* 1: 15–29

Geertz, Clifford (1975) *The Interpretation of Cultures*, London: Hutchinson

Genette, Gérard (1982) *Figures of Literary Discourse*, Eng. trans., Oxford: Blackwell

Gergen, Kenneth J. (1994) 'Mind, text, and society: self-memory in social context', in Neisser and Fivush

Gergen, Kenneth J. and Mary M. (1986) 'Narrative form and the construction of psychological science', in Sarbin

Giddens, A. (1984) *The Constitution of Society: Outline of the Theory of Structuration*, Cambridge: Polity

(1989), 'Modern urbanism', chapter 17 in *Sociology*, Cambridge: Polity

(1991) *Modernity and Self-identity: Self and Society in the Late Modern Age*, Cambridge: Polity

Gramsci, Antonio (1971) *Selections from the Prison Notebooks*, Eng. trans., London: Lawrence & Wishart

Grigsby, John (1992) 'Milton Keynes', *Daily Telegraph* 23 January

Gudeman, Stephen and Rivera, Alberto (1990) *Conversations in Colombia: the Domestic Economy in Life and Text*, Cambridge: Cambridge University Press

Hall, Stuart (1991) 'Old and new identities', in King, A. (ed.) *Culture, Globalization and the World-system*, London: Macmillan

(1992) 'The question of cultural identity', in Hall, Stuart, Held, David and McGrew, Tony (eds.) *Modernity and its Futures,* Cambridge: Polity

(1997) (ed.) *Cultural Representations and Signifying Practices,* London: Sage

Hamer, David (1990) *New Towns in the New World: Images and Perceptions of the Nineteenth-century Urban Frontier,* New York: Columbia University Press

Hanne, Mike (forthcoming) (ed.) *When Plot meets Knot: Narrative and Metaphor across the Disciplines*

Hannerz, Ulf (1980) *Exploring the City: Inquiries toward an Urban Anthropology,* New York: Columbia University Press

Hardy, Barbara (1968) 'Towards a poetics of fiction: an approach through narrative', *Novel* 2: 5–14

Hardy, Dennis (1991a) *From Garden Cities to New Towns: Campaigning for Town and Country Planning, 1899–1946,* London: Spon

(1991b) *From New Towns to Green Politics: Campaigning for Town and Country Planning, 1946–1990,* London: Spon

Hareven, Tamara K. (1977) 'Family time and historical time', *Daedalus* 106: 57–70

Harvey, David (1988) *Social Justice and the City* 2nd edn, Oxford: Blackwell

(1989) *The Urban Experience,* Oxford: Blackwell

Horton, Robin (1993) *Patterns of Thought in Africa and the West,* Cambridge: Cambridge University Press

'Housing at 1 and 2, Fishermead, Milton Keynes' (1977), *The Architects' Journal* (11 May): 877–91

Howard, Ebenezer (1898) *To-morrow: A Peaceful Path to Real Reform,* London: Swan Sonnenschein

(1902) *Garden Cities of To-morrow,* London: Swan Sonnenschein (revised version of Howard 1898; also reprinted 1946, London: Faber and Faber)

Howell, Signe (1986) 'Formal speech acts as one discourse', *Man* 21: 79–101

Hymes, Dell (1981) *'In Vain I tried to Tell You': Essays in Native American Ethnopoetics,* Philadelphia: University of Pennsylvania Press

(1982) 'Narrative form as a "grammar" of experience: Native Americans and a glimpse of English', *Journal of Education* 164 (2): 121–42

Inglis, Fred (1993) *Cultural Studies,* Oxford: Blackwell

Johnstone, Barbara (1990) *Stories, Community, and Place: Narratives from Middle America,* Bloomington: Indiana University Press

Josselson, Ruthellen and Lieblich, Amia (1993) (eds.) *The Narrative Study of Lives,* Newbury Park: Sage

Kalcik, Susan (1975) '. . . like Ann's gynecologist or the time I was almost raped', in Farrer, Claire R. (ed.) *Women and Folklore,* Austin: University of Texas Press

Karen [Kipping], Norine, John (1985) *'Showing Off': a Selection of Illustrated Poetry,* Milton Keynes: the authors

Kasinitz, Philip (1995) (ed.) *Metropolis: Centre and Symbol of our Times,* Basingstoke and London: Macmillan

Keith, Michael and Pile, Steve (1993) (eds.) *Place and the Politics of Identity*, London and New York: Routledge

Keller-Cohen, D. (1994) (ed.) *Literacy: Interdisciplinary Conversations*, New York: Hampton Press

Kemper, Robert V. (1991) 'Urban anthropology in the 1990s: the state of its practice' and 'Trends in urban anthropological research: an analysis of the *Journal of Urban Anthropology* 1972–1991', *Journal of Urban Anthropology* 20: 211–23, 373–84

Kitchen, Roger (1974) 'Moving to Milton Keynes', *New Society* 29 (22 August): 478–80

(1975) 'More than a "meet and greet" job at Milton Keynes', *Community Care* (26 February): 13–15

Kuper, Adam (1992) (ed.) *Conceptualizing Society*, London and New York: Routledge

(1994) 'Culture, identity and the project of a cosmopolitan anthropology', *Man* 29: 537–54

Labov, William (1972) *Language in the Inner City: Studies in the Black English Vernacular*, Philadelphia: University of Pennsylvania Press

Landau, Misia (1991) *Narratives of Human Evolution*, New Haven: Yale University Press

Langellier, K. M. (1989) 'Personal narratives: perspectives on theory and research', *Text and Performance Quarterly* 9 (4): 243–76

Langness, L. L. and Frank, Gelya (1981) *Lives: an Anthropological Approach to Biography*, Novato Calif.: Chandler and Sharp

Lanser, Susan Sniader (1981) *The Narrative Act: Point of View in Prose Fiction*, Princeton: Princeton University Press

LaRue, L. H. (1995) *Constitutional Law as Fiction: Narrative in the Rhetoric of Authority*, University Park Pa.: Pennsylvania State University Press

Lasch, Christopher (1984) *The Minimal Self: Psychic Survival in Troubled Times*, London: Pan

Lash, Scott and Friedman, Jonathan (1992) (eds.) *Modernity and Identity*, Oxford: Blackwell

Layder, Derek (1996) 'Contemporary sociological theory', *Sociology* 30: 601–8

Lévi-Strauss, Claude (1963) 'The structural study of myth', in *Structural Anthropology*, New York: Basic Books

(1969–81) *Introduction to a Science of Mythology*, 4 vols., Eng. trans., New York: Harper & Row

Linde, Charlotte (1993) *Life Stories: the Creation of Coherence*, New York and London: Oxford University Press

Llewelyn-Davies in association with Pell Frischmann (Milton Keynes), Milton Transport Management, Landscape Town & Country (1992) *Milton Keynes Expansion Study: Final Report*, Milton Keynes: for Commission for New Towns, Buckinghamshire County Council, Milton Keynes Borough Council, Aylesbury Vale District Council

Llewelyn-Davies Weeks Forestier-Walker & Bor (1968) *Milton Keynes Plan: Interim Report to the Milton Keynes Development Corporation*, London: Llewelyn-Davies Weeks Forestier-Walker & Bor

Lord, Albert (1960) *The Singer of Tales*, Cambridge Mass.: Harvard University Press

Lüthi, Max (1987) *The Fairytale as Art Form and Portrait of Man*, Eng. trans., Bloomington: Indiana University Press

Lyotard, Jean-François (1984) *The Postmodern Condition: a Report on Knowledge*, Eng. trans., Manchester: Manchester University Press

MacIntyre, Alasdair (1985) *After Virtue*, London: Duckworth

Mackay, Hugh (1997) (ed.) *Consumption and Everyday Life*, London: Sage

Malinowski, B. (1948) 'Myth in primitive psychology', in *Magic, Science and Religion and Other Essays,* New York: Doubleday

Marks, Laurence (1992) 'City of sky and myth', *Observer Review* 19 January

Massey, Doreen (1993) 'Power-geometry and a progressive sense of place', in Bird *et al.*

   (1995) 'Making spaces, or, geography is political too', *Soundings* 1: 193–208

McCabe, Allyssa and Peterson, Carole (1991) (eds.) *Developing Narrative Structure*, Hillsdale: Erlbaum

McCloskey, Donald N. (1990) *If You're so Smart: the Narrative of Economic Enterprise*, Chicago and London: Chicago University Press

Metcalfe, A. W. and Bern, J. (1994) 'Stories of crisis: restructuring Australian industry and rewriting the past', *International Journal of Urban and Regional Research* 18 (4): 658–72

Meyrowitz, Joshua (1985) *No Sense of Place*, Oxford: Oxford University Press

Middleton, D. and Edwards, D. (1990) *Collective Remembering*, London: Sage

Milton Keynes Borough Council (1993) *People and Housing in Milton Keynes: a Profile of Settlements from the 1991 Census*, Milton Keynes: Chesterton Consulting for the Milton Keynes Borough Council and the Commission for the New Towns

Milton Keynes Development Corporation (1970) *The Plan for Milton Keynes,* Wavendon: Milton Keynes Development Corporation (two volumes and ten technical supplements)

   (1975) *New City: Milton Keynes 1975*, Milton Keynes: Milton Keynes Development Corporation

   (1988) *Community Facilities: Development Strategy: Policy Statement*, Milton Keynes: Milton Keynes Development Corporation

   (1990) *Press Briefing Papers* [Briefing pack for the media, eleven papers], Milton Keynes: Milton Keynes Development Corporation

   (1992a) *The Planning of Milton Keynes*, Milton Keynes: Chesterton Consulting for Milton Keynes Development Corporation

   (1992b) *The Milton Keynes Planning Manual*, Milton Keynes: Chesterton Consulting for Milton Keynes Development Corporation

Mink, L. O. (1987) *Historical Understanding*, Ithaca: Cornell University Press

Mishler, Elliott G. (1986) *Research Interviewing: Context and Narrative*, Cambridge Mass.: Harvard University Press

Mitchell, W. J. T. (1981) (ed.) *On Narrative*, Chicago: University of Chicago Press

MKDC. *See* Milton Keynes Development Corporation

More, Thomas (1937) *Utopia* (Ralph Robinson's trans.), ed. H. B. Cotterill, London: Macmillan (first published in Latin 1515/16)

Morley, David (1993) 'Active audience theory: pendulums and pitfalls', *Journal of Communication* 43 (4): 13–19

Morris, Brian (1994) *Anthropology of the Self: the Individual in Cultural Perspective*, London: Pluto Press

Mumby, Dennis K. (1993) (ed.) *Narrative and Social Control: Critical Perspectives*, Newbury Park: Sage

Mundy, Hawtin (1984) *No Heroes, No Cowards*, Milton Keynes: The People's Press

Munzer, Marina E. and Vogel, John (1974) *New Towns: Building Cities from Scratch*, New York: Knopf

Myerhoff, Barbara (1980) 'Telling one's story', *The Center Magazine* 13 (2) (March): 22–40

Mynard, Dennis and Hunt, Julian (1994) *Milton Keynes: a Pictorial History*, Chichester: Phillimore

Neisser, Ulric (1994) 'Self-narratives: true and false', in Neisser and Fivush

Neisser, Ulric and Fivush, Robyn (1994) (eds.) *The Remembering Self: Construction and Accuracy in the Self-narrative*, Cambridge: Cambridge University Press

Official City Atlas: 1994: Milton Keynes (1994) Reading: GEOprojects (UK) Ltd for Commission for the New Towns, Milton Keynes

Oring, Elliott (1987) 'Generating lives: the construction of an autobiography', *Journal of Folklore Research* 24 (3): 241–62

Osborn, Frederic J. and Whittick, Arnold (1977) *New Towns: their Origins, Achievements and Progress* 3rd edn, London: Routledge and Kegan Paul

Osborne, John (1994) 'Philistines who need a lesson in the language', *Mail on Sunday*, 7 August

Ouroussoff, Alexandra (1993) 'Illusions of rationality: false premises of the liberal tradition', *Man* 28: 281–98

Packwood, Anita (1986) *Coming Out: Poems*, Milton Keynes: the author

Pahl, Ray (1970a) *Whose City? and Other Essays on Sociology and Planning*, London: Longman

   (1970b) *Patterns of Urban Life*, London: Longman

   (1995) *After Success. Fin-de-Siècle Anxiety and Identity,* Cambridge: Polity

Paulme, D. (1976) *La Mère dévorante: essai sur la morphologie des contes africains*, Paris: Gallimard

Personal Narratives Group (1989) (ed.) *Interpreting Women's Lives,* Bloomington: Indiana University Press

Plummer, Ken (1983) *Documents of Life: an Introduction to the Literature of a Humanistic Method*, London: Allen and Unwin

(1995) *Telling Sexual Stories: Power, Change and Social Worlds*, London: Routledge

Polanyi, Livia (1979) 'So what's the point?', *Semiotica* 25 (3/4): 207–41

Polkinghorne, Donald E. (1988) *Narrative Knowing and the Human Sciences*, Albany: State University of New York Press

Prince, Gerald (1982) *Narratology: the Form and Functioning of Narrative*, Berlin, New York and Amsterdam: Mouton

(1987) *A Dictionary of Narratology*, Lincoln, Nebr.: University of Nebraska Press

(1989) 'Narrative', in Barnouw, Erik (ed.) *International Encyclopedia of Communications*, New York and Oxford: Oxford University Press

(1994) 'Narratology', in Groden, Michael and Kreiswirth, Martin (eds.) *The Johns Hopkins Guide to Literary Theory and Criticism*, Baltimore and London: Johns Hopkins University Press

Propp, Vladimir (1968) *The Morphology of the Folktale*, Eng. trans., 2nd edn, Austin: University of Texas Press

Reyna, S. P. (1994) 'Literary anthropology and the case against science', *Man* 29: 555–81

Rice, Ouida (1982) (comp.) *Village Memories, Glimpses of Village Life during the First Fifty Years of this Century as Seen through the Eyes of the Villagers of Woughton-on-the-Green*, Milton Keynes: The People's Press

Ricoeur, Paul (1984–8) *Time and Narrative*, 3 vols., Eng. trans., Chicago: Chicago University Press

Riessman, Catherine Kohler (1990) 'Strategic uses of narrative in the presentation of self and illness', *Social Science and Medicine* 30 (11): 1195–200

(1993) *Narrative Analysis*, Newbury Park: Sage

Rimmer, Dave (1986) 'The non-place urban realm', *Harpers & Queen* (February): 78–80

Robertson, George, Mash, Melinda, Tickner, Lisa, Bird, Jon, Curtis, Barry, and Putnam, Tim (1994) (eds.) *Travellers' Tales: Narratives of Home and Displacement*, London: Routledge

Roe, Emery (1994) *Narrative Policy Analysis: Theory and Practice*, Durham N.C. and London: Duke University Press

Rorty, Amelie Oksenberg (1987) 'Persons as rhetorical categories', *Social Research* 54 (1): 55–72

Rosenwald, George C. and Ochberg, Richard L. (1992) (eds.) *Storied Lives: The Cultural Politics of Self-understanding*, New Haven and London: Yale University Press

Rubin, David C. (1996) (ed.) *Remembering our Past: Studies in Autobiographical Memory*, Cambridge: Cambridge University Press

Salaman, Graeme (1997) 'Culturing production', in du Gay, Paul (ed.) *Production of Culture/Cultures of Production*, London: Sage

Samuel, Raphael and Thompson, Paul (1990) (eds.) *The Myths We Live By*, London and New York: Routledge

Sandelowski, Margarete (1991) 'Telling stories: narrative approaches in qualitative research', *Image: Journal of Nursing Scholarship* 23 (3): 161–6

Sanjek, Roger (1990) 'Urban anthropology in the 1980s: a world view', *Annual Review of Anthropology* 19: 151–86

Sarbin, Theodore R. (1986) (ed.) *Narrative Psychology: the Storied Nature of Human Conduct*, New York: Praeger

Savage, Mike and Warde, Alan (1993) *Urban Sociology, Capitalism and Modernity*, Basingstoke and London: Macmillan

Schafer, R. (1992) *Retelling a Life: Narration and Dialogue in Psychoanalysis*, New York: Basic Books

Scholes, R. and Kellogg, R. (1966) *The Nature of Narrative*, London: Oxford University Press

Schwab, William A. (1992) *The Sociology of Cities*, Englewood Cliffs N.J.: Prentice-Hall

Scott, Alan (1995) Review [of S. Watson and K. Gibson (1994) (eds.) *Postmodern Cities and Spaces*, Oxford and Cambridge Mass.: Blackwell], *International Journal of Urban and Regional Research* 19 (3): 468–9

Seidler, Victor J. (1994) *Recovering the Self: Morality and Social Theory*, London and New York: Routledge

Sennett, Richard (1973) *The Uses of Disorder. Personal Identity and City Life*, Harmondsworth: Penguin

Sherzer, Joel (1990) *Verbal Art in San Blas*, Cambridge: Cambridge University Press

Sherzer, Joel and Woodbury, Anthony C. (1987) (eds.) *Native American Discourse: Poetics and Rhetoric*, Cambridge: Cambridge University Press

Shotter, John and Gergen, Kenneth J. (1989) (eds.) *Texts of Identity*, Newbury Park: Sage

Shuman, Amy (1986) *Storytelling Rights: the Uses of Oral and Written Texts by Urban Adolescents*, Cambridge: Cambridge University Press

Simmel, Georg (1903) 'The metropolis and mental life', in Levine, Donald N. (1971) (ed.) *Georg Simmel on Individuality and Social Forms*, Chicago and London: University of Chicago Press

Smith, Barbara Herrnstein (1981) 'Narrative versions, narrative theories', in Mitchell

Spencer, Jonathan (1989) 'Anthropology as a kind of writing', *Man* 24: 145–64

Stanley, Liz (1992) *The Auto-biographical I: the Theory and Practice of Feminist Auto/biography*, Manchester: Manchester University Press

Stanley, Liz and Morgan, David (1993) (eds.) *Auto/biography in Sociology*, Special issue, *Sociology* 27 (1)

Stone, Vera (1981) *I'm Off: Adventures of a Concrete Cow*, Milton Keynes: the author

 (1985) *'I'm Off Again': More Adventures of Millie Moo the Concrete Cow*, Milton
 Keynes: the author

Street, Brian (1993) (ed.) *Cross-cultural Approaches to Literacy*, Cambridge: Cambridge University Press

Stromberg, Peter G. (1993) *Language and Self-transformation: a Study of the
 Christian Conversion Narrative*, Cambridge: Cambridge University Press

Tedlock, Dennis (1972) *Finding the Center: Narrative Poetry of the Zuni Indians*,
 New York: Dial

 (1983) *The Spoken Word and the Work of Interpretation*, Philadelphia: University of Pennsylvania Press

The Times (1992) 'Paradise mislaid', 24 January

*This Place has its Ups and Downs, or, Kids Could Have Done it Better, a Collection
 of Children's Impressions about Life in Milton Keynes* (1977) Milton Keynes:
 The People's Press

Thrift, Nigel (1997) '"Us" and "them": re-imagining places, re-imagining identities', in Mackay

Titon, Jeff Todd (1980) 'The life story', *Journal of American Folklore* 93 (369):
 276–92

Tonkin, Elizabeth (1990) 'History and the myth of realism', in Samuel and Thompson

 (1992) *Narrating our Pasts: the Social Construction of Oral History*, Cambridge:
 Cambridge University Press

Toolan, Michael J. (1988) *Narrative: a Critical Linguistic Introduction*, London:
 Routledge

Turner, Jane and Jardine, Bob (1985) (eds.) *Pioneer Tales: a New Life in Milton
 Keynes*, Milton Keynes: The People's Press

Turner, Victor (1982) *From Ritual to Theatre: the Human Seriousness of Play*,
 New York: Performing Arts Journal Publications

Urban, Greg (1991) *A Discourse-centered Approach to Culture: Native American
 Myths and Rituals*, Austin: University of Texas Press

Van Maanen, John (1988) *Tales of the Field: on Writing Ethnography*, Chicago and
 London: University of Chicago Press

Wallman, Sandra (1984) *Eight London Households*, London: Tavistock

Ward, Colin (1978) 'Innovationsville', *New Society* 46 (30 November): 524–5

 (1993) *New Town, Home Town: the Lessons of Experience*, London: Gulben-
 kian Foundation

Waterman, P. W. (1979), 'Milton Keynes, the official view', *The Architect* (December): 12–16

Watson, Lawrence C. and Watson-Franke, Maria-Barbara (1985) *Interpreting Life
 Histories: an Anthropological Inquiry*, New Brunswick: Rutgers University
 Press

Watson, Sophie and Gibson, Katherine (1995) (eds.) *Postmodern Cities and*

Spaces, Oxford and Cambridge Mass.: Blackwell

Weber, Eugen (1989) '. . . And God made the town', *The American Scholar* 58: 79–96

West, Bill (1992) *Remember Wolverton, Stratford and Bradwell: the Story of Three Towns in a Council 1919–1974*, Whittlebury: Baron for Quotes Ltd

White, David (1980) 'What's really so bad about Milton Keynes?', *New Society* 52 (17 April): 95–8

White, Hayden (1973) *Metahistory*, Baltimore: Johns Hopkins University Press
    (1987) *The Content of the Form: Narrative Discourse and Historical Representation*, Baltimore: Johns Hopkins University Press

Whitmore, Colin (*c.* 1989) *Exploring Milton Keynes*, Milton Keynes: City Discovery Centre

Williams, Raymond (1975) *The Country and the City*, St Albans: Paladin

Worthington, Kim (1996) *Self as Narrative*, Oxford: Oxford University Press

Wright, K. W. *et al.* (1979) (comp.) *Fenny Stratford Album*, Milton Keynes: The People's Press

Yankah, Kwesi (1995) *Speaking for the Chief: Okyeame and the Politics of Akan Royal Oratory*, Bloomington and Indianapolis: Indiana University Press

Yow, Valerie Raleigh (1994) *Recording Oral History: a Practical Guide for Social Scientists*, Thousand Oaks, London and New Delhi: Sage

Zukin, Sharon (1992) 'Postmodern urban landscapes: mapping culture and power', in Lash and Friedman

Index

References to Figures are in *italics*, and pseudonyms of personal narrators are within quotation marks.

chronicle 10, 191
  see also story
circulation, mode of 9, 12, 174
  academic urban tales 21–3
  concrete cows tales 45–6
  garden city tales 39
  humanistic–historical tales 47–54
  personal stories 73–81
  planners' tales 35–6, 37
citizens, in stories, *see* 'people, the'
city, the
  abstract tales of 14–23
  as created through multiplicity of
    stories 1, 3, 9, 165–71, 176–80
  definition of 1, 190
  as formulated through personal
    stories 155–64
  the 'good city' 23, 34, 38–41
  as inimical to humanity, *see* binary
    opposition myth
  liberalising role of, *see* freedom
  as narrated in tales of a specific city
    24–55, 155–64
  as natural setting for human life
    158–64, 175–6
'classic' urban theory, as story 14–23,
  173
Clifford, James 12, 190
Cohen, Anthony 21, 58, 190, 192
coherence in stories 9, 10–11
  academic urban tales 18–20
  concrete cows tales 44–7
  garden city tales 37–9
  personal tales 101–6, 118
  planners' tales 33–6
  see also plot
coincidences, in stories 90–1
commumication of stories, *see*
  circulation; performance
communicative event 12, 73–5
community, as theme in stories 16, 19,
  21, 34, 36, 38, 41, 124, 131–8, 152,
  153–5, 164, 171, 174, 175–80

  see also binary opposition myth
conclusions, *see* endings
concrete cows 44–51, *45*, *51*, 54, 55,
  157, 163, 165–6, 170–1, 173–9
consumption, as theme in stories 21,
  100, 174
contexts for story-telling 7, 12, 22,
  35–6, 38–9, 73–81, 174
  see also communicative event
continuity, sense of, in stories 174,
  176–80
  in personal tales 99, 101–2
control, personal, in stories 81, 114–19
  see also individuals
conventions, in story-telling 9, 11–13,
  173–7
  academic urban tales 21–3
  concrete cows tales 45–7
  humanistic–historical tales 49–54
  personal tales 57–9, 73–81, 89–93,
    98–106, 114–23, 138, 147–64
  planners' tales 35–6
country/countryside, *see* binary
  opposition myth; 'green' city;
  rural/urban juxtaposition
Cowper, William 47
cultural studies, urban stories in
  14–23
'Cunningham, Andrew' 103, 117, 149,
  161–2, 183
'Curtis, Ruth' 155, 184
cyclical time 101–2, 173, 177

'Dale, Lucy' 115, 119, 124–31, 135,
  136, 147, 148, 152, 154, 155, 161,
  184
'Dawson, Brenda' 2, 59–72, 73–8, 89,
  90, 98, 104, 114, 116, 119, 148,
  155, 156, 159, 161, 162, 184
delivery of stories, *see* circulation;
  performance; style
destiny, as theme in stories 25–36, 55,
  175